PENGUIN PLAY

CAUGHT YAPPING

Abhishek Mukherjee is the head of special content at Wisden.com. He co-authored *Sachin and Azhar at Cape Town* and *The Great Indian Cricket Circus*; he also won the Anandji Dossa Award for the Cricket Statistician of the Year in 2019–20. Mukherjee used to be the assistant editor at the *Wisden India Almanack* and the chief editor at *CricketCountry*. He has written for several media houses, including the Cricketer, Moneycontrol, Quint and Yahoo! Cricket. His X (Twitter) handle is @ovshake42.

ADVANCE PRAISE FOR THE BOOK

'What this book and Abhishek Mukherjee provide are the eyes of the previously unseen. He is not rewriting history; he is simply telling the stories from the other side that weren't recorded correctly'—**Jarrod Kimber, cricket writer, analyst, commentator, author, film-maker and podcaster**

'The cricketing equivalent of *A History of the World in 100 Objects*. Well-chosen quotes, and even better stories about the context and the aftermath. Highly recommended!'—**Joy Bhattacharjya, cricket analyst, Cricbuzz; CEO, Pro Volleyball League; director, 2017 FIFA U-17 World Cup; and former team director, Kolkata Knight Riders**

'An innovative approach . . . Succeeds in throwing light on the many historical dimensions hitherto left unexplored by the predominantly Anglo-Australian narratives of the game'—**Arunabha Sengupta, author of *Elephant in the Stadium* and *Cricket Across Dark Waters***

Caught Yapping

A HISTORY OF CRICKET IN 100 QUOTES

Abhishek Mukherjee

PENGUIN
PLAY
An imprint of Penguin Random House

PENGUIN PLAY

Penguin Books is an imprint of the Penguin Random House group of companies whose addresses can be found at global.penguinrandomhouse.com

Published by Penguin Random House India Pvt. Ltd
4th Floor, Capital Tower 1, MG Road,
Gurugram 122 002, Haryana, India

Penguin Random House India

First published in Penguin Play by Penguin Random House India 2025

10 9 8 7 6 5 4 3 2 1

ISBN 9780143463405

Typeset in Garamond by MAP Systems, Bengaluru, India

www.penguin.co.in

Rituparna,
for the quotes that make life worth living

Foreword

There is something magical about listening to a chat in Hindi, Urdu or Bengali, and hearing the English words 'flipper', 'googly' or 'leg slip'. That's the language of cricket now—one of the many Asian languages with an English word thrown in. We know the sport has changed, but much of the history is still from the English-speaking viewpoint.

It is more than just the words. Think about cricket sweaters. They are thick, have long sleeves, and are usually made of coarse wool. They are somehow heavy, chunky and box-like all at once. People from non-cricket nations wear this; to them, it doesn't say cricket—it says England.

What other country would devise a summer sport and then make a uniform that included something for cold weather? The cricket sweater is not the only thing cricket has because England created the sport.

The bats are made of English willow. What would cricket be like without this magical tree that is somehow a hardwood species but has softwood tendencies? It allows for a stiffness that has great impact resistance. Baseball has three major kinds of trees that make up their bats. In cricket, we have just this one, dense and light, English willow, or to use its scientific name, *Salix alba 'Caerulea'*. All these years later, this is still cricket's tree, with most today grown out near Chelmsford in Essex.

And we haven't even got to tea. India and Sri Lanka have a great relationship with the beverage, but English cricket has made it an official break.

If you want to intellectualize it, cricket is a construct of the English class system. Amateurs were often batters because there was less work in that, and in true aristocratic style, they were often paid more than the professionals. And guess what job those professionals were paid even lesser to do? Bowling. The hard yards, day after day, running in only to be rebuffed by the landed gentry with the bat.

The fielding positions sound like P.G. Wodehouse wrote them. There is more sexual innuendo in some of the terms than a *Carry On* film: Are you a happy hooker to fine leg when you want to stop a maiden?

Of course, I am talking about England, but what about Britain? You could debate whether cricket is the most English of sports, you cannot on whether it is the sport of the empire. John Mangan once wrote of cricket, 'the umbilical cord of Empire linking the mother country with her children'. Cricket was used by the British to civilize the colonies in a way other sports were not. You could be taught to be a proper member of society through the sport, hence the term 'Gentlemen's Game'.

Of course there is an inherent lie there, as we know that not everyone can be a gentleman. In cricket of the 1800s, the people who were given that title were from a particular elite part of society. If anything, cricket was teaching you to be subservient to the elites. Listen to the man chosen to lead your team based on his family connections. Also, cricket wasn't being taught to people in order for other nations to be good at it, but more to learn the societal norms of the British.

So, cricket grew as a sport and a tool of the empire at the same time. Making it the most political sport there has ever been.

But the children of imperialism have grown up. Women are no longer banned from the game; they make money from it. India once considered Douglas Jardine for their first captain, now it runs cricket politically and financially. And England have now lost to Afghanistan and the Netherlands at cricket; they aren't even Commonwealth nations.

There is no doubt cricket is changing. Japan and Thailand sending teams to the U-19 men's and senior Women's World Cup is huge. The Brazilian women's side were the first to be paid even before their men's team was. We live in a world where a Nepalese kid can watch YouTube and be paid to bowl leg-spin around the world.

So, the game has changed, but the history has stayed the same: English. This comes from the amount of newspapers and media money that they have as much as their control over other cricket nations. It means when we go back to old cricket stories, we read them the way the English saw them.

There is this idea that revisionist history is some kind of bad idea. You cannot change history, the doubters will say. What this book does—and what Abhishek Mukherjee has always provided—is the eyes of the previously unseen. He is not rewriting history; he is simply telling the stories from the other side that weren't recorded correctly.

The children of the empire have grown up, and they want their history back. Because cricket is a part of nation-building, this is not just about sport; it is about identity.

This book is 500 years of history, told from the quiet side. Because they've now found a voice through writers like Abhishek Mukherjee.

Jarrod Kimber

Author's Note

Had this book been restricted to cricket on the field, it could potentially have been a hundred scorecard entries. After all, nothing speaks about the game more than the score—which is why they provide the ticker during live telecasts.

Of course, this book is about famous matches and about legends whose cricketing deeds will be talked about for as long as the sport is played. But it is not *only* about them, or what happened on the field. Cricket, after all, is not played in a vacuum.

This book is also about heroes who turned the playing arena into battlefields where they took on social barriers and oppressive regimes. About letters that stopped cricket when it went on for longer than it should have. About telegrams that salvaged international relations.

About reverse swing and reverse sweep and other wonderful innovations. About legendary umpires and scoring methods. About the helmet and the Decision Review System. And about coverage of the sport on radio and television and the internet.

About the changing shape of the cricket bat and the stigma around revolutionary bowling actions. About the ball-by-ball commentary that united a planet at the cost of melted servers. About the live-streaming of the sport that came as a glimmer of hope to millions amidst one of the greatest global crises of the twenty-first century.

About people who owned personal teams, be it in the eighteenth century or the twenty-first. About visionaries who changed the sport forever. About players who prompted changes to the Laws of Cricket. About the people who ran the great game getting it wrong, sometimes through inaction, often through deliberate discrimination. And about sterling individuals who prompted action and righted those wrongs.

Why Quotes?

There are tales that scorecards do not tell, stories of heroes and villains, rises and falls, temptations and conflicts, inclusions and exclusions.

The sport has inspired considerable literature, and continues to do so, perhaps more than most other sports. Cricket's stories lie in these innumerable volumes and letters and dusty archives of newspapers, magazines, journals and periodicals and the wonders of the internet.

Then there are words the people of cricket have told their peers or adversaries on the field; words uttered at press conferences or in the commentary box or from the comfort of their home. As a medium, spoken words predate written history. They also do not enjoy the additional security of the editor's pen.

In this book, I have tried to chronicle the history of cricket, and history means little without the people. And what better way to tell you the story of the people than use their own words?

Why Another Book?

The long, rich history of cricket has been narrated many times. The voices have almost always been either from England, where the sport originated, or Australia, the great rival. Such myopic narration was normal in a sport largely played by England and her colonies and dominions.

It is not the same world anymore. Cricket is a global sport now. No longer is the ICC run from the confines of Lord's. The narratives created over centuries from the ivory towers of the cricket establishment need to be reassessed and retold. This book tries to do that.

This and That

The chapters are chronologically arranged based on the events the quotes describe—and not the date when the words were said. For instance, Bernard Bosanquet's words in Chapter 20 are from a monograph he wrote in 1925, but the incidents he describes took place in 1897.

In some cases, the on-field action has taken a backseat. Two quotes, used in two chapters (58 and 59), were from a timeless classic of a Test match, but neither focuses specifically on the game, as what happened off the field was far more impactful.

It is worth a mention that in any other sport, this course of events in Chapters 46 and 72 would perhaps have been deemed too insignificant to become part of history. Their bizarre relevance can be attributed to cricket's unfounded, embarrassingly hollow sense of moral superiority.

Disclaimers

Quotes are tricky. They change over time. Written words are easier to reproduce (though digging into eighteenth-century newspapers and periodicals would have been quite a task without the internet), but spoken words can change with every telling.

When Frank Worrell had a word with Wes Hall in the dying stages of the Brisbane tie (Chapter 54), they were the only two people who knew the exact words. Neither can be blamed if a word or two got altered over time over their (and others') many retellings.

Thankfully, there have not been many of these conflicts around the quotes in this book. The exact versions were often available. For the rest, I have tried to retain the essence of the quotes as much as possible.

Cricket used to have its share of sexist terms, from 'batsman' to 'nightwatchman' to 'third man' to 'twelfth man'. Our vocabulary is more inclusive today. While reproducing quotes, I have kept the words in their original. However, in the narrative connecting the quotes, I have avoided the archaic terms and used the current vocabulary.

Section 1

The Dawn of Cricket

Chapter 1

'HEE AND DIVERSE OF HIS FELLOWS DID RUNNE AND PLAY AT CRECKETT AND OTHER PLAIES.'

John Derrick, Queen's Coroner of Surrey,
at a court of law in Guildford, 27 January 1598 (as per the Gregorian calendar. The corresponding Julian calendar date was 17 January 1597).

The years mentioned in this chapter are according to the Gregorian calendar even for the days before Gregory XIII.

The early days of cricket are shrouded in mystery. 'The youths at cricks did play/throughout the merry day,' wrote Joseph of Exeter in 1180. The 1301 wardrobe accounts of Edward II mention playing '*creag et alios ludos*' (creag and other games). Some speculate that these are references to cricket, but there is little substance to these claims.

John Major, former British Prime Minister and cricket historian, has questioned Joseph's 'cricks' ('sounds more eighteenth-century than twelfth') in *More Than a Game: The Story of Cricket's Early Years*, while educationalist and cricket historian Derek Birley suggested that 'creag' might have been a variation of 'craic' ('enjoyable social time'). All that aside, there is no reason for the sport to make these random appearances before disappearing for centuries.

However, we do find a sudden influx of cricketing references in the early seventeenth century. In 1611, teams from the Downs and the Weald played an organized cricket match at Chevening, Kent. In the same year, Bartholomew Wyatt and Richard Latter, parishioners at Sidlesham, had to serve penance and pay a 12-pence fine for playing cricket on a Sunday.

Despite being little more than village amusement, cricket gained popularity in the 1600s. Yet, the century before that hardly mentions it … until 1598. That year, John Derrick, the fifty-nine-year-old Queen's Coroner of Surrey, was called upon to provide testimony at a court in Guildford.

In 1593 (or 1594), one William Wyntersmoll had withheld an acre of land from the town of Guildford—only to find an enclosure built there, by one John Pavrishe, forty years ago. Wyntersmoll took the matter to court.

But long before that, in 1509, Robert Beckingham, a Freeman of the City of London, had left a bequest in his will to 'make a free scole at the Towne of Guildford'. The Free School was founded, and, following a 1552 order from Edward VI, renamed the Royal Grammar School as well as moved to High Street, where it still stands. John Derrick was an alumnus of this school.

At the court, he stated that fifty years ago, the land 'lay waste and was used by the inhabitants of Guildeford to saw timber in and for saw-pitts' before adding that 'being a scholler in the ffree schoole of Guildeford hee and diverse of his fellows did runne and play at creckett and other plaies'.

Derrick's 'creckett' is universally accepted as cricket. Since he reminisced about incidents from fifty years ago, it appears that the Surrey schoolboys had almost certainly been playing cricket around 1550.

It took an adult to put that into words, though.

This is acknowledged by cricket historians as the first authentic mention of cricket.

Chapter 2

'THE MIDDLE OF LAST WEEK A GREAT MATCH OF CRICKET WAS PLAYED IN SUSSEX; THERE WERE ELEVEN OF A SIDE, AND THEY PLAYED FOR FIFTY GUINEAS APIECE.'

Foreign Post, 7 July 1697.

In John Derrick's early days, cricket was mostly restricted to children in the Weald, an area consisting of parts of—by today's definition—Hampshire, Surrey, Sussex and Kent. However, grown-ups had taken it up by the turn of the century.

At Sidlesham in 1611, two clergymen were fined 12 pence each for playing cricket on Easter Sunday 'instead of attending divine service in their parish church'. Men of their profession would be serial offenders for at least the first half of the 1600s.

However, as cricket spread, many quickly identified it as a viable option for betting—somewhat like cockfighting and horse racing, but with human beings in the arena. The aristocrats were invariably the ones with the largest stakes: if they did not play themselves, they bet large sums on others.

In the time of Charles II (1660–85), 'it became the thing in London society to make matches and form clubs'. Indeed, London became the hub of all cricketing activity.

Betting on sport became so rampant that Charles II had to pass an act against 'deceitfull disorderly and excessive Gameing' to restrict the stakes to £100—still a very large sum of money. Innkeepers typically profited heavily from matches as well, by serving refreshments as well as putting up the players. These matches also invited heavy wagers on the outcome.

The consequences were not necessarily peaceful. John Major mentions how Thomas Reynolds, Henry Gunter and Eleanor Lansford, 'only spectators at a game of cricket' at Sussex, were charged with 'riot and battery' for assaulting Ralph Thurston. Major speculated that betting could have been a reason. *Sussex Cricket in the Eighteenth Century*, edited by Timothy McCann, puts the year as 1693.

Ugly fights resurfaced time and again at cricket, almost always over betting. At the Strand in 1749, 'serious riots' broke out when a group of sailors accused a 'brothel-keeper' of cheating, noted Derek Birley in *The Willow Wand*. During a 1774 match at Kent, played for 1000 guineas, 'a great battle amongst the spectators' resulted in several of them getting injured.

The Licensing Act of 1662 was decreed in 1695, thereby establishing freedom of the press in Great Britain. This was significant, for newspapers could now report on cricket. In 1697, the *Foreign Post* ran the first known report of a cricket match from which the quote above is drawn.

The sum—50 guineas per player (not team)—perhaps justified the 'great match' tag. The contest was of historical significance in more ways than one, for this was the first *known* eleven-a-side cricket match.

Cricket coverage in the media became common over time, but they were different from their twenty-first-century counterparts. Advertisements invariably focused on, along with the itinerary, the sums at stake. Reports were more about the biggest winners from the day's bets and the respective sums and less about the cricket.

By 1743, the *Gentleman's Magazine* actually complained that advertisement of cricket matches 'is a most notorious breach of the laws, as it gives most open encouragement to gaming—the advertisements most impudently reciting that great sums are laid'. Not that it had an impact.

Cricket 'in the old times', thus, used to be entirely about money.

Chapter 3

'WEE HAVE BEAT SURREY ALMOST IN ONE INNINGS.'

Charles Lennox, a letter to a friend, September 1742.

We discussed the famous eleven-a-side match of 1697 in the previous chapter. One of the twenty-two players was Charles Lennox, the First Duke of Richmond and an illegitimate son of Charles II.

His son, also Charles Lennox, was the Second Duke and a cricketer just as passionate. Keeping in tune with the nobility of the era, he built his own team. Sure, money was a major reason, but defeating rival lords also earned prestige.

Lennox was as serious as anyone in this. His scouting methods are not clear, but he ended up hiring the best professionals in England. Thomas Waymark, the first great all-rounder in cricket history, was a prime example. Not only did Lennox find him but he also had him on the payroll as his groom.

With income taken care of, Waymark was available to play cricket for Lennox when he wanted to. He grew in stature as a cricketer—to the extent that cricket matches would be postponed if Waymark fell ill. No, the 'game bigger than individual' notion did not hold in the supposed pristine past of cricket.

But Lennox's legacy did not stop at building his own team. Ahead of a two-match series against Alan Brodrick's side in 1727, Lennox insisted the two men wrote a list of Articles of Agreement according to which the match would be played. We shall return to these in the next chapter.

Four years later, Lennox's team hosted Thomas Chambers's side at Richmond Green for 200 guineas. As an aside, this was the earliest match whose team scores are still available.

Lennox's team made 79 and 72. Having scored 119 in the first innings, Chambers's side needed only 33. They needed 8–10 'notches' (runs) with 4–5 wickets in hand when time ran out.

The crowd was far from happy with this result, because they had staked a lot of money. Lennox was partly to blame, because his late arrival had delayed the start. In the violent riot that ensued, some Sussex players had shirts torn off their backs.

A disgruntled Lennox retired to the village of Slindon, only to resurface in 1741. He had stopped playing after breaking his leg in 1733, but away from the cricketing limelight, he was ready with the first outstanding team in cricketing history.

All-rounder Richard Newland, the first known left-handed cricketer, was the best in England until the arrival of Robert

'Long Robin' Colchin later that decade. Richard and his brothers, Adam and John, formed the nucleus of this side. They had a colleague in Edward 'Cuddy' Aburrow Sr, a smuggler. Lennox was clearly not one to leave his best bowler out of the side for such transgressions.

In 1741, this Slindon side beat Portsmouth in front of more than 5000 people in Hampshire. The following year, Lennox challenged the Duke of Newcastle ('poor little Slyndon [*sic*] against almost your whole county of Surrey', to quote from *Sussex Cricket in the Eighteenth Century*).

This was no ordinary affair. Lennox had been recruiting cricketers from all over Sussex for a decade. He had built the first genuinely strong representative county side, though they had been playing under the name of Slindon. He had elevated a village sport to an inter-county affair. Nearly a century later, in 1839, the oldest of the existing eighteen first-class county clubs would be founded … in Sussex.

'Surrey' stood no chance in this match at Merrow Down. 'Wee have beat Surrey almost in one innings,' wrote Lennox to his wife, Sarah. In return, the Duchess expressed how she wished 'the Sussex mobb had thrash'd the Surrey mob'.

This win was part of a long streak, where Slindon played forty-three matches and lost only once. Their famous run ended when the London Club beat them in 1744, that too not once but twice. There was a third match, where Slindon beat London. For this occasion, Lennox had the proceedings chronicled. This is the oldest known cricket scorecard. He was a man of many firsts.

There had been 'county' teams before Lennox. 'Kent' had played 'Surrey' at Dartford on 29 June 1709 for a sum of £50. However, Lennox should be credited for building a representative 'county' team of this quality, one that found sustained success to this extent.

Chapter 4

'THE GAME AT CRICKET AS SETTLED BY THE SEVERAL CRICKET-CLUBS PARTICULARLY THAT OF THE STAR AND GARTER IN PALL-MALL.'

Consensus reached upon by 'noblemen and gentlemen members' of the London Cricket Club in 1744. Printed by W. Read in 1755.

It is now time to return to the 1727 agreement between Charles Lennox, the First Duke of Richmond, and Alan Brodrick, the

Second Viscount Midleton. Ahead of a series between their two sides, the two men wrote a code by hand. The teams were supposed to abide by these during the match.

For decades, cricket has been playing according to rules passed on by word of mouth. Even if anyone had written them down, the records do not survive. Lennox and Brodrick can, thus, be credited with the first codes of cricket.

Today's cricketers may find some of these rules unusual. Matches were twelve a side and not eleven. The wickets were 23 (not 22) yards apart. The umpire carried a 'stick', which the 'batt man' had to touch—instead of reaching the popping crease—to complete a run. Still, it was not a bad first attempt.

This written code, however, did not get universal acceptance. Then, in 1744, members of the London Cricket Club got together to create an updated version. These are universally accepted as the first Laws of Cricket, though they were not printed until 1755. The printed edition mentions that the Laws were 'settled' by 'several cricket-clubs, particularly that of the Star and Garter in Pall-Mall'.

The Laws were classified into six major sections: The Game at Cricket; Laws for the Bowlers, Four Balls an Over; Laws for the Strikers, or Those That Are Inn; Bat, Foot, or Hand, Over the Crease; Laws for the Wicket-Keepers; and Laws for the Umpires.

The pitch was reduced to 22 yards, while the umpire's stick was replaced by the popping crease (3 feet 10 inches from the wicket). At the same time, there is a curious restriction on the wicketkeeper who 'shall not, by any Noise, incommode the Striker'.

The authority of the umpires—they are referred to as 'sole judges' several times throughout the Laws—was firmly established, through phrases like 'his Determination shall be absolute' and 'no Person shall have any Right to question him'.

Dismissals like 'obstructing the field' ('If he runs out of his Ground to hinder a Catch, it's out') and 'hitting the ball twice'

('If a Ball is nipp'd up, and he strikes it again wilfully, before it came to the Wicket, it's out') are as old as the Laws themselves, but there was no leg-before wicket (LBW). We shall come to that.

There was also 'two Minutes for each Man to come inn when one is out', but no defined penalty even if the two-minute window was over. Timed out was a thing of the future.

The Laws of Cricket have undergone numerous changes over time, but they are not too different from the 1744 set.

Chapter 5

'FOR HONEST LUMPEY DID ALLOW/ HE NE'ER WOULD PITCH BUT O'ER A BROW ... SO SURRY DID THE VICT'RY AGAIN/BY LUMPEY, FORTUNE, ART, AND RAIN.'

The *Gentleman's Magazine*, November 1773.

While the magazine had used the spelling 'Lumpey', cricket historians have largely stuck to 'Lumpy'. Perhaps the nickname never had a definitive spelling. I have used the latter here.

No one can say for certain why the 'short, stout, genial, and straightforward' Edward Stevens got the iconic nickname of 'Lumpy'. Ashley Mote cited three possible reasons: the 'lumpiness' in his face; the man polishing off an enormous apple pie all by himself at a Hambledon Club dinner; and his ability to deliberately land the ball on lumpy pieces of the pitch to make it shoot.

I am inclined to believe the last one, because Lumpy was an incredible bowler renowned for, among other aspects, metronomic precision. A famous story involves the great bet of the Burway Ground at Chertsey: Lumpy landed the ball four times in four attempts on a feather placed on a pitch to earn £100 for his patron, the Earl of Tankerville.

Tankerville kept his greatest professional cricketer on the payroll—not only for the matches but round the year. Lumpy worked in the garden on Tankerville's Walton-on-Thames estate—but spent most of his time honing his skills and improving his accuracy.

Some of Lumpy's famous exploits came against the Duke of Dorset, whose team had a rivalry with Tankerville's. Lumpy's domination in this 'match-up' prompted the *Gentleman's Magazine* to write on Dorset: 'His Grace for bowling cannot yield/To none but Lumpey in the field.'

To understand the quote that forms the title of this chapter, it is important to know the cricket pitch of the era. The concept of mowing grass and rolling pitches still lay in the future. Sheep were often used to graze on the grass until at least one strip was clear enough to be called a pitch. Sometimes they used scythes. The bowling side eventually chose the pitch for the day.

Lumpy was a master at this. Easily the finest bowler of the side, he chose to bowl from over a 'brow' (slope), landed the ball on lumps, and made them shoot. He also read the batters well enough for Tankerville to allow him to change the field. It was unthinkable for an aristocrat of the era to allow a professional to do this. Additionally, after dropping a catch off Lumpy, Tankerville would sometimes compensate the heavy drinker in bottles.

Lumpy figured out that the good-length ball—neither short enough to wait nor close enough to take on the full—could wreak havoc, because the batters did not have a chance against unpredictable bounce or the movement with their hockey-stick-like curved cricket bats.

Bowlers before Lumpy—underarm, of course—merely rolled the ball along the ground. Lumpy bowled in the air, controlled the trajectory, and made it land where he wanted it to. When the ball shot or lifted off a length, most batters stood little chance.

Lumpy revolutionized underarm bowling. In David Harris of Hambledon, younger by twenty years and quicker, there was a worthy heir. Their careers overlapped, and Harris developed on Lumpy's work. He would 'bring it from under his arm by a twist, and nearly as high as his arm-pit, and with this action push it' to generate astonishing pace. Underarm bowling would attain great heights over the next few decades, but Lumpy was the one who started it all.

Lumpy also prompted a change to the Laws of Cricket. Playing for All England at the Artillery Cricket Ground, Finsbury, in 1775, he beat the bat of John Small, the first great batter in history and his famous rival, not once or twice but thrice. Every time the ball passed *between the stumps*—there were only two of them, spread wide apart, with one bail on top. The unfairness of it eventually led to the introduction of the middle stump.

It is impossible to tell how many wickets he captured. Scorecards are available mostly from 1772, when Lumpy was thirty-seven and had played numerous matches. When they finally began to score games in detail, some chronicled only the batters and the scores. Then they began to register the bowler, but in case of a catch or a stumping, they recorded only the fielder or wicketkeeper.

In other words, today's 'A caught X bowled Y' was recorded as merely 'A caught X'. Y did not feature at all.

Lumpy, thus, took many more than his recorded 305 wickets (from eighty-three first-class matches). Since the balls bowled or runs conceded by the bowler were not recorded, we do not have an average or strike rate either.

Cricket, however, does celebrate him as the first great bowler and a pioneer on many counts. When Dorset commissioned an 'itinerant painter' called Almond to paint all his house helps in 1783, Lumpy—despite being a Tankerville employee—was among them. This, according to the venerable Rowland Bowen, is the 'earliest known portrait of a man famous only for his cricket'.

Chapter 6

'HERE LIVES JOHN SMALL/MAKES BAT AND BALL/PITCHES A WICKET, PLAYS AT CRICKET/WITH ANY MAN IN ENGLAND.'

Signboard outside John Small's (1737–1826) house and workshop, Dragon Street, Petersfield.

We briefly met John Small in the previous chapter. Small famously hit 138 for Hampshire against Surrey at Broadhalfpenny Down in 1775, not only the first-ever hundred in first-class cricket but, at that point, the highest recorded score in *any* cricket. To achieve the latter, Small went past the 107 by John Minshull (also known as John Minchin), who was on the fielding side that day.

Some sources suggest Small made 136, but the Reading Mercury, *which provides the most complete description of the match, mentions 138.*

If that sounds impressive, it is important to note that Small had made 'more than 140' for Hambledon against Kent in 1768—though it is not clear whether he did it in a single innings or across two innings.

Documentation was scant back then, and often unreliable. Small's first *recorded* match was in 1764, but Derek Birley mentions him playing since 1755. Since scorekeeping became common only in 1772, his first-class record (3346 runs at 16.73) is grossly understated. They also do not include his exploits in the myriad single-wicket or double-wicket or five-a-side matches.

'As active as a hare', Small also prowled at cover or mid-wicket, and the Hambledon captain often consulted his brilliant mind on the field. But Small's legacy is as the first outstanding batter in the history of cricket, and the man who revolutionized batting more than anyone in the sport.

Small was the 'first who turned the short run to account': indeed, sharp singles of the tap-and-run nature were not very popular before him. On the uneven grounds, he 'formulated a method of scoring runs heavily'.

But perhaps most importantly, this 'sure guard of wicket' shaped defensive batting. He was the first to stand upright in his stance while batting. Bowlers of the era (Lumpy and David Harris, in particular) had figured out that pitching on a good length provided an advantage against the hockey-stick-like curved bats that could handle neither bounce nor movement on primitive pitches. Harris's pace and extra bounce made things even more difficult.

So, Small—also a bat manufacturer—carved the broad, straight blade that has remained a constant since. Equipped with this new device, he pioneered the straight-batted defensive stroke. To make drives and pulls more efficient, he also added the 'shoulder' to the bat. Batters edged the ball more than before—with age, Small himself became one of them—but they also scored far more runs.

To comprehend the enormity of his impact, one needs to picture the pre-Small batters: they stood in any way they wanted to with a curved stick, usually made of *a single piece* of ash or cider; then, with scant concept of technique, they scythed hard with little focus on occupying the crease or keeping the scoreboard ticking.

Small changed that. He would not have looked out of place in a cricket match today. His innovation and adaptation also influenced two law changes.

The straight bat made the forward defensive stroke popular, and one can see why. When the bowlers used to roll the ball along the ground, the batters could play as late as possible, from the crease. They did not need to reach out. But now, they began to lunge forward to smother the ball to counter any possible threat.

While revolutionary, this had a pitfall. The batters adopted the 'shabby' practice of thrusting their leg forward and letting the ball hit them. To combat this, the 1774 Laws ruled 'if the striker puts his leg before the wicket with a design to stop the ball, and actually prevent the ball from hitting his wicket by it' as out. LBW was born.

In September 1771, Thomas White strode out to bat for Chertsey against Hambledon at Laleham Burway with a bat as wide as the wicket. Hambledon bowler Thomas Brett wrote a proposal, which was countersigned by Small and captain Richard Nyren. The new law, a direct outcome of the Monster Bat Incident, restricted the width of the blade to 4.25 inches, which stands till date.

After Small came William Fennex, who not only mastered forward play but could also drive the ball. Fuller Pilch would place his front-footed drives wherever he wanted to. The Grace brothers, E.M. and W.G., began to hit across the line. Batting progressed.

The batting stalwarts of the future might have pushed the giant into obscurity, but there is little doubt that when they picked up their first bat, they were merely following John Small's path.

Section 2

Pioneers and Rebels

Chapter 7

'WE WILL NOT PLAY THE THIRD MATCH BETWEEN ALL ENGLAND AND SUSSEX.'

Declaration by Fuller Pilch, Tom Marsden, William Ashby, William Mathews, William Searle, James Saunders, Thomas Howard, Will Caldecourt and Thomas Beagley, 1827.

Well until the late eighteenth century, bowling used to be underarm. Tom Walker of the Hambledon Cricket Club can be credited as the first bowler to try roundarm in the late eighteenth century. In roundarm, the bowler can raise his arm up to shoulder level (think Lasith Malinga, well … almost). It was not encouraged by the authorities.

There were multiple attempts at a revival, most prominently by John Willes of Kent in the 1810s. There are stories of him picking it up from his sister Christiana, who, restricted by her hooped skirts, had to bowl with her arm away from her body. This story is probably not true, for hooped skirts had gone out of fashion by then.

Willes's roundarm attempts in minor matches prompted the Marylebone Cricket Club (MCC) to legislate in 1816 that the ball must be 'bowled (not thrown or jerked), and be delivered underhand, with the hand below the elbow'. The penalty would be a no-ball.

But Willes would not stop. On 15 July 1822, he became the first bowler in the history of first-class cricket to be called for throwing—at Lord's, no less. Willes immediately left the ground 'in high dudgeon', mounted his horse, and never returned to first-class cricket.

All that made for terrific drama, but it also triggered a movement—though like all successful movements, it needed an influential person. Among those who tried to imitate the form of bowling was Jane Austen's nephew G.T. Knight, whose efforts resulted in three 'Experimental Matches' between Sussex and 'England' for 1000 guineas; roundarm bowling would be considered legal for these.

Knight himself played in the series for 'England', but the centre of attraction was Sussex's roundarm stars, William Lillywhite and 'Jem' Broadbridge, who bowled Sussex to a 2–0 lead. After the second defeat, nine 'England' batters (listed above) signed a declaration: 'We, the undersigned, do agree that we will not play the third match between All England and Sussex, which is intended to be played at Brighton in July or August unless the Sussex bowlers bowl fair—this is, abstain from throwing.'

The nonet was no ordinary group. They were some of the best cricketers of the era. Foremost among them was Fuller Pilch, the finest batter until W.G. Grace. It took some convincing from Knight for them to relent. 'England' won the third match, but the die had been cast.

Lillywhite and Broadbridge continued to bowl roundarm even after the series until the MCC relented in 1828, allowing bowlers to release from elbow level. There were cries in the media. John Nyren had no qualms in expressing his extreme opinion on the matter. In *The Young Cricketer's Tutor*, he titled the last chapter 'Protest against the Modern Innovation of Throwing, Instead of Bowling the Balls'. There, his rant culminated in a warning: if roundarm was allowed, 'the elegant and scientific game of cricket will decline into a mere exhibition of rough, coarse horse play'.

It was of no use. The lure of the more potent roundarm was far too strong for it to be not legalized. That finally happened in 1835: 'If the hand be above the shoulder in the delivery, the umpire must call "No Ball".'

But why would bowlers stop at that? Why not run in and release the ball from *above the shoulder level* to generate even more pace? Thus, it was a revolution all over again, with bowlers refusing to abide by even this restriction.

Things peaked in August 1862—John Lillywhite (William's son!) no-balled Edgar Willsher of 'England' *six times* during a match against Surrey at The Oval for bowling overarm. Willsher left the ground in protest with eight other 'England' professionals, though their two amateur colleagues—captain Edward Walker and Charles Lyttelton—stayed put. Play resumed the next day, but only after Lillywhite had been replaced.

Finally, in 1864, the MCC amended Law 10 to legalize overarm, marking what cricket historians often call the beginning of the modern era. Roundarm bowling continued for a few decades—W.G. himself was a practitioner—but cricket would not be the same again.

Chapter 8

'YOU MAY AMPUTATE MY LIMB, BUT DIE I WILL, SOONER THAN LOSE THE WHOLE LIMB.'

Alfred Mynn, August 1836.

Alfred Mynn was a 6 foot 1 man who weighed between 18 and 20 stone (multiply by 6.35029 for kilograms) and believed that 'beef and beer are the thing to play cricket on'. The Lion of Kent, they used to call him.

Coached by John Willes—we remember him from the previous chapter—Mynn was a champion all-rounder of the first half of the nineteenth century. Despite the frame, he could bowl very fast with a roundarm action and could hit the ball extremely hard.

Mynn had arrived at Leicester to play for South (of England) against North, an important match of the times that drew several top names. During the pre-match practice, 'a Leicestershire professional' hit a ball that hit Mynn on the ankle. Lesser mortals would have opted out of the match, but Mynn decided to play.

Before the game, Mynn went to the Anchor Inn, where his ankle was bandaged. South batted first, and it was not until the second morning that he walked out with a runner. He made 21 not out as South were bowled out for 165. Samuel Redgate, one of the finest roundarm fast bowlers of the era, claimed 5 wickets.

North made 110. Despite the condition, Mynn not only bowled but even got 2 wickets. By the third day, his leg 'had swollen alarmingly, and a normal being would have withdrawn from the match', but all that could not prevent him from coming out to bat at one-down and slamming 125 not out in five hours in a total of 314. 'It mattered not what length I bowled him—the better I bowled, the harder he hit me away,' admitted Redgate. An outstanding hundred played in agonizing pain.

But Mynn's teammates underwent emotions of a different nature as the great man returned to the pavilion and removed his trousers: 'The leg, usually the size of Goliath's, was grotesque from swelling and inflammation.' He had to be rushed to the hospital, but how to transport a giant who was unable to move?

They tried a stagecoach—a wagon drawn by horses, usually four—but with an immobilized leg, Mynn could not get inside. Eventually they had to tie him to the roof. After a 100-mile journey on terrible roads, he was finally admitted to Angel Tavern in London. They moved him to St Bartholomew's, where it was deemed necessary to 'amputate the thigh at hip joint'.

Mynn would have none of it. The doctors had to operate on him. It went well. 'When I saw the surgeons enter the room, old fellow, I collected all my thoughts and requested that before they began, they would leave the room for a few minutes so that I might say my prayers,' Mynn admitted to Nicholas Felix the day after the surgery. It went well.

News of the incident spread slowly in that era of archaic communication. The match at Leicester had got over on 25 August, but few were aware when Kent travelled to Brighton to play Sussex from 12 September without their 'Lion'—even though they were led by Alfred's brother Walter. When the news got out, the odds on Kent promptly dropped from 2:1 to 3:2. But by the time Mynn returned to cricket two seasons later, everyone in the cricket fraternity had knowledge of it. It sparked a batting revolution.

Mynn adapted upon his return, though it periodically affected his batting. In 1841, he was bowled by James Dean of Sussex. 'In consequence of the immense padding which he is compelled to wear, to protect his "game leg", he lost his wicket by a ball from Deane [*sic*], striking his pad and turning in upon his wicket,' reported the *Maidstone Journal.*

But he continued to play at first-class level until 1859—and retired as one of the greatest cricketers of the era. William Jeffrey Prouse immortalized him with his lines: 'Proudly, sadly will we name him—to forget him were a sin/Lightly lie the turf upon thee, kind and manly Alfred Mynn!'

Until Mynn's injury, purists used to look down scornfully at leg guards (much like their counterparts did a century and a half later when the first helmets came into vogue). Felix, that great innovator, was probably the first to put them on while batting; Fuller Pilch often used them; but they were not common.

But in the aftermath of the Mynn incident, cricketers began to embrace this curious protective gear. Over time, they became an essential part of the batter's kit. Frederick Gale claimed that Mynn gifted W.G. Grace a pair of his leg guards—the Doctor wore them during his dubious quadruple hundred, of which we shall read more—but this story remains unverified.

By then, leg guards were widely known as pads, just as they are today.

Chapter 9

'THE GREAT MEETING OF THE WHIGS IN CANAL STREET. THE "NATIONAL PERFORMERS".'

New York Herald, 28 September 1844.

By the early nineteenth century, cricket was being played across British colonies, mostly by Britishers posted in faraway lands—India, Australia, Hong Kong, Argentina. But each of the early cricketing hubs were too far away from each other for cricket matches that could be deemed 'international'. It took two countries with a land border to start that.

In the United States, the sport is as old as at least 1709. The Dutch had been playing a game of hitting the ball at New Amsterdam, but there is no evidence of that being cricket. The Americans also invented a cricket spin-off called wicket—a version featuring one-day matches, three innings and thirty fielders that even George Washington played. Even after the US distanced itself from many things British after independence in 1776, cricket remained surprisingly popular.

Meanwhile, in neighbouring Canada, in 1785, cricket was being played in Ile-Ste-Helene, where the Montreal Exposition buildings stand today. There is evidence of cricket being played *on ice* when two ships were trapped near the island of Igloolik in North Canada in the 1820s. In a way, cricket in Canada is older than Canada itself, for the dominion was formed only in 1867.

In 1840, a man called Phillpotts sent out an invitation to the St George's Club in New York for a cricket match in Toronto. The Americans crossed Lake Ontario by steamer and reached the Toronto Cricket Club, only to find that the entire thing had been a hoax.

Nevertheless, the Canadians turned out to be excellent hosts. They hosted their tired neighbours and even arranged a cricket match, on 4 September at Caer Howell in Toronto. The match, played for $250, was accompanied by a brass band. In attendance was, among others, George Arthur, the governor of Upper Canada. The New Yorkers won the match, but the result was incidental.

New friendships had been formed on this tour. In August 1843, two St George's members, on a trip to Canada, met the Torontonians and invited them for a return game. Unlike the accidental contest of 1840, the 1844 match was not a hurried-up friendly encounter.

'The Eleven of the St George's should be *bona fide* members of the Club at the time of the challenge was put forth,' the New Yorkers assured. In their report, the *Anglo American* called this an 'unjust and unfair' deal, as there was no such restriction on Toronto. However, in a subsequent letter, St George's president R.N. Tinson admitted that the club had lost six major cricketers for various reasons.

The Torontonians agreed to be flexible. The match was on. It was billed as 'United States of America versus the British empire's Canadian Province', but it was far from being representational of the entire nations. The Canadian team was essentially members of the Toronto Cricket Club (though some correspondence indicates the possibility of players from Guelph Cricket Club and Upper Canada Cricket Club). The Americans, however, were picked from clubs in New York, Philadelphia, Washington DC and Boston.

This two-day contest, played for $1000 at the St George's Cricket Club ground (in today's Manhattan), was the first international cricket match.

In front of at least 5000 people, the tired Canadians batted first and made 82 and had the USA at 61–9 by stumps. Rain washed out the entire second day's play, and the teams agreed to a reserve day. The USA made only 64 and bowled out Canada for 61 before reaching 58–9.

They needed another 24, but George Wheatcroft, their No. 3, had not arrived at the venue on the final day. He did show up, but twenty minutes after the match had been awarded to Canada. The Americans wanted the game to resume, but it was too late …

Thus began not only the oldest international rivalry in cricket but also in any sport, though the game is not recognized by the ICC. The two countries now clash for the K.A. Auty Cup, though the format switches between multiple days, 50-over and Twenty20.

Chapter 10

'I SHALL PLAY SIDES, STRONG OR WEAK, WITH NUMBERS OR WITH BOWLERS GIVEN, AND SHALL PLAY ALL OVER THE COUNTRY, TOO–MARK MY WORDS–AND IT WILL MAKE GOOD FOR CRICKET AND FOR YOUR TRADE TOO.'

William Clarke to James Dark, 1846.

William Clarke played most of his cricket in the second quarter of the nineteenth century, as an underarm bowler who spun the ball away from the right-hander. He played in an era when many, including his coach William Lambert, were switching to roundarm. But Clarke, a master at using the air and the undulated grounds as well as reading the opposition batters, continued to back his strength.

His 3157 recorded wickets came at only 6.29 apiece. In first-class cricket, he had 797 wickets at 10.32 and took 83 five-wicket hauls in 143 matches. He could bat a bit. Remarkably, he did all this with one eye, for the right eye had been lost to an accident. Clarke batted by sound, not sight, his teammate George Parr would say.

Yet, on-field feats (or founding the Trent Bridge Cricket Ground) were far from being Clarke's greatest legacy. That journey began when, to move away from a dysfunctional marriage, he took a job at the MCC and moved from Nottingham to London.

Here, he understood two things. One, the MCC paid the professionals very less. And two, he was not the only cricketer who thought on these lines. He addressed both by forming his own team, the All England Eleven (AEE), in 1846. The next year, he announced, much to the surprise of MCC proprietor James Dark, that his team would play cricket against anyone who would pay them to.

Clarke was different from the previous private team-owners. A bricklayer's son, he had risen in life through marriage, cricketing skills and business acumen. He was not using cricket to go one-up on fellow earls and barons; he meant business. 'He was the first man to make a fortune out of cricket. He was also the first to see that a fortune was to be made out of it,' wrote John Arlott.

Unlike most teams, the AEE did not have a home ground. Taking advantage of the railways, that new marvel of science, they played everywhere in Britain, even in Edinburgh and Glasgow. It was a nomadic team in the true sense.

This was not a motley crew of inept barons and their staff. We mentioned Parr, but Clarke also got, among others, William Lillywhite, Fuller Pilch, William Caffyn, John Wisden, Nicholas Felix, Alfred Mynn, Joseph Guy, William Hillyer, James Dean, Julius Caesar (his real name: not a pseudonym), James Grundy, Thomas Lockyear—some of the biggest names of the era.

During a match, he was impressed by the fielding of a thirteen-year-old Bristol boy called E.M. Grace at long-stop and gifted him a bat, and his mother Martha a copy of William Boland's *Cricket Notes*. E.M. and his younger brother W.G. would both play for the AEE, albeit after Clarke's death.

Clarke was not merely the owner but also the captain, manager, agent and talent scout of the team. This was common, but what set him apart was that he was their main bowler as well: he claimed 2385 wickets for the AEE alone.

Until this point, the MCC used to control the narratives of the sport, decide the proceedings, and—like today—own the Laws of Cricket. Clarke shook English cricket to its core by taking the game out of London and making it professional.

Clarke was not choosy about hectic schedules or poor playing conditions. It could be a village or two or three villages at the same time. It could be an XI of AEE against an XI, a XVI, even a XXII of local players. Since the money was good, the professionals were happy to move away from the MCC-ruled world of cricket. This is not very different from today's players foregoing internationals for franchise cricket.

In their characteristic pink polka-dotted trousers—contrary to popular belief, cricketers taking the field in whites was not common until the last quarter of the nineteenth century—the AEE were the first true cricket franchise.

But an inevitable problem arose. By 1852, Wisden and Dean of the AEE became unhappy with the way Clarke ran the team, particularly with the substantial percentage he used to pocket. They formed a new franchise, the United All-England Eleven, on Clarke's principles.

Clarke could not stop them from playing, but he managed to come to an agreement that these 'rebels' would never play for or against any of his teams. The two teams did clash on the field—but only after Clarke's death. Since the best professionals in Britain—in the world—were involved in these matches, they were arguably the highest level of cricket. Up to 10,000 would turn up for these matches.

Clarke's legacy outlasted him. In fact, franchises are taking over the world of cricket.

Chapter 11

'IN OFFERING OUR FIRST EDITION OF THE CRICKETERS' ALMANACK TO THE PATRONS OF THE NOBLE GAME, WE HAVE TAKEN GREAT PAINS TO COLLECT A CERTAIN AMOUNT OF INFORMATION, WHICH WE TRUST WILL PROVE INTERESTING TO ALL THOSE THAT TAKE PLEASURE IN THIS GLORIOUS PASTIME.'

Wis*den Cricketers' Almanack*, 1864.

John Wisden was only 5 foot 6, and at the time of debut, only 44 kilograms. But he defied that slight frame to emerge as a much-feared roundarm fast bowler with a lethal off-cutter. Playing for the South (of England) at Lord's in 1850, Wisden bowled all ten North batters—a feat without an encore in first-class cricket.

Between 1852 and 1855, Wisden coached cricket at Harrow, and owned a 'cricket and cigar' shop at 2 Coventry Street with Fred Lillywhite. In 1859, he went on the first-ever overseas cricket tour by an English side, to North America.

Rheumatism ended Wisden's playing days in 1863. Not too long afterwards, the *Bradford Observer* advertised the launch of an almanack on 8 February 1864. Thus began the journey of the *Wisden Cricketers' Almanack.*

This was by no means the first of its kind. MCC scorer and archivist Samuel Brichter's annual records were published between 1791 and 1805—a time when, on an average, only 400 books 'of all types' were published in England every year. Henry Bentley's Correct Account of All Matches 1786–1822 *was published in 1823, and had two supplements. Fred Lillywhite's* The Guide to Cricketers *was still in vogue when the first edition of* Wisden *came out. None of them, however, had* Wisden*'s longevity.*

The first edition was a humble 112-page, paper-bound pink booklet, edited by 'compilers' W.H. Crockford and W.H. Knight. It bore the rather long title of *The Cricketers' Almanack for the Year 1864, being Bissextile or Leap Year, and the 28th of the Reign of Her Majesty Queen Victoria.* From the sixth edition, the apostrophe to denote possession was moved to the end of the second word and it became *Cricketer's.*

It included 'full and accurate Scores of the Matches between the Two Elevens', stripped to the bare minimum, devoid of accompanying reports or explanation; the Laws, 'as revised by the Marylebone Club'; and 'Scores of 100 and upwards, from 1850 to 1863'.

But that was not all. To make up the page count, the almanack accommodated outright random topics. These varied from games like horse racing, rowing, bowls, quoits, knurr and spell; the English Civil War; the trial of Charles I; and even 'The Sikhs defeated at Aliwal by Sir Harry Smith, 1846' and 'Interest due on India bonds'.

Published every year since then, it is the longest-running annual in the history of any sport. No catastrophe—near-liquidation in 1937, two World Wars (including the 1944 fire when a German bomber attacked the headquarters and destroyed its records), COVID-19—has been strong enough to make it skip a year.

This first edition was priced at a shilling. Today, a copy of the same edition costs upwards of £10,000. Collecting Wisden editions, both as cricketana and investment, remains a prestigious, if expensive, cricketing hobby.

Some traditions, like the myriad records and the obituary section, continue to exist. The 1917 edition featured a sombre 106-page 'Deaths in the War' section that Sydney Pardon referred to as 'the Roll of Honour' in his editorial.

Beginning 1889, Wisden began to honour the leading cricketers of the previous English summer. That continues to date. The salmon-pink cover has been replaced by bright yellow, but the size has remained the same. In 1938, the Wisden cover bore Eric Ravilious's woodcut image of two cricketers—this continued until 2003, since when they have used a cricketer's photograph.

Perhaps most significantly, Wisden's stature as the authoritative, independent voice on the sport has helped it earn the moniker of the 'Bible of Cricket', though the almanack itself has never used the phrase.

Chapter 12

'OH, MAKE IT 400.'

W.G. Grace to W. Skelton and W. Wainwright, scorers, on 12 July 1876.

Words on W.G. Grace may fill an entire library, so it is better to come straight to the point. To begin with, not only was he the finest English cricketer of the 1870s, but he was miles ahead of anyone else.

There were several reasons behind this. Grace was the first to play both off the front foot and the back, unlike his 'specialist' predecessors. He was an excellent athlete (the popular photographs of his stout frame are mostly from his later days). His appetite for runs was perhaps matched only by Don Bradman's in later years. And no one travelled as much to play cricket—at least by land—before aeroplanes were invented.

One must remember that he was not merely a specialist batter. In first-class cricket, Grace had 54,211 runs, 2809 wickets and 873 catches. He is fifth, tenth and second on the corresponding charts even today.

Grace topped the runs charts for every season from 1868 to 1877 apart from 1875, when he served at St Bartholomew's Hospital. In 1871, he scored ten hundreds when no one got two. He also made more than twice as many runs as anyone else, as he did in 1876.

In 1876, he made 3669 runs at 59.17, claimed 211 wickets at 16.98, and held 77 catches. In first-class cricket alone, the numbers read 2622 runs at 62.42, 130 wickets at 18.90 and 46 catches. His summer included an eight-day phase when he amassed 839 runs including the *first two* first-class triple-hundreds—a feat made even more astonishing by the heatwave that hit England that year.

No one had ever seen a cricketing phenomenon like that. His runs and wickets, his strapping physique and his generous facial hair made him perhaps the most recognizable face in England of the time. In Victorian England, he was everywhere. He was the face of cricket.

Grace took advantage of his stature to the fullest. He was an amateur—he was a doctor—but he made substantial money from his private team, the United South of England Eleven (USEE). He paid the professionals £5 a match and kept the rest. He invariably had his way when it came to money, and why not? The organizers were known to double the ticket price when he was at the crease! Unfortunately, he also made the most of his power on the field as well. Not all the several anecdotes surrounding him ('They have come to watch me bat, not you, umpire', for example) are established, but the Grimsby incident is well documented.

This was a match against twenty-two locals, all of whom fielded when Grace batted. It did not matter. He did survive a 'plumb lbw' on 6, but that was it. By stumps he was on 130. A telegram arrived for him on the second morning. He had become a father for a second time.

Play was stopped (who would argue with him?). Out came the champagne for everyone. Grace raised a toast to wife Agnes, announced that he would like to break a record, and resumed. By stumps, he was 314. The Hull XI had come to watch the match. During the second afternoon, they asked whether they could lend Grimsby their bowlers. No, said Grimsby.

Grace had already hurt his team's chances of a win (they needed to take 21 wickets per innings), but he continued to bat even on the final day. Naturally, the crowd did not show up.

Not that he cared. He gave a chance on 380 but 'Loco' Clark dropped him. Grace finally left the crease with an hour and a half to go before the scheduled close of the match—but only because the Laws of Cricket forced him to: the USEE were bowled out, for 680, leaving him stranded.

He dragged himself towards the pavilion and asked for his score. They informed him that he had made 399 not out.

In the famous high-pitched voice—it startled many the first time they heard him—he ordered from downstairs: 'Oh, make it 400.'

By then, several Grimsby fielders had climbed into the scorers' cupola. Sam Haddelsey exclaimed, 'Oh, make it 400, he jolly well deserves it!' Haddelsey's teammate Bob Lincoln did not even wait for the scorers: He leant over the scorer, added a single and went on to add, 'This is an absolute fact, and should once and for all settle the vexed question as to whether he scored 400 or not.'

Till date, Grace's score shows as 400 not out and the USEE's as 681 because *the opposition wanted it that way.*

Few things sum up the Grace phenomenon like this incident. This was a man capable of amassing 399 in perfectly legitimate ways on an underprepared surface with twenty-two fielders on the ground. This was also a man greedy enough to bat on for no purpose other than increasing his own score, and someone who had no qualms about bullying the scorers.

A genius with cricketing abilities far ahead of his contemporaries. Yes. A brazen bully. Yes to that too.

Section 3

Tests and Contests

Chapter 13

'THE AUSTRALIANS CAME DOWN LIKE A WOLF ON THE FOLD/THE MARYLEBONE CRACKS FOR A TRIFLE WERE BOWLED/OUR GRACE BEFORE DINNER WAS VERY SOON DONE/ AND GRACE AFTER DINNER DID NOT GET A RUN.'

Punch, 1878.

It had not yet been a century since the First Fleet had arrived on the Australian shores with the British settlers. As the settlers began to spread across the vast continent, so did the sport. By the 1860s, English and Australian sides were touring each each other.

A group of English cricketers had toured Australia in 1876–77. Two of the matches they played were subsequently given 'Test' status. Back home in England, however, all this had little impact. When the Australians came over in 1878, the consensus was that they would never be able to compete against a group of the best English cricketers.

The feeling was fuelled after their tour opener, where Alfred Shaw (11–55) and Fred Morley (8–72) were enough to bowl out the tourists for 63 and 76. Nottinghamshire won by an innings inside two days. Rampant racist remarks ('Why, they bean't Black at all; they're as White as wuz', 'Those three chaps have Black blood in them') were indicative of the general attitude towards the colonials.

When Australian captain Dave Gregory alighted from the train at Nottingham, a man noticed his black beard and skin browned by the Australian sun and remarked, 'Ah, here's one's a 'arf caste any'ow.' 'I hear you're going to play the ni**ers on Monday,' the Reverend Arthur Ward asked A.G. Steel, the English cricketer.

The second match was at Lord's, where the cream of the English cricket fraternity had assembled to watch the tourists play—and lose against—a very strong MCC side. Shaw and Morley, the tormentors from Trent Bridge, were both there.

It had rained before the match. Batting was not going to be easy. W.G. Grace, the greatest cricketer of the era, made only 4, but 'Monkey' Hornby and Arthur Ridley took the score to 27–2. Then Dave Gregrory brought on Fred Spofforth, the first outstanding bowler in Australian history.

In a whirlwind spell of fast bowling, Spofforth routed the MCC for 33. After conceding 2 in his wicketless first over, he finished with figures of 5.3–3–4–6. When the crowd recovered from their shell-shocked stupor, they 'mobbed' Spofforth and Harry Boyle (3–14).

But the MCC could bowl too, especially Shaw (5–10) and Morley (5–31), and the Australians could make only 41. This time Gregory did not delay Spofforth's advent. As he steamed in, the historic ground waited … surely their champion could not fail for the second time in a day?

The first ball zipped past Grace's bat. The second ball took a bail on its way. As the leviathan walked back for a duck, an ecstatic Spofforth 'jumped about two feet in the air and sang out: "Bowled! Bowled! Bowled!"' After the match, he would repeatedly ask his teammates, 'Ain't I a demon?', giving birth to an iconic nickname.

The MCC never recovered from that blow. Even an innings defeat seemed imminent when they lost their first four wickets for one run. Despite avoiding that ignominy, they could make only 19 against Spofforth (4–16) and Boyle (6–3). The Australians lost only one wicket in the chase.

The entire thing was over within a day, though the exact duration varies from four and a half hours to six from account to account. Even after all these years, the match aggregate of 105 runs remains the lowest in a first-class match where all four innings have been played.

Punch parodied Lord Byron's 'The Destruction of Sennacherib' in its entirety to describe this match. The first four lines are in the quote above.

The match did not get Test status (no match on the tour did), much to the dismay of trivia-mongers: George Bailey, who played here for Australia, never played a Test match—but his great-great-grandson of the same name did in 2013–14. Test cricket narrowly missed a cricket connection separated by four generations.

The assignments of 'Test' status to teams was somewhat arbitrary for a long time. Arthur Gilligan (in 1926–27) and Lionel Tennyson (1937–38) led strong English teams to India, but they did not get Test status. However, matches between expatriates and a motley group of English cricketers of varied quality in 1888–89 were recorded as the first Test matches in South Africa. Cricket is full of whimsical allocation of such hallowed status.

Cricket was never the same again. The Australians, especially Spofforth, had established their credentials in England. And in 1878, the opinion of the English cricket fraternity was all that mattered in cricket.

The USA and Canada might have played the first international match back in 1844, but this Lord's game set off cricket between England and Australia, the first great rival nations in the sport.

Chapter 14

'IN AFFECTIONATE REMEMBRANCE OF ENGLISH CRICKET, WHICH DIED AT THE OVAL ON 29TH AUGUST 1882. DEEPLY LAMENTED BY A LARGE CIRCLE OF SORROWING FRIENDS AND ACQUAINTANCES. R.I.P. N.B.–THE BODY WILL BE CREMATED AND THE ASHES TAKEN TO AUSTRALIA.'

Reginald Shirley Brooks ('Blobbs') in the *Sporting Times*, 1 September 1882.

Four years had passed since Fred Spofforth had destroyed the cream of English cricket at Lord's. The Australians had returned in 1880, and again in 1882. There was one Test match on each tour, at The Oval. During the latter, history would be created in more ways than one.

Australia made only 63, but Spofforth (7–46) restricted England to 101. Opening batting, Hugh Massie then made 55 in 60 balls—every run worth perhaps twice as much in a Test match this low-scoring.

Australia were 114–6 when their captain Billy Murdoch played a ball to the leg-side. Wicketkeeper Alfred Lyttelton picked it up and threw it to W.G. Grace at short point. Assuming the ball was dead, non-striker Sammy Jones left his crease to 'garden' the pitch.

Grace ran him out: 'I just taught the young lad a valuable lesson.'

Spofforth, next man in, was fuming even after Australia's 122-run innings was over. He invaded the England dressing-room and unleashed a verbal volley in colourful language. He concluded with 'this will lose you the match' (there are variants of this quote, but the essence remains the same).

Appreciable sentiments, undoubtedly—but defending 85 against England was no easy task. Spofforth knew he would have to replicate his heroics from Lord's 1878. With the team score on 15, he clean-bowled 'Monkey' Hornby and Dick Barlow with consecutive deliveries, but at 51–2, it was England's match to lose.

But Spofforth struck again, and Harry Boyle took out Grace for 32. 'Bunny' Lucas and Lyttelton hung on grimly for nearly an hour, but for a mere 13 runs. Then Spofforth struck four times in quick succession to leave England reeling at 75–8.

It is not clear why Hornby had held back C.T. Studd, the formidable bat, until No. 10. Perhaps it was because Studd was under the weather that day. When his turn came, he had to stand at the non-striker's end, for Spofforth had taken a wicket with the last ball of his over. His match figures stood at 14–90.

Boyle removed Billy Barnes with the second ball. Last man Ted Peate, a rank tail-ender, had to see out the second half of this 4-ball over. He cleared 2 of the remaining 10 runs with a hit to square leg. The logical thing would have been to play out the last ball and leave it to Studd, but Peate went for another hoick and was bowled.

'Mr Studd was so nervous I did not feel I could trust him to score the runs,' he explained.

Nearly a century and a half has passed since, but no team has defended a target as low as 85 in Test cricket. Yet, the legacy of The Oval 1882 runs deeper than the world record, Spofforth's superlative performance, the gentleman who died of tension in the stands that day or the one who gnawed through his umbrella handle.

The media tore into the English cricket team. On 29 August, *Cricket* published a mock obituary of English cricket that ran: 'Sacred to the Memory of England's Supremacy in the Cricket-Field, Which Expired on the 29th Day of August, at The Oval. Its End Was Peate.'

A more famous obituary, by Reginald Shirley Brooks (under his pseudonym, 'Blobbs'), appeared in the *Sporting Times* two days later. It forms the subject of this chapter. This obituary concluded with 'the ashes will be taken to Australia'.

The word 'ashes' (spelt with a small 'a' at this point) stuck, despite the *Sporting Times* being known to thrive on 'its profusion of coarse and scurrilous scraps of tittle-tattle, representing "society journalism" in its most degraded form'.*

When England next toured Australia, in 1882–83, captain Ivo Bligh promised to bring the 'Ashes of English cricket' back home. Murdoch, the home captain, vowed to retain them. When

* Alexander Andrews, 'Chapter XXIII', *Chapters in the History of British Journalism.*

England won that series, Florence Morphy—who later married Bligh—and her friends presented him with a small terracotta urn that Bligh 'always regarded as a personal gift'.

For more than a century, it was believed that the coveted urn contained the ashes of a burnt bail. However, in 1998, Morphy's daughter-in-law confirmed that her mother-in-law had only burnt a veil of hers. While it ruins the story, the version is more believable, for no one had witnessed the burning, and a veil is far easier to reduce to ashes without getting noticed than a bail.

This is the Ashes urn that rests in the Lord's Museum, and whose replica is celebrated by fans of both countries.

More than a decade before the Modern Olympics, the Ashes were underway.

There have been phases when one of the two sides was among the weakest in the world (it held for both sides for a part of the 1980s). Despite the hype around it, the contest is no longer the most outstanding in Test cricket.

On 3 January 2022, Gideon Haigh wrote in *The Times* that the Ashes 'arrogates to itself outsized significance'. He called 'the Ashes as cricket's equivalent of *The Simpsons*, felt by aficionados to have peaked about season ten, but still profitable, and thus continuous, in season 33'.

Yet, despite the advent of the World Cup in all three formats, the Ashes remain the Holy Grail for many fans in both nations.

Chapter 15

'THE MEETING WAS, WE UNDERSTAND, NOT QUITE UNANIMOUS, BUT A MAJORITY WERE IN FAVOUR OF IGNORING DRAWN GAMES ALTOGETHER AND SETTLING THE QUESTION OF CHAMPIONSHIP BY WINS AND LOSSES.'

Annual meeting of county secretaries, 10 December 1889.

Clubs representing cricket teams from counties were there by the nineteenth century, leading to obvious speculations around the 'best county'. Rowland Bowen put the first use of the phrase 'County Championship' to 1837, though there was no concept of an official competition. Teams largely played each other based on mutual consent.

From the 1860s, leading publications began to name the best team of the summer. In the 1870s, the newspapers picked up the idea. In 1873, eligibility conditions for the cricketers became formalized, enabling the players to represent counties by virtue of birth or residence and barring them from switching team mid-season.

Inter-county matches drew massive crowds. Around the late 1880s, bank-holiday matches between Surrey and Nottinghamshire, the two best sides, were 'generating an excitement as great as cricket had ever known'. With a formal structure in place, a full-fledged championship was only a matter of time.

When the secretaries of all counties met in December 1889 to draw up the fixtures for the summer of 1890, the representatives of the eight 'leading counties' mulled over the idea of the first-ever county championship in a private meeting.

While 'not quite unanimous', the consensus was that the champion would be determined by 'wins and losses': every win would fetch a point; every defeat a negative point; and a draw, nothing.

The first County Championship comprised only eight counties. Six of these were major cricketing powerhouses—Surrey, Middlesex and Kent in the south and Yorkshire, Lancashire and Nottinghamshire in the north. They were joined by Sussex, the oldest of the county clubs (founded in 1839); and W.G. Grace's Gloucestershire. Six points from fourteen games—nine wins, two draws, three defeats—made Surrey the first-ever champion.

Until now, high-profile cricketing fixtures invariably featured the upper echelons of society—Eton versus Harrow, Oxford versus Cambridge. Professional leagues, while often superior in quality of cricket, did not have the glamour of these high-society contests. Gentlemen (amateurs) versus Players (professionals) games, the pinnacle of pan-England cricket, was defined by the social divide.

The County Championship did not address this completely. The amateurs and the professionals used different dressing-rooms and gates. It was unthinkable of a professional cricketer to lead a county. Yet, it was English cricket's first approach at bridging the social gulf, albeit an 'illusory' one. The English summer found its most significant contest.

Somerset joined in 1891. By 1921, there were seventeen teams. That count has not changed barring the incorporation of Durham in 1992. Over time, matches have increased in number, then decreased. Three days have become four. The points system has undergone numerous changes. Overseas cricketers joined the fray. Shorter formats found their way to the heart of the summer. The league is now split into two divisions where teams are promoted and relegated.

But for over thirteen decades, the County Championship has defined the English summer, perhaps more than the Ashes, which—despite its international flavour—is not an annual event.

Chapter 16

'YOUNG LADY PLAYERS WANTED ... MUST BE OF GOOD ADDRESS AND APPEARANCE, RESPECTABLE, STRONG, ACTIVE, NOT UNDER 5FT. 6IN. IN HEIGHT OR OVER 22 YEARS OF AGE.'

Advertisement placed by Edward Michel in the *Leeds Mercury*, 1890.

The first recorded women's cricket match was played between Bramley and Hambledon at Gosden Common in 1745. 'The girls bowled, batted, ran and catched as well as most men could do in that game,' reported the *Reading Mercury*. Two years later, Charlton and Singleton clashed with West Dean and Chilgrove in a 'long expected' contest. Delayed by a pitch invasion, this match was extended to the next morning due to crowd trouble.

However, barring the odd game—including one in 1768 played over a barrel of ale and a plum cake—women's cricket remained largely confined to 'high society', on private grounds, not in front of large crowds.

In 1777, John Sackville, the Third Duke of Dorset, did ask, 'Why should not the ladies play it as well as we?' to the editor of the *Lady and Gentleman's Magazine* but his interests were very unlikely to be noble. As Roy Case noted in *The Pebble in My Shoe: An Anthology of Women's Cricket*, Sackville 'liked his women sporty', and his support for women's cricket was 'just one of his many endeavours in assisting women to participate'.

Two years after playing in the first Eton versus Harrow match, Lord Byron—his physical handicap (a deformed right foot) could not curb his enthusiasm for the sport—wrote about 'cricket's manly toil'.

But when the women played, their cricket did invoke interest. In 1811, Hampshire beat the Surrey Heroines in a three-day match played for 500 guineas a side at Ball's-pond, Newington. The wager was placed by 'two noblemen'. A reasonable crowd braved poor weather to show up. The cricketers were between fourteen and sixty (Ann Baker, the oldest, was 'the best runner and bowler' for Surrey, and donned ribbons (true blue for Hampshire, orange and blue for Surrey). In *Skirting the Boundary*, Isabelle Duncan calls this the first women's match between two counties *and* the first where the names of the cricketers were listed.

Unfortunately, these remained one-off contests. Women's cricket became sporadic for two reasons. Duncan elaborates on how the Industrial Revolution resulted in the gradual disappearance of cricket from working-class women, for they were 'too worn out to play cricket by long hours labouring at machines'. At the same time, 'the increasing strict Victorian moral attitudes' prevented the women in the upper echelons from playing the sport.

'The women so far forgot themselves as to enter upon a game of cricket, and by their deportment as well as frequent applications to the tankard, they rendered themselves objects such as no husband, brother, parent, or lover could contemplate with any degree of satisfaction,' reported the *Nottingham Review* in 1833, summing up the mentality of the era towards women playing cricket.

White Heather Club, the first-ever women's cricket club, was founded at Nun Appleton as late as in 1887, but the members were 'mostly Yorkshire ladies with enough money to pay their own expenses'. Women were finally playing *some* cricket, but not professionally.

Then, in 1889, a French-American railway manager called Edward Michel founded the English Cricket and Athletic Association Ltd syndicate, and began to advertise for players who would play exhibition cricket matches in the summer of 1890. He called them the 'Original English Lady Cricketers'.

Michel assured that the cricketers would be 'elegantly and appropriately attired' and his venture would be 'in all respects select and refined'. The applicants needed written consent from parents or guardians, and character references.

The conservative cricket fraternity sprang into action. A syndicated column that appeared in several newspapers hoped that this venture 'will not succeed', for the author believed that 'exhibitions by professional female cricketers and lawn-tennis players will be positively painful'.

None of that deterred Michel. From 200 applications, his syndicate shortlisted thirty and split them into two teams, called (somewhat unimaginatively) the Reds and the Blues, led respectively by Violet Blanche Westbrook of Godalming and

Daisy Stanley of Chetnole. Some players switched between the two teams over time.

Michel left no stone unturned to make his venture a success. He used a part of his £2000 budget to get Surrey professionals like George Hearne and Maurice Read as coaches, and a matron to chaperone the players. But most significantly, the cricketers were professionals: Michel paid them £10 a week during training and between £25 and £30 during matches.

The Reds and the Blues played all over England. Matches started between half past one and two and got over by six, in time for evening activities like 'lawn tennis, fencing, boxing, musical drill, and the "wonderful performing weasels"'*

Fifteen thousand attended the first match, at Liverpool. The official attendances, where known, almost always exceeded 2000. Imitators quickly jumped on the bandwagon. In October 1890, the *Era* ran an advertisement for the Gardiners Original Lady Cricketers. Stanley herself formed the All England Lady Cricketers in February 1891.

There was predictable backlash in an era when *men* playing cricket for a livelihood was frowned upon. Some referred to the Original English Lady Cricketers as 'amazons'. While celebrating upper-class women's matches at country houses as 'quite an institution', the *Graphic* had 'little sympathy' for the women 'who are touring round the country making money out of their skill'.

So rampant was sexism in the era that in 1898 (1897 according to another source), Alfred Reader manufactured a blue cricket ball (the Laws never mentioned what colour the ball should be) at the request of A.W. Gamage Ltd of London, for the women, who might 'swoon' at the sight of a 'blood-coloured ball'. It was discontinued once it turned out to be difficult to see against the sky.

---

* Judy Threlfall-Sykes, *A History of English Women's Cricket, 1880–1939.*

The harshest criticism came from W.G. Grace, the biggest name in contemporary English cricket. 'If the lady cricketers expected to popularise the game among women, they failed dismally ... Cricket is not a game for women, and although the fair sex occasionally join in a picnic game, they are not constitutionally adapted for the sport,' he insisted in *'W.G.': Cricketing Reminiscences and Personal Recollections.* Grace had not been supportive of the cricketing career of even his daughter, Bessie: 'A real good bat, a splendid fielder, and a fair under-hand bowler . . . but as she is now seventeen, her cricket days are over', he had told the *Pall Mall Gazette* in June 1895.

Michel's teams folded after two seasons amidst financial turmoil. The pioneering cricketers, who were not paid their full amounts, remain largely forgotten. But over time, Grace's 'not constitutionally adapted' remark proved to be woefully off target.

Chapter 17

'GIVE ME THE BALL, MR STODDART, AND I'LL HAVE T'BOOGERS OUT BEFORE LOONCH.'

Bobby Peel to 'Drewy' Stoddart, 20 December 1894.

England and Australia had been competing for the Ashes for over a decade. There had been some classic contests, but it was not until England's 1894–95 tour of Australia that Test matches became the centrepiece of cricket.

The first Test, at the Sydney Cricket Ground, has its own place in history, for it was the first time that a team won after following on. Only thrice has this been emulated.

Syd Gregory made 201 and George Giffen 161 in Australia's 586. Giffen then claimed 4–75 and 4–164 to bowl England out for 325 and 437 (they were 296–6 at one point). With only 177 to win, Australia were 113–2 at stumps. With 30 on the board, Giffen was one of the unbeaten batters.

Giffen was as confident as any of his teammates when he woke up, but then captain Jack Blackham broke the news at the Baden Hotel, where they were staying, his face 'as long as a coffee pot': 'It had been pouring half the night, George.'

The English hotel was in a different mood, for their left-arm spinner Bobby Peel was a master on a wet wicket of 'stiff black soil' that dried rapidly as the sun 'shone bright and hot'. Unfortunately, Peel had five teeth extracted before the Test, had had an ordinary game, and really, there was little chance of a win. He lay in his room, stone drunk.

Captain 'Drewy' Stoddart knew it could not be done without Peel. He put the Yorkshireman under a cold shower. A rejuvenated Peel famously announced doomsday for Australia.

In his first over, he 'cut a flake out of the pitch half as big as his hand' when he bowled. Giffen made 41. Joe Darling got 53. But it was never going to be enough against Peel (6–67). England won by 10 runs.

Wisden praised this timeless classic as 'probably the most sensational match ever played either in Australia or in England'. It set the tone for what David Frith called 'the first great Test series'. Blackham refused to be interviewed after this game, during which he had also picked up an injury that brought his Test career to an abrupt end. Giffen took charge mid-series.

England were bowled out for 75 in Melbourne but won by 94 runs and went two-up, but Australia squared the series with massive wins in Adelaide and Sydney. It came down to the decider.

By then, the Test series had captured the imagination of cricketers, media and fans of both nations. Cables were sent to England to keep the fans updated on cricket news. Never before had an overseas series been followed with such fervour in England. There are stories of even Queen Victoria being kept abreast of the on-field proceedings.

As Giffen noted, both captains felt the heat by the time they walked out to the toss: 'He [Stoddart] was as white as a sheet, and I have been told that the pallor of my own countenance matched his.'

The enormous Melbourne Cricket Ground (MCG) was full. Scores and live updates were cabled all over the country. People had been designated to post them up for everyone.

Australia made 414 and England 385. In the fourth innings, England had to chase 297. England were 28–1 when the day's play began, and Stoddart fell first ball. But Jack Brown of Yorkshire strode out to play an innings for the ages. He made 140 in a stand of 210—at that point a world record Test stand for any wicket. Albert Ward stood at the other end with 93, and England won by 6 wickets.

Peel had taken the last wickets in England's first two wins of the series. Here, he fittingly hit the winning runs. In front of the cheering crowd, Giffen choked as he shook Stoddart's hand: 'It's hard to have to congratulate you, Stoddy, old boy.'

Stoddart was hailed as a hero back home. 'Then wrote the queen of England/Whose hand is blessed by God/I must do something handsome/For my dear victorious Stod,' ran the eulogy in *Punch.* His new wax model at Madame Tussauds was 'the talk of the summer 1895 season'.

The 'primacy of Test cricket', now finally and firmly established, would continue for decades.

Section 4

Era of Many Firsts

Chapter 18

'LOOK HERE, NOSS, WHAT YOU NEED IS A TONIC. I OFTEN HAVE ONE MYSELF. I'LL MIX YOU ONE.'

Harry Trott to Frank Iredale, Trent Bridge, 27 June 1896.

Frank Iredale's maiden tour of England seemed headed for a disaster. Eleven first-class matches and nineteen innings later, he had reached 50 only once. He came into this game, against

Nottinghamshire, with 3, 0, 0, 0, 6, 0, 1 in his seven previous innings. After a first-innings 13 here, he was predictably nervous.

The Australians needed only 170 to win the match. Iredale should open, decided captain Harry Trott, and offered him a 'tonic' to soothe his nerves: Iredale returned with 94 not out. Fortified by generous helpings of the 'tonic', he made four hundreds in his next eight innings, including one in the Old Trafford Test match. He was a transformed man. Only much later did Trott admit that he had given Iredale brandy and soda.

This was one of many stories about Trott, the first great Test captain. The mode of his appointment may seem unusual today. As was the norm in Australian cricket back then, the selectors used to choose the squad, but the players voted for the captain. George Giffen proposed Trott's name ahead of the 1896 Ashes tour; Hugh Trumble seconded it; and a 'not eager' Trott accepted the role.

'Probably the best captain Australia ever had,' felt Ranjitsinhji, who played against him in the Ashes. 'The best I have played under,' admitted Clem Hill, another first-timer to England on that 1896 tour like Iredale. Hill himself later led Australia. 'Incomparably the best captain the Australians have ever had,' summed up *Wisden*.

But perhaps the greatest compliment came from the postal department, where Trott used to work as a mail sorter and mail carrier. When other public servants complained about him taking leaves to play cricket, the postal chief reminded them that 'Harry Trott is a national institution'.

Trott revolutionized cricket like few had. Until him, the norm used to be—it may sound bizarre today—to keep bowlers on for as long as possible. In the eight Tests they played together, Charlie Turner bowled 43 per cent of the balls for Australia and J.J. Ferris 39 per cent; the captains refused to take them off. Trott changed that. He understood 'the gruelling nature' of the bowlers' work and rotated them. He also rested bowlers when they had off days. With him, nothing was predetermined.

He used 'match-ups'—albeit intuitively—over a century before the term entered cricket lexicon. 'Time and time again, he got a champion batsman's wicket by putting on a bowler he knew the batsman did not like,' recalled Hill. Indeed, Trott always 'seemed to sum up the exact pace of the pitch' and used his bowlers accordingly.

If a partnership brewed, he kept shuffling his bowlers to ensure the batters did not get set. In the same Old Trafford Test where Iredale got a hundred, Trott realized that an ageing W.G. Grace's footwork had slowed down. Despite being a slow leg-spinner, Trott took the new ball against the wind, dragged Grace and his partner 'Drewy' Stoddart outside the crease, had both men stumped, and promptly took himself off.

Then there were the flexible field placements. Until then, captains often placed their fielders in fixed positions and seldom moved them irrespective of the batter or the bowler. Trott 'seemed to possess a mental chart of the chief strokes and the strong and weak points in each opposing batsman', noted John Corbett Davis in the *Sydney Morning Herald*.

The English cricketers struggled to come to terms with Trott's ahead-of-the-times left-field thinking. 'I like a captain to have a settled plan. He just seemed to do whatever he thought at the moment. Some of our chaps found it rather upsetting,' felt Bill Storer, who kept wicket in five Tests against Trott.

More cultural shock awaited the English cricket fraternity. While the professionals in England were not allowed to address their amateur captains by their names, the touring skipper was 'Trotty' to all.

The Iredale incident was an instance of Trott's exceptional ability to handle his players. He studied their 'whims and fancies' and knew how to get the best out of them. On the same tour, Hill dropped Grace, no less, *off Trott.* The captain ensured it did not affect the youngster: 'Don't let that upset you, son. Everyone on this field has dropped catches.'

Calm, affable, genial with an infectious sense of humour, Trott led Australia to five wins in eight Tests, all in the Ashes. Before the Wars, none of his compatriots had captained in more matches against England with a win–loss ratio better than his 1.667.

He also set templates that captains follow even today.

Chapter 19

'IN ASKING MR RANJITSINHJI TO PLAY, THE LANCASHIRE CLUB UNDOUBTEDLY CAST A REFLECTION ON THE MCC.'

The Field, July 1896.

Kumar Shri Ranjitsinhji had become a phenomenon in England in the 1890s. The nation had seen batters pile on enormous scores at astonishing rates—who better than W.G. Grace?—but such delectable stroke-making was alien to them. The mystique of the East, the royal connections—everything added to the aura.

Ranji had to endure racism in his early days, at Cambridge and Sussex, but most of that was behind him by 1896. His supreme batting abilities, combined with his royal status, ensured that. After all, he was rich enough to play as an amateur.

From his first seven innings in the summer of 1896, Ranji made three hundreds and never got out for under 26. When he got a fourth hundred in mid-June, there were speculations of him making it to the England XI for the ongoing Ashes. The *Leader* (Melbourne) even included him in their likely XI for the Lord's Test.

But that did not happen. MCC president Lord Harris was not keen on 'birds of passage' playing for England. This was hypocritical, as Harris was himself born in St Ann's, Trinidad.

Harris had served as the governor of the Bombay Presidency until the year before. When he left, a collation of newspaper clippings was published with the words 'never during the last hundred years has a Governor of Bombay been so sternly criticised and never has he met with such widespread unpopularity'.

'It is in the matter of patience that I think the Indian will never be equal to the Englishman,' he would go on to write in his 1921 autobiography. A man like that was unlikely to select an Indian for an English side.

The Times near-echoed Harris: 'Although the Indian Prince has learnt all his cricket in England he could scarcely, if the title of the match were to be adhered to, have been included in the English eleven.'

England won at Lord's by 6 wickets. The second Test was scheduled at Old Trafford. As per the prevalent rules, the right to select the XI there was with the Lancashire County Cricket Club and not the MCC. Lancashire did not have a problem with Ranji, who had by then become the first amateur to score a thousand runs in the season.

But Ranji now put forward a condition: he would play only if the Australians agreed. That was sorted out easily: Touring captain Harry Trott assured that he would be 'delighted' if Ranji played. 'If eleven Indians came to England and learnt cricket, and were good enough, the dear old Mother Country might have a coloured English representative team,' he added.

We have met the very likeable Trott in the previous chapter. It is pertinent to mention here that this remarkable stance might have to do with him being the grandson of a freed slave.

So, Ranji debuted at Old Trafford in a Test match we have mentioned in the previous chapter. He made 62 and, after England followed on, 154 not out, the first hundred against the Australians that summer. 'It is safe to say that a finer or more finished display has never been seen on a great occasion, for he never gave anything like a chance,' reported the usually neutral *Wisden.*

There was effusive praise from other quarters as well. Among them was eminent writer and MCC member Home Gordon. This did not go down well with the other MCC members, noted Simon Wilde in *Ranji: The Strange Genius of Ranjitsinhji.* One of whom reprimanded him for praising 'a nigger showing us how to play the game of cricket'. Another insisted he be expelled for 'having the disgusting degeneracy to praise a dirty Black'.

None of that could stop Ranji. He averaged 44.95 across fifteen Tests, including an excellent tour of Australia in 1897–98. He captained Sussex; and eventually retired with nearly 25,000 runs in first-class cricket.

But Ranji's significance was more than that. A number of Parsis had played cricket for about half a century before him, but he was the first face of Indian cricket—perhaps Indian sport—outside the nation.

Of course, none of that convinced Harris. In 1906, four years after Ranji had played his last Test match, Harris observed that 'Indians have a good eye and rather long arms, but do not possess the patience and resolution of the Anglo-Saxon'. One doubts if even Sunil Gavaskar or Sachin Tendulkar, both of whom have held the world record for most Test runs at various points, would have broadened his narrow visions.

Chapter 20

'IT SOON OCCURRED TO ME THAT IF ONE COULD PITCH A BALL WHICH BROKE IN A CERTAIN DIRECTION AND WITH MORE OR LESS THE SAME DELIVERY MAKE THE NEXT BALL GO IN THE OPPOSITE DIRECTION, ONE WOULD MYSTIFY ONE'S OPPONENT.'

Bernard Bosanquet, writing in the 1925 *Wisden Almanack* about an 1897 incident.

Few expected South Africa to compete in the 1905–06 home series against an Ashes-winning England. The tourists, however, should have looked at their defeat against Transvaal more seriously. Chasing 176, they made only 115 against Reggie Schwarz (5–34) and the greatest all-rounder of the era, Aubrey Faulkner (3–62). Schwarz had also taken 4–80 in the first innings and Faulkner 3–46.

Schwarz and Faulkner, leg-spinners both, were among the five South African debutants in the first Test match of that series, at Johannesburg. Two others were Bert Vogler and batting all-rounder Gordon White. Both bowled leg-breaks as well.

South Africa won a Test match for the first time. It had taken them thirteen Tests and sixteen years to achieve this. In fact, they thrashed England 4–1. Schwarz returned 18 wickets at 17.22, Faulkner 14 at 19.42, Vogler 9 at 22.23 and White 2 at 15.

Let us take some time out to understand this. Most Test teams hesitate to pick two leg-spinners in a Test XI; South Africa used four of them to win their first-ever Test series (though White was really picked for his batting). That was because all of them had mastered a novel craft: the googly.

England had no clue against this innovation, popularized—if not pioneered—by Bernard Bosanquet, one of their own. Schwarz had learnt this craft from him.

Born in Kent, Schwarz had migrated to Johannesburg to work as Abe Bailey's secretary. He was part of a side that Bosanquet led to North America in 1901. The duo then clashed during South Africa's 1904 tour of England. In his greatest season, Bosanquet put the googly to great use to claim 132 wickets at 21.62 (to go with 1405 runs at 36.02).

At Lord's, Bosanquet took 9–107 to bowl out the South Africans for 194. Schwarz did not get a wicket, but Bosanquet's sorcery caught his eye. Until this point, he was a batter who bowled some leg-spin, but now he decided to give it a shot.

Against Oxford, Schwarz got 5–27—all bowled. He followed that with 5–48—all bowled or leg-before—against Middlesex, Bosanquet's team. He finished the tour with 65 wickets at an impressive 18.26. More significantly, he brought the googly home.

The googly might have been new to Schwarz, but it had debuted in the County Championship in 1900. Playing for Leicestershire, the *left-handed* Samuel Coe had made 98 against Middlesex at Lord's. He was facing Bosanquet, once a bowler of genuine pace but now a practitioner of leg-breaks.

Bosanquet tossed the ball up. Coe stepped out to cash in on what he clearly thought was a gift, but the ball landed, *went the other way*, beat Coe's bat, and—in Bosanquet's own words—*bounced four times* on its way to wicketkeeper William Roberts. So stunned was Coe by this that he forgot to return to the crease—and was duly stumped.

'The incident was rightly treated as a joke, and was the subject of ribald comment, but this small beginning marked the start of what came to be termed a revolution in bowling,' Bosanquet recollected.

Was this the first googly in history? Perhaps not, but it is unanimously accepted that Bosanquet's dismissal of Coe was the first instance in professional cricket.

Bosanquet had been practising the googly for three years before that dismissal. While playing twisti-twosti, a game in which the player would bounce a tennis ball on a table to ensure the opponent at the other end could not catch it, he had accidentally discovered how it worked in 1897. He had also figured out that the one-two trick, of a leg-break followed by a googly, 'would mystify one's opponent'.

He moved on from the tennis ball at twisti-twosti to the soft ball at stump-cricket to the cricket ball. During Oxford's matches in 1899, he would demonstrate it at the lunch intervals—as a party trick.

After conquering Coe, he tried his new trick outside England. He had fond memories of the first googly bowled in Australia, to a well-set Victor Trumper: 'Two leg-breaks were played beautifully to cover, but the next ball (delivered with a silent prayer), pitching in the same place, saw the same graceful stroke played—and struck the middle-stump instead of the bat!'

While 'googly' and 'wrong 'un' are the commonly used phrases, Bosie (or Bosey)—named after the man who made it mainstream—remained in vogue for years.

Chapter 21

'A CRICKETER IN FRANCE IS A STRANGER IN A STRANGE LAND LOOKED UPON WITH MINGLED AWE AND CONTEMPT BY THE AVERAGE FRENCHMAN.'

A contemporary journalist, 1900.

The first international match could well have been England versus France. In 1789, two years after they were founded, the MCC arranged a tour of the country 'in conjunction with' the Duke of

Dorset, then Britain's ambassador in Paris, and the Duke of Leeds, then the Foreign Secretary. The English cricketers even travelled to Dover. However, before they could begin their voyage across the English Channel, they met the Duke of Dorset; he had been fleeing from the French Revolution.

More than a century after this, Baron Pierre de Coubertin considered cricket for the inaugural edition of the Modern Olympics, at Athens in 1896. Cricket was listed in the *Des Jeux Olympiques de 1896*, the provisional programme for the event, published in January 1895. Had cricket been played in 1896, it would have followed the *les règlements* (the regulations) of the MCC; it would also have been the only team sport that year. Unfortunately, there were not enough entries.

The Paris Olympics of 1900 was not exactly flooded with entries either. Of the four teams, Belgium and the Netherlands withdrew. And the British and French teams were not quite full-strength either.

Of them, the French team bore a more 'official' look. All member clubs of the Français de Sports Athletiques formed the selection pool, but the cricketers were really chosen from the Union Club and the Standard Athletic Club, formed in 1890 by British expatriates who had been working on the Eiffel Tower. Philip Tomalin, their captain, was the main driving force behind the match.

Elsewhere, Harry Donne had founded the Devon and Somerset Wanderers, also known as the Devon County Wanderers, 'almost exclusively from Castle Cary Cricket Club and alumni of Blundell's School in Somerset'. It was a group of amateurs whose selection often depended on 'who could get a fortnight off from work'.

They were on a tour of France at this point, to—among other things—play cricket. They ended up playing as Great Britain. They had two first-class cricketers, Montagu Toller, 'a well-built

Devonian', and Alfred Bowerman, in a contest featuring 'distinctly average club cricketers'. Donne himself played as well.

It was a blessing that their opponents were Englishmen (though there was one F. Roques), for they struggled with the language throughout the tour. At least one Great Britain cricketer ordered '*café au lait* with milk'.

The two-day match was at the 20,000-seater Municipal Velodrome de Vincennes, where the banked cycling track 'formed an unusual boundary' in front of a sparse crowd. To add to the list of oddities, the sides added an extra player. This was a decision so last-minute that the scorers had little option but to write the additional names on the pre-printed scorecards by hand.

Despite the informal nature and the quality of the cricketers, this *match de cricket France contre Angleterre* was hyped up through 'posters and handbills', though these did not mention the word 'Olympics'.

As for the match, Great Britain made 117 and 145–5 declared and bowled out France for 78 and 26. For the winners, Frederick Christian claimed 7 wickets in the first innings, as did Toller in the second, for 9 runs. A contemporary journalist noted that the French were 'too excitable to enjoy the game' and could not be 'persuaded to play more than once'.

The aftermath was more interesting than the game. After being awarded medals and miniature Eiffel Tower replicas, the cricketers took the coach back to the hotel, only to find the driver was too drunk to drive. The replacement driver was intoxicated as well, but he still took charge. Predictably, the coach crashed. Thankfully, no one was seriously injured.

To add to the surreal nature of the contest, neither side was aware of the enormity of having won Olympic medals. For that, they had to wait until 1912, when the International Olympic Committee compiled the list of events for the five editions.

Despite there being no international cricket in 1900, the authorities never assigned this match first-class status (Test status was perhaps unthinkable). However, it is worth mentioning that cricket was not the only sport where a club won the gold medal for Great Britain at the 1900 Olympics. Upton Park Football Club won it in football (here, too, they beat Club Français—a French side—in the final), and the Osborne Swimming Club of Manchester in water polo.

Cricket has since been part of the Commonwealth Games at Kuala Lumpur 1998 and Birmingham 2022, and at the Asian, South Asian, Southeast Asian, African and Pacific Games. However, it is not until Los Angeles 2028 that it will make a reappearance at the Olympics.

Chapter 22

'HOW THE DEVIL CAN YOU PLAY A BALL THAT COMES AT YOU LIKE A HARD THROW-IN FROM COVER-POINT?'

Sammy Woods, 1901.

It is not clear exactly when bowlers figured out that they could move the new ball in the air. Left-arm *underarm* bowler Noah Mann Sr of Hambledon was an expert of 'swerve bowling' in the 1770s and 1780s. The chief exponents in the roundarm generation were two left-armers: Edmund Hinkly of Surrey and Kent; and Frank Allan, who played a Test match for Australia in 1878–79.

As a craft it was not in vogue, but the legalization of overarm bowling in 1864 opened a world of possibilities. By the end of the nineteenth century, bowlers in three continents had, perhaps independently, taken notice of this curious phenomenon.

Bart King of Philadelphia was perhaps the first truly great bowler to master it. By then, the US had drifted towards baseball, reducing the once-popular cricket to pockets around Philadelphia. King was the greatest cricketer to have emerged from the nation.

King knew how to swerve a ball from his early baseball days. He figured out that 'under certain unpredictable conditions the ball would respond, and suddenly swing in at an angle or tangent to the flat trajectory of my fast ball'. He also discovered that a new, shiny cricket ball, while favourable, was not necessary for this movement.

King's biographers Stephen Musk and Roger Mann dispute baseball's role in this in Bart King of Philadelphia. *Among their reasons was the timeline: Overarm pitching in baseball became legal in 1887, only two years before King switched to cricket: 'Bart deserted baseball before pitching made significant progress into an aggressive science and, as a result, it is not certain how many "transferable skills" baseball would have been able to offer him.' At the same time, it can be argued that two years is substantial in an athlete's short career.*

The impact of baseball notwithstanding, King studied these 'unpredictable conditions' using a 'trial and error method'. He noticed that wind and weather assisted the movement of the cricket ball in the air. He then found the ideal run-up, and the role of the wrist and fingers.

Yet, not only did King ace the swerve but he also learnt how to hide his grip. His most devastating ball swerved into the right-hander. They used to call it the angler back then. Today, we would have called it the inswinger.

When a strong Australian side toured the US in 1896, the Philadelphians beat them by an innings. King claimed 8 wickets, and the Clark brothers, Percy and Walter—both pacers—shared the rest. 'It was the fact of their bowlers playing us with baseball curves that upset our batsmen,' confessed George Giffen.

King toured England with the Gentlemen of Philadelphia in 1897, 1903 and 1908. After the first tour, *Wisden* wrote about how he made 'the ball swerve in the air in the manner of the baseball pitchers'.

It is worth a mention that Fred Spofforth had almost certainly mastered the swerve in Australia before King. However, unlike King, Spofforth used it sparingly, for it 'sometimes affected his length'. Besides, he also questioned that 'swing bowlers would not be just as successful if they did not swerve at all'.

However, it was the legendary Yorkshireman George Hirst who made the swerve popular. Hirst's all-round skills made him an asset to even a very strong Yorkshire side, but he was predominantly a batter. With the ball, he was at best an accurate seamer. Between 1896 and 1900, he had taken 394 wickets at 25.12. But in the summer of 1901, he unleashed the swerve and claimed 183 wickets at 16.38.

As astonishing as the numbers was the impact he had on the batters. 'The most technically gifted batsmen were reduced to impotence and could make no more of this queer business than their own tail-enders,' noted A.A. Thomson in *Hirst and Rhodes*.

England had seen the swerve before. Walter Wright (Nottinghamshire and Kent) and John Thomas Rawlin (Yorkshire and Middlesex) could both 'impart this then curious flight to a new ball'. Australian captain Billy Murdoch had a long stint for Sussex. At best a part-timer, he never bowled in Australia, but in

England, he was 'used sometimes to bowl two or three overs at the beginning of an innings on account of his peculiar gift'.

None of them used the swerve to devastating effect. Perhaps only Albert Trott, another Australian who played in England, did that to some extent ('took a great many wickets with a swinging yorker'). But barring King, none of them wreaked havoc like Hirst. If we go by Thomson, Hirst's swing was 'more deadly and more frequent' than even King's.

Hirst finished with 2742 wickets at 18.73 in first-class cricket to go with his 36,356 runs at 34.13. This included twenty-four Test matches. When he claimed 9 wickets in his final series, the 1909 Ashes, *Wisden* remarked how he 'was making the ball swerve in his most puzzling fashion being masterly'.

Hirst was determined to not divulge the secret behind the swerve ('Sometimes it works and sometimes it doesn't,' he maintained). Neither did he like being at the receiving end of it. In 1911, Frank Foster of Warwickshire repeatedly hit Hirst on the thigh with his left-arm swerve bowling. Hirst responded by threatening to throw his bat at the youngster.

But the craft caught on, and Hirst's role behind that is undeniable. Today, it is one of the best friends of the new-ball bowler. We call it 'swing' now.

Chapter 23

'IF HE HAD POSSESSED THE ENTHUSIASM FOR THE GAME … HE MIGHT HAVE MADE A NAME FOR HIMSELF, HIS NATURAL GIFTS AS A BOWLER BEING SO REMARKABLE.'

Sydney Pardon, *Wisden Almanack*, 1903.

Among all bowlers with 150 Test wickets, Syd Barnes still has the best bowling average (16.43). One may argue that he used to play in a different era, but he claimed a mind-boggling 7 wickets per Test match. Some still hesitate to leave him out of all-time World XIs.

It is difficult to classify Barnes the bowler. He bowled fast-medium, but he could also bowl off-breaks and, without using his wrist, a ball that turned from the leg to the off. The 'Barnes Ball', they used to call the last one. Was it the leg-cutter or an early *doosra*? When David Frith met him in the 1960s, Barnes said, 'I spun it', with all conviction. He was a pacer-spinner, perhaps, then.

Barnes could also extract steep bounce and vary pace without visible change of action; he could move the new ball in the air; and his accuracy was legendary. Arguably the greatest fast-medium-paced bowler of all time, he would have been a superstar even today. Yet, that was not the only thing that made him stand out.

Barnes played only 133 first-class matches across thirty-six years (including a thirteen-year gap), of which only 20.3 per cent were Tests. For perspective, among all English cricketers to have played twenty-five Tests before the Wars, Test matches did not amount to even 9 per cent of their first-class careers.

This leads to two obvious questions. Why did Barnes play so little domestic first-class cricket? And given that he did, how did he hone his skills?

Between 1894 and 1896, he played only four times for Warwickshire. He preferred playing for Rishton in the Lancashire League, which offered a better financial deal. This was bold, for this was an era when the County Championship was the inevitable stepping stone towards professional cricket.

But Barnes chose a job that paid more, including a bonus for five-wicket hauls, for less work. Of course, the batters were inferior. In club and league cricket, he had 4069 wickets at a ridiculous 6.03, and he could play until sixty-five. But the level of cricket was certainly enough for him to retain his skills.

So good was Barnes that he was picked to tour Australia in 1901–02 despite having played virtually no county cricket. He had impressed England captain Archie MacLaren in the nets.

Once there, Barnes took 19 wickets at 17 apiece in three Tests: he bowled only 7 overs in one of these.

Then he played for Lancashire, taking 226 wickets across two seasons at 19.41. But he returned to the Lancashire League, this time to play for Church. One can see why. While Lancashire paid him £3 a week, Church offered twice as much for playing only on Saturdays. On the other days, he played for Staffordshire in the Minor Counties Championship (1441 wickets at 8.15).

This did not go down well with many in the establishment. How could one turn his back on the County Championship, the centrepiece of the English summer, the supposed great unifier of amateurs and professionals? The national selectors stopped picking him for the Test matches. After a lone outing in 1902, he had to wait until England's 1907–08 tour of Australia to play Test cricket again.

'We don't understand you. You only play when you like,' Lord Hawke once told him. *Wisden* editor Sydney Pardon, who considered league cricket a 'menace', was not happy either—though he had to acknowledge Barnes's immense skills.

Not that Barnes cared. He was making money. And so devastating was he as a bowler that he could not be ignored after a point. They had to recall him to the Test side. When England won the Ashes in Australia in 1911–12, he took 34 wickets at 22.88. In next summer's Triangular Tournament at home, he added another 39, at 10.35.

On the matting wickets in South Africa in 1913–14, he had 10–105, 17–159 (still the second-best match haul), 8–128, 14–144 in the first four Test matches. The 49 wickets remain a record for a series to this day. He then requested the authorities to pay for his wife's accommodation during the fifth Test. When they refused, Barnes opted out of the match.

One of the greatest bowlers of all time was never picked for England again. He was past forty-seven when Test cricket resumed after the War, but he troubled international sides long after that. At fifty-five, he took 12–118 against the touring West Indians *for Wales*. At fifty-six, he claimed 19 wickets in two *first-class matches* against the South Africans.

As Don Bradman plundered runs in England in 1930, the desperate selectors considered recalling Barnes, thirty-five years older than Bradman, for the decider at The Oval. That did not happen, but Barnes finished the summer with 89 League wickets for Rochdale at 8.22.

Had he played in the County Championship, Barnes would have played more than the 27 Tests that he did. He would have been celebrated for the legend he was. After all, he played in an era when stalwarts of the County Championship became icons despite having ordinary Test careers.

But Barnes chose to secure his future, and the authorities invariably had a problem with that. Over a century later, cricketers are still criticized for following that path.

Chapter 24

'THERE'S NO REASON IN THE WORLD WHY YOU SHOULDN'T GET THE JOB.'

Monty Noble to Bill Ferguson, December 1904.

Bill Ferguson had a mundane day job at the Sydney Directory. He wanted to travel. He knew that the Australian national cricket team travelled a lot, but he also knew that he was not good enough to make the cut. So, he applied for the roles of baggage master and scorer for the touring party to England for the 1905 Ashes.

He first prepared an application. Next, he visited a clinic in Macquarie Street and requested the dentist to fill, cap, extract—

basically do anything if it allowed him to spend time there. He spent a fortune on gold fillings, but he could spend hours talking to the dentist. When Ferguson spoke of his ambition, the dentist assured him.

The dentist was none other than Monty Noble, one of Australia's greatest cricketers and captains. He introduced Ferguson to Frank Laver, the manager for the tour, and Victor Trumper, the superstar of the side. Ferguson applied to Laver. He was on board for a salary of £2 a week and train fare to the grounds. If they did not like him, they would terminate the contract after a week.

Much to his father's chagrin, he quit a 'secure' job, paid £17 for his way to England, and embarked on one of the longest, most illustrious careers in the history of cricket.

But before that, it is important to mention Johann Gottlieb Jackschon, who began his scoring career in the late 1880s, and received a medal from Lord Sheffield for his solo scoring effort in the Sydney Test match of 1891–92. Reports of the match mentioned balls faced by several batters.

Here is how he summed up Trumper's 101 for New South Wales against Victoria in 1905–06: 'Victor received 67 balls only. He played 61, missed six, 18 fours, two threes, four twos, and nine singles. He made 51 off 28 balls from [Jack] Saunders, 19 off six from [Frederick] Collins, 16 off 12 from [Frank] Laver, 9 off 15 from [Arthur] Christian, and 6 off 6 balls from Tom Warne.' Information at this level would not have looked out of place in the computer era.

For centuries, cricket scorers used to count only the runs scored by the batters and *how long* they batted, with scant mention of *how many balls they faced*. In a monograph in the winter 2015 edition of *Between Wickets*, legendary cricket statistician Charles Davis, an authority on ball-by-ball scoring, cited several sources that establish Jackschon as the pioneer of balls-faced data in Australia.

Richie Benaud and Bill Frindall have both mentioned English scorer John Atkinson Pendlington using the linear scoring method during a match between C.I. Thornton's XI and the touring Australians at Scarborough in 1893. During the match, he presented his method to W.G. Grace.

The linear scoring method is different from the conventional scoresheet. Here, a batter at the crease is assigned a column, and every over a row; this makes it easier to compute the balls faced by batters as well as head-to-head records between batters and bowlers.

Davis argues the claims of Benaud and Frindall for lack of sufficient evidence. Indeed, until 1994, there was no mention of Pendlington barring 'an unidentifiable article' in a newspaper in 1914. On the other hand, there is little doubt over Jackschon—who predated Pendlington—chronicling balls faced by batters.

We shall now turn to Ferguson, who improved on linear scoring. It is not clear whether he improved on Jackschon, but Ferguson did chronicle the balls faced by the batters—though they 'rarely made it into print'. His successors in Australia did not use it. In England, scoring methods 'would not modernise' for decades. As late as in the 1980s, official MCC scorecards lacked the parameter.

Today, it is considered among the most important parameters in cricket analytics.

But that was not all that Ferguson did. Cricket historian B. Sreeram noted that during the 1905 Ashes, the *Manchester Guardian* published diagrams of the cricket field, noting every scoring shot played during every major individual innings. Today's wagon wheels, in other words. These diagrams became more detailed over the course of the series, but they did not bear the identity of the chronicler.

This was also Ferguson's first tour of England. Over the years, he maintained numerous wagon wheels, but as Davis explains, the *Manchester Guardian* diagrams were probably not his work. The nameless statistician's diagrams featured concentric circles for every possible scoring shot (1, 2, …). Ferguson never used them. The English diagrams stopped appearing after 1906.

Wagon wheels appeared in Australian newspapers during the 1907–08 Ashes as well, but these were different from Ferguson's style. In fact, there is no evidence of him using them before The Oval Test match of 1912—a fact corroborated by English scorer Keith Booth.

What Ferguson did was to take wagon wheels—they were called Ferguson's Charts back then—to an astonishing standard. He did everything manually, but such was his accuracy that Douglas Jardine and Don Bradman, two of the finest cricketing brains, were among those who sought his help. He maintained charts for Test matches, Sheffield Shield and Grade Cricket. Cricketers of all levels dug into his charts to analyse their errors.

That he did everything all by hand makes Ferguson's legacy even more remarkable. In 1948, King George VI asked Ferguson whether he used 'an adding-machine' when Bradman batted. Ferguson did not need to.

His reputation convinced other boards (England, South Africa, and in 1946, India) to invite him to score in Test matches *not involving Australia.* In all he scored in 208 Tests. The only time he was perhaps flustered was during the 1939–40 ten-day Test at Durban, when his scorebook had reached its last five pages, and a replacement could not be found!

In 1951, he was awarded the British Empire Medal for services to cricket. In the twenty-first century, Davis used Ferguson's scorebooks to build his databases.

But scoring was only one half of the Ferguson legacy. A baggage handler for Australia on forty-three tours spanning more than five decades, to England, South Africa, New Zealand and the West Indies, he had the distinction of not losing or misplacing a single piece of luggage.

'A wizard at his job,' admitted Bradman. 'There will never be another to compare with him.'

Chapter 25

'INTER-RIVALRY WITHIN THE EMPIRE CANNOT BUT FAIL TO DRAW TOGETHER IN CLOSER FRIENDLY INTEREST ALL THOSE MANY THOUSANDS OF OUR KINSMEN WHO REGARD CRICKET AS THEIR NATIONAL SPORT.'

Abe Bailey to Francis Lacey, 1907.

Abe Bailey was a Randlord—one of several South Africans who controlled gold and diamond mining in the country. He was one of the richest men in the world, and famously crossed the Equator more than a hundred times. An active politician, his real interest was in sports—boxing, horse racing, fox hunting, pheasant shooting and cricket. He even played first-class for Transvaal, though in Bailey's time, cricket in South Africa was run like a private club of British expatriates.

He was also a staunch imperialist who dreamt of establishing his beloved South Africa in the Mother Country. For that, he knew South Africa had to make a mark in the supposedly British sport. At only twenty-four, Bailey had witnessed South Africa being thrashed by England in 1888–89. 'We must set ourselves to beat the Englishmen on equal terms,' he had told Bernard Tancred, the best South African batter.

Bailey worked hard on his promise. He appointed the legendary English bowler George Lohmann as Transvaal coach. In 1902–03, he assured the reluctant Australians £2000 for a month-long trip; they played Test cricket in South Africa for the first time.

His role in establishing South Africa as the third force in world cricket is undeniable. We have seen how their googly bowlers spun South Africa to their maiden Test and series win, against England at home in 1905–06. When some South African cricketers cited financial reasons to pull out of the return tour, in 1907, he paid them £80 per head.

The tour went ahead, and South Africa won seventeen matches and lost four. Bailey wrote to MCC secretary Francis Lacey later that year: he wanted to form a committee with the three Test-playing nations and launch an 'Imperial Contest' between them in 1909.

This 'contest' did not take place, for an Ashes series had already been planned for that summer, but Bailey's wallet ensured a meeting featuring representatives of the three teams during the Lord's Test match. They formed the Imperial Cricket Committee—the earliest form of the ICC.

Being part of the British empire was a mandatory condition for being an ICC member at that point. The ICC retained its name until 1965 before switching to the International Cricket Conference. In 1989, they became the International Cricket Council.

All that does make Bailey come across as a very rich visionary with a keen interest in cricket, but that was only part of the story. The US used to be a strong team back then. The Gentlemen of Philadelphia, especially their superstar fast bowler Bart King, had impressed in England the previous summer. They won four and lost six first-class matches, a record better than most South African sides and even a couple of Australian sides on tours of England. They were not invited to the ICC.

Neither were India, although the Parsees had toured England in 1886 and 1888, beaten touring England sides in the early 1890s, and held their own against the European cricketers based in the nation. India had also produced Ranjitsinhji. Also snubbed were the West Indies, who had impressed on their England tour of 1900 and had again toured in 1906.

Bailey, you see, was a bigoted racist. In an ESPNcricinfo article in 2006, Gideon Haigh mentioned that Bailey called the Asiatic population 'the white ants of South Africa, destroying the foundations of our institutions and the roots of the livelihood of the white race', and believed that South Africa should 'not allow any Native to take the place of any White man'. He was all 'for the white race being on top of the black'.

It is worth a note that neither England nor Australia minded any of this. Rowland Bowen described that as 'an early illustration of the power of South African gold in influencing policies in Britain'.

The first ICC was thus a league of three White nations, all part of the British empire. By the time India and the West Indies were inducted in 1926 (along with New Zealand), Bailey had moved away from the ICC.

Bailey should be credited with the formation of the ICC and elevating South Africa to the highest level. At the same time, this enabled South Africa to enjoy full membership status despite playing only the White nations—England, Australia and New Zealand—until they were banned in 1970. He built a legacy, but one that enabled the abnormal.

Chapter 26

'YOU'VE BEEN ASKING FOR A PUNCH ALL NIGHT AND I'LL GIVE YOU ONE.'

Clem Hill to Peter McAlister, 3 February 1912.

Cricketers have fought with the administration for years. Indeed, why should cricket be any different from other sport? Yet, few tussles have been as ugly as the Big Six Incident of early 1912.

England were touring Australia that summer. The series stood at 1–1. As captain, Clem Hill was also part of the three-member Australian selection committee. Ahead of the third Test, Hill cabled to the other selectors, board members Peter McAlister and

Frank Iredale: he wanted Charles Macartney and Jimmy Matthews for Bill Whitty and Roy Minnett.

A left-arm spinner who had taken 11–85 in the Headingley Test of 1909, Macartney had been focusing on batting for some time. The last time he played a Test, against South Africa the previous summer, he had scored 137 and 56—but had been left out of the first two Tests. Hill wanted him for Minnett, who had made 90 on debut but failed in the second Test.

It was a fair call, but McAlister responded with an astonishingly rude cable: 'If Iredale agrees with you as to Macartney's inclusion, I favour yourself standing down not Minnett.'

The ridiculousness of this suggestion needs to be understood. The leading run-scorer in Test cricket at the time, Hill—the first truly outstanding left-handed batter in international cricket—would hold that world record for another twelve years. In the first Test, he had made 46 and 65. He was in form.

On the other hand, the board had appointed McAlister selector and treasurer ahead of the 1909 Ashes tour. The latter was a new post, for it was customary of the manager to deal with expenses, and Frank Laver—we shall return to him—had already been named manager for the tour. McAlister had not stopped there. Despite his limited playing abilities (and being forty years old), he had named himself vice-captain on that tour.

McAlister's telegram successfully 'galvanized' the cricketers. Hill called a meeting where he invited every team member (except Warren Bardsley: 'too cosy with the board'). The players stood behind their captain. There would be a protest, of course, but the youngsters should not be jeopardized. Instead, it should be led by six 'certainties': Hill, vice-captain Warwick Armstrong, Victor Trumper, Vernon Ransford, Hanson Carter and 'Tibby' Cotter—the Big Six.

For the match, Hill managed to get Matthews in the team but not Macartney. Minnett got 38 runs and 2 wickets as England won by 7 wickets to go 2–1 up in the series.

But the Australian cricketers had more on their minds. For the upcoming 1912 tour of England, the cricketers wanted Laver again, but the board did not like him. They had asked for his accounts once the team had returned from the 1909 tour. When Hill requested an independent audit of Laver's books, William McElhone, chair of the board, had simply said: 'It is not a question of books: it is a question of Mr Laver having been disloyal to the board.'

The board appointed George Crouch as the manager instead. When the topic had come up on the eve of the second Test, board treasurer Henry Rush had simply said, 'It will be unnecessary for them [the players] to appoint a manager.' When board member Justin Foxton reminded him of Regulation 9, Rush had responded with, 'Oh, we swept Regulation 9 away last night.'

Unfortunately for the board, the entire episode had become public. The cricketers already knew how the board was set on curbing them. Now, after the third Test, the Big Six signed a petition, demanding Laver's appointment. It ended with, 'Failing compliance with our requests, we have to inform you with much regret none of us will be available for selection or to play if selected.'

The board did not budge. Secretary Sydney Smith Jr responded: 'While the Board is anxious at all times to send the best team possible, still, at the same time, I am sure it will not permit any number of cricketers to dictate the terms and conditions on which a visit is to be made, or if a manager is appointed the terms and nature of his engagement.'

One must remember that this response came at the back of McAlister's disrespectful telegram. The cricketers had had a strained relation with the board for some time; the proverbial straw finally broke the camel's back. On an overseas tour, they would now not get a manager they could be comfortable with; they would have to contend with a board's man.

It was under these circumstances that the selection committee met at Sydney six days before the fourth Test. Neither Hill nor McAlister bothered to act in a civil manner.

McAlister had a go at Hill's leadership over the last two Tests. 'The Australians wouldn't have gone to England under you,' Hill snapped back.

'I am a better captain than you and Trumper put together. You are the worst captain I have ever seen,' responded McAlister.

Hill had had enough. He threw a punch at McAlister. The two men then flung themselves at each other. Iredale and Smith tried to separate them, and even had to restrain Hill from hurling McAlister out of the third-storey window.

Once they could be separated, Hill resigned on the spot as selector and stormed out of the room with McAlister yelling, 'Come back and fight, you coward.'

'Very few blows were struck. It was more like a wrestling match,' ran Iredale's version to the press. 'Mr Smith and I did our best to part them, but they were all over the place, and when the big table was upset, I was pinned in a corner. It lasted about twenty minutes. Hill, who was using his weight, would bore in on McAlister, who was bleeding profusely.'

Incredibly, the meeting went on. They did not pick Macartney, but for some reason, retained Hill as captain. After a standing ovation at the toss, Hill made only 22 and 11, and in the final Test, 20 and 8. England won both to take the series 4–1. Recalled for the fifth Test, Macartney scored 26 and 27 and got a wicket.

Crouch went as manager for the 1912 tour of England. All six cricketers withdrew from the tour despite a barrage of letters from the fans to the newspapers (some even attached cheques to fund their trip!). Without the Big Six and with a manager they did not want, Australia had a predictably disastrous tour on the field and off it. Once back home, Crouch 'lodged a scathing complaint' against some of the players. The animosity was mutual.

Hill, Trumper, Ransford and Cotter never played Test cricket again. Bright's Disease claimed Trumper in 1915. Cotter was killed during the First World War. Carter played Test cricket for a year after the War, and at first-class level for some time after that. Armstrong, however, continued to torment the Australian board and the English cricket fraternity for some time.

Chapter 27

'NINE TESTS PROVIDE A SURFEIT OF CRICKET.'

Daily Telegraph, 1912.

Abe Bailey had proposed a triangular tournament for the English summer of 1909. That did not happen, but when the ICC was formed, they included Bailey's idea in their first-ever Future Tests Programme (FTP).

This FTP would cover two cycles—from 1909 to 1913 and from 1913 to 1917. Every team would tour every other team once during the cycle. And there would be triangular tournaments in

1912 and 1916, where every team would play three three-day Tests against every other team. Rival boards would share revenue for every Test.

The three Tests between England and Australia would also be contested for the Ashes.

Since the ICC had only three members at this point, it was technically the first-ever World Cup. It was a great idea on paper, but as we saw in the previous chapter, Australia went without the Big Six (see Chapter 26). The cricketers who went fell out with the board-appointed manager, George Crouch.

South Africa, on the other hand, arrived without Percy Sherwell, their captain, and Bert Vogler, a major practitioner of the googly, their main strength. Among the ones who toured, many struggled, for the matting wickets back home had not prepared them for the wet English summer.

Even England appointed forty-year-old C.B. Fry, who had not toured Australia the previous winter, as captain. Fry was a man of curious ideas. During a tournament of this length, he met the selectors only once.

But what really spelt doom was the weather. The summer of 1912 was the wettest since 1766. Two of the three Anglo-Australian Tests—the marquee events—were hit badly. The Lord's Test did not reach a third innings on a pitch Fry criticized as 'pure mud', while only 13 overs were bowled in the second innings at Old Trafford.

England won three of their first five Tests. Australia, two. South Africa were thrashed in five of their six matches—two by an innings, two by 10 wickets, and one by 174 runs. They drew the other because it rained.

It was then decided that the last Test, England versus Australia at The Oval, would be played 'to a finish even if it takes a week'. They even announced a tie-breaking Test in case Australia won.

England made 245 amidst rain. Australia reached 90–2 before Syd Barnes (5–30) and Frank Woolley (5–29) shot them out for 111 on a pitch 'better suited to water polo'. Fry then made 79 out of England's 175 as Gerry Hazlitt took 7–25. England needed only a draw, but they went a step better: they bowled out Australia for 65 in 22.4 overs as Woolley claimed 5–20 and Harry Dean 4–19. The anticlimactic end summed up the tournament.

There were minor highlights. In the tournament opener, at Old Trafford, Australian Jimmy Matthews did the hat-trick in each innings of the Test against South Africa. Poor Tommy Ward, Matthews's third victim in each innings, remains the only batter to register a king's pair on Test debut. Interestingly, Matthews never played Test cricket after the tournament, but Ward kept wicket in twenty-three Tests.

During the second Australia–South Africa Test, at Lord's, George V became the first reigning monarch to watch Test cricket. But even that could not inspire any interest.

The tournament was largely a disaster. The Tests, especially the three Australia–South Africa clashes, generated little revenue.

The organizers tried their best with the three neutral matches. They scheduled the Old Trafford Test on Whit Monday and the Trent Bridge Test on the August Bank Holiday, but to no avail. Few neutrals wanted to watch cricket between a depleted side and an underperforming one.

The tournament yielded £12,463 4s. 2d. After the expenses were paid for, the Australians received £2986, the South Africans £1878 10s., and the MCC £4465 16s. 2d (the England Tests obviously generated more revenue). The tourists earned less than they had on some previous tours.

In his *Wisden* editorial, Sydney Pardon was sympathetic towards the organizers: 'The Fates fought against the Triangular Tournament. Such a combination of adverse conditions could hardly have been imagined ... The result is that the experiment is not likely to be repeated for many years to come—perhaps not in this generation.'

It was prophetic. Cricket had to wait until the 1973 Women's World Cup for the next multi-nation tournament.

Chapter 28

'I THINK THE TIME HAS ARRIVED WHEN THE COUNTY CRICKET SEASON SHOULD BE CLOSED.'

W.G. Grace's letter, published in the *Sportsman*, 27 August 1914.

Archduke Franz Ferdinand, heir presumptive to the Austro-Hungarian throne, and his wife were shot dead by an assassin in Sarajevo, Bosnia and Herzegovina on 28 June 1914. Soon, Austria-Hungary declared war on Serbia. Russia backed Serbia.

Germany supported Austria-Hungary. France pledged support to Russia. Germany invaded Belgium for easy access to France.

Belgium sought support, citing the 1839 Treaty of London that bound Britain, France and Germany to protect their neutrality in war. Britain declared war on Germany and Austria-Hungary. The Great War (later known as the First World War) was in motion. Every fit man was summoned to the front. Normal activity came to a halt.

There were calls for cricket to be abandoned. The army took over The Oval in July, but cricket limped along through August, though there was little interest. The people did not care for cricket anymore. The *Kentish Express* did not mince words: 'It will be a relief to everyone when this fiasco called county cricket comes to an end. The people don't want cricket, won't have cricket.'

'No good purpose can be saved at the moment by cancelling matches,' felt the MCC, even as the players were being summoned to the front (in all, 210 first-class cricketers fought in the Great War).

Then, on 27 August, *the Sportsman* published a letter from W.G. Grace, no less: '… it is not fitting at a time like this that able-bodied men should be playing cricket by day and pleasure-seekers look on …'

Two days later, Field Marshal Lord Roberts told a thousand volunteers of the City of London Regiment: 'I respect and honour you more than I can say. My feeling towards you is one of intense admiration. How very different is your action to that of the men who can still go on with their cricket and football, as if the very existence of the country were not at stake…'

The MCC responded with a statement which spoke of how 'the continuation of first-class cricket [was] hurtful to the feelings of a section of the public'. The tone-deafness of the message was evident in the use of 'a section of'.

Francis Lacey was the MCC secretary during this time. 'The committee felt that any tendency towards scare or morbidity should be resisted and an outward show of "carrying on" was allowed,' he would admit years later, in the 1931 *Wisden.*

Four matches began on 31 August. In one of these, Gloucestershire could field only ten men (Alf Dipper had already enlisted). Two of the matches ended in two days, and a third on the third morning. The fourth, between Sussex and Yorkshire at Hove, ambled to tea on the last day amidst lack of enthusiasm before being called off as 'the men's hearts were barely in the game'.

At the MCC committee meeting on 9 November that year, Surrey would be declared champions for a points percentage of 74 per cent. Few cared.

Colin Blythe, who headed the wickets chart that summer, was killed by shrapnel during the Battle of Passchendaele three years later. One of the greatest ever Kent cricketers, he was only thirty-eight.

Major Booth (his name was Major) of Yorkshire had been a Wisden Cricketer of the Year in 1914. In July 1916, he was hit by a shell on the Somme and died in the arms of Yorkshire colleague Abe Waddington. Waddington survived the war, but the incident tormented the feisty fast bowler for the rest of his life.

Percy Jeeves of Warwickshire was killed at High Wood near Montauban-de-Picardie in the same Battle of Somme. He never played a Test, but Plum Warner had predicted great things about him, and it was him that another Plum—P.G. Wodehouse—had named his iconic character after.

'Batting so remarkable and individual as his, has not been seen since Ranjitsinhji and Trumper first delighted the cricket world,' *Wisden* had written of Kenneth Hutchings of Kent in 1907. At thirty-three, he was killed by an artillery shell at Ginchy.

Reggie Schwarz and Gordon White had played key roles when South Africa had beaten England in 1905–06. Schwarz died at forty-three at Etaples of a Spanish flu epidemic a week after the Armistice of 1918. White, thirty-six, wounded at Khan Jibeit near Jerusalem, had died in Gaza three weeks before him.

'Tibby' Cotter, that express Australian fast bowler and part of the Big Six (see Chapter 26), was thirty-three when he was killed at Beersheba, Israel. There are multiple 'conflicting stories' about how he died, which his biographer Max Bonnell has evaluated and was unable to arrive at a conclusion: 'Choosing between these stories involves more than weighing up the evidence: it means who you want Tibby Cotter to be.'

In 1899, thirteen-year-old Arthur 'A.E.J.' Collins had scored 628 not out for Clark's House against North Town. It remained the highest score in recorded cricket until 2016. At twenty-nine, he was killed in action in Ypres. Norman Callaway had scored 207 on first-class debut in the last Australian season before the War. He was summoned before he could play another match. At twenty-one, he was killed in action at Bullecourt, Pas-de-Calais.

Hardit Malik, the first Indian to fly as a pilot with the Royal Flying Corps in the World War, lived to tell the tale. Having played five times for Sussex before the War, he made an appearance in 1914 and continued to play in the Lahore Tournament for both the Sikhs and the Hindus.

But perhaps the most astonishing story was of Middlesex cricketer Harry Lee, part of the 13th battalion that suffered casualties at Aubers Bridge. His corpse could not be found; he was presumed dead; and his parents held a memorial service. But Lee was there, in no man's land, a bullet having fractured his left femur. The first stages of gangrene had set in. The Germans sent him to Valenciennes in a cattle train where he lay on a sack of straw in near-unbearable pain before finally transferring him to a Red Cross train. He somehow survived this ordeal, but one of his legs became permanently shorter than the other. Yet, he was back to cricket by 1917. In 1930–31, fifteen years after his parents had held his funeral, he made his Test debut, against South Africa.

Wisden saw a spike in sales as anxious parents and loved ones searched frantically for obituaries. They did not honour five cricketers in 1916 or 1917 and named schoolboys in 1918 and 1919. Cricket was played in Australia, New Zealand and India, but in England, it was mostly restricted to war fundraising games and school matches.

After the Armistice, the Australian soldiers who had fought in Europe formed the Australian Imperial Force Touring XI and played forty-six matches across Britain, South Africa and in their home country. Some from this side—Herbie Collins, Jack Gregory, 'Nip' Pellew, Johnny Taylor, Bert Oldfield—went on to become household names.

The County Championship resumed after the War, but England, hit far worse than Australia, took longer to recover. At cricket, they lost the next two Ashes series 0–5 and 0–3.

W.G. Grace did not survive the war.

A younger Grace would almost certainly have been at the front, but the great man had aged. He had lost his daughter, Bessie, and a son, Bertie. He was not the champion cricketer of his youth anymore, full of vigour and abundant energy.

Grace accepted an invitation from Archie MacLaren and Alec Hearne for a fundraising cricket match. Too unwell to play, he walked around the ground with his younger son, Charles, with a collecting box in hand.

The relentless German air raids on England took a toll on him. On 9 October 1915, he suffered a stroke while working in the garden. Four days later, the Germans targeted Woolwich Arsenal. Grace grew more agitated. He was spotted shaking his fist at the Zeppelins.

He died of a heart attack on 23 October. He is not listed as a World War victim.

Section 5

Giants and Trailblazers

Chapter 29

'THE MORE YOU PLAY THIS GAME, THE MORE YOU WILL FIND OUT THAT YOU WILL BE GIVEN OUT MANY TIMES WHEN YOU ARE NOT OUT AND VICE VERSA.'

Warwick Armstrong to Arthur Gilligan, 1921.

John Arlott had defined 'Australianism' as a 'single-minded determination to win … within the laws but, if necessary, to the last limit within them'. No one embodied this more than

Warwick Armstrong. He would have made Steve Waugh's 'mental disintegration' seem almost juvenile.

Before all that, it needs to be mentioned that Armstrong was among the surprisingly few Australian world-class all-rounders. He made 2863 Test runs at 38.68 and took 87 wickets at 33.59 despite missing out during the First World War years. In first-class cricket, he averaged 47 with the bat and 20 with the ball.

The methods were ugly. His leg-breaks seldom turned. Sometimes he would wheel away for hours with nagging accuracy. His batting was laboured, even awkward. All that fit into his image, for he demonstrated that great cricketers need not be attractive in an era when writers used to wax eloquent about amateurish aesthetics. Gideon Haigh called Armstrong 'the first modern cricketer'.

At 133 kilograms (140, according to some), he was one of the heaviest international cricketers. The boat-like shoes (32 cm x 18 cm) matched the tent-like shirt (85 cm x 26 cm). The Big Ship, they called him. This did not affect his cricket. He bowled 733 overs on his final tour and took exactly 100 wickets, at 14 apiece. He also scored over a thousand runs at 42, which was also his age at the time.

He led Australia ten times across two series, both Ashes, at home in 1920–21 and in England in 1921. In the first, Australia recorded the first-ever 5–0 sweep. In the second, they won the first three Tests and drew the other two. On that England tour, they did not lose to any of the counties either.

Armstrong remains the only captain to stay undefeated in a career of ten or more Tests. But with him, more than the *what*, it was more about the *how*.

He had been a nuisance on the 1909 tour of England, long before he became captain. At Leeds, Jack Hobbs set off for a run, slipped, dislodged a bail, left, realized midway that he had completed the stroke before the act, asked the umpire and was ruled not out.

The Australians protested ('The chief offender was Warwick Armstrong who got very nasty and unsportsmanlike'). Two balls later, Charles Macartney bowled a straight delivery. Hobbs simply stood there holding his bat and was bowled middle-stump ('I did not know whether I was standing on my head or my heels,' Hobbs would later admit in *My Cricket Memories*).

Armstrong's gamesmanship had managed to ruffle one of the most unflappable batters of all time.

At The Oval, debutant Frank Woolley walked out to bat for the first time in Test cricket. Armstrong bowled trial balls down the side of the pitch—these used to be legal—for several minutes. At least one of these ran to the boundary behind the wicketkeeper. Everyone waited until it was returned. 'It was rather a trying time for me, especially as it was my first Test innings,' admitted Woolley. He made only 8.

Between 1909 and the Great War, Armstrong took on the Australian administrators. He argued with the Victoria Cricket Association (VCA) over payments and was forced to apologize. As we have seen, he was part of the Big Six of 1912.

The VCA sacked Armstrong and asked Arnold Seitz, 'a stooge at a gerrymandered player's vote', to lead Victoria, but named Armstrong stand-in captain *for one match* next season. Armstrong demanded a full-time role. The VCA refused. Armstrong resigned *after the first session.* The VCA gave in next season, 1914–15, and Armstrong promptly led Victoria to their first title in seven seasons.

All that was before the war. When cricket returned, so did Armstrong, now older and bulkier, to bully England. Initially elected captain for one Test, he left a mark straight away. While awaiting his turn to bat, he sat padded up in the members' bar, sipping whisky with his friends. He then scored 158.

When Australia toured England, rain reduced the Old Trafford Test to two days. On the first, England declared their innings at 5.50 p.m.. According to Law 54 back then, teams could not declare inside the last 100 minutes of day one of a two-day match.

When wicketkeeper Hanson Carter pointed this out, Armstrong's eyes probably lit up in glee. He sat on the pitch, waiting for the Englishmen to return. When they did, Armstrong, who had bowled the last over, bowled the one after the commotion as well. Illegal, of course, but the umpires never noticed. Later, when asked whether it was deliberate, Armstrong merely 'smiled and looked away'.

He refused to declare against Kent despite a 439-run lead. He was not going to entertain the crowd: 'There's a Test coming on and I'm not overworking my bowlers for anybody.' Kent president Lord Harris commented that he would be 'very happy to see ten of the Australian team again'.

In the Oval Test, he asked his part-time bowlers to bowl whenever they wanted to and retreated to the boundary, ostensibly showing no interest. The barracking had as much impact as 'a peashooter on the Great Pyramid'.

He probably thrived on booing. Once, he was about to throw a ball in a Sheffield Shield match when a spectator shouted, urging him to 'throw it in'. Armstrong walked slowly to the slips and softly lobbed the ball back to the bowler.

Against Sussex, Jack Gregory thought he had edged a ball and walked. Non-striker Armstrong asked the umpire and recalled Gregory, who then smashed 53. Fielding captain Arthur Gilligan criticized Gregory for not playing 'the right game'. Armstrong used the quote of this chapter to explain how it evened out in the long run.

Walking after being ruled not out is a curious cricketing concept, started—according to Derek Birley—in English county cricket by the amateur captains who would 'set their honour code above the authority of the humble umpires'. It was not as common in Australia or even in the league cricket in north England.

The English did not take to him too kindly. They were shaken by him, his antics. 'Hard-bitten', 'grim' and 'pitiless', they called him and his team. But he got a hero's welcome back home. Even Prime Minister Billy Hughes hailed this 'king of sport', comparing him to Julius Caesar.

Chapter 30

'GILLIGAN PROMISED TO STATE OUR CASE WHEN HE RETURNED TO LORD'S.'

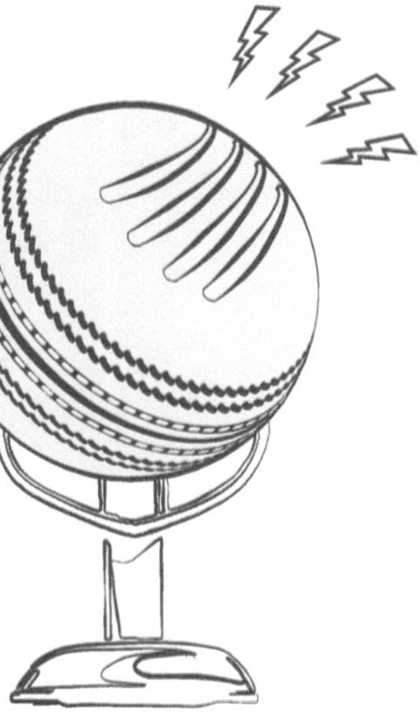

Anthony de Mello, referring to a conversation in early 1927.

Throughout the book, I shall refer to the community as the 'Parsis', the standard spelling today, instead of the colonial 'Parsees'. However, I shall use 'Parsees' while referring to the team.

There was a fundamental difference between the early all-India cricket teams and other contemporary national representative sides. Australia, South Africa and New Zealand were dominated by cricketers of European origin. The West Indies did include Black cricketers, but the White Europeans called the shots. The Indian team, on the other hand, consisted solely of native cricketers.

The first reference to cricket in India was in 1721, by one Clement Downing. The Parsis of Bombay were the first Indians to play cricket. They were also the first from the nation to tour England, in 1886 and 1888.

They fared poorly on the tours, but at home, they soon began to defeat English teams. When G.F. Vernon brought a side over in 1889–90, the Parsees were the only side to beat them. When Lord Hawke brought a stronger unit in 1892–93, they beat them too. That same season, they defeated a team of Europeans based in India.

M.E. Pavri was a Parsi star of the era. In the first of the two matches against the Europeans, he took 2–3 and 7–34; and scored 21 in a chase of 77. In the second, he had 2–18 and 6–36. A fast bowler, he had 275 wickets at 15.04 in all recorded matches. He also played once for Middlesex, in the 1895 County Championship.

The second contest between the Parsees and Europeans triggered the annual bilateral Presidency match between the Parsees and the Europeans. With the Hindus joining in 1907–08 and the Muslims in 1912–13, it expanded to the Bombay Quadrangular—for years the premier Indian tournament. A fifth team, The Rest, would be inducted in 1937–38.

Despite the growing popularity of the sport in the nation, Indian cricket could not earn respect. On the 1911 tour of England, an All-India team won two, drew two and lost ten first-class matches. With 75 wickets at 20, Palwankar Baloo was their hero on that tour. Baloo's struggles extended beyond on-field hurdles: he had to battle the curse of untouchability to earn a place in a representative national XI.

The ICC, a three-member White-only club since 1909, invited the West Indies, New Zealand and India to their 1926 meeting.

There, they assured to extend membership to 'governing bodies of cricket in countries within the Empire to which cricket teams are sent, or which send teams to England'. That winter, Arthur Gilligan led an MCC squad to India.

At this point, India did not have a cricket board. Despite the odd victory against touring sides, the illustrious career of Ranjitsinhji, and the advent of Duleepsinhji, India were yet to impress the global cricket fraternity. All that changed on a December morning at Bombay Gymkhana later that year.

Gilligan's team had been undefeated in all twelve first-class matches on the tour till then. Now, against the Hindus, they put up 363. C.K. Nayudu walked out at 67–2. And mayhem followed.

Nayudu lofted Stuart Boyes on to the roof of the pavilion, and twice more into the adjacent tents. He had also hit three fours by then. Ewart Astill dropped Nayudu—and paid a heavy price. Nayudu's next four sixes, the last two off consecutive balls, were off Astill.

Against Maurice Tate, the best English bowler, he hit only fours. His idea of caution, perhaps. But two consecutive balls from Bob Wyatt landed on the roof of the Gymkhana. Another six came off Jack Mercer.

Nayudu blasted 153 in 100 minutes with thirteen fours and eleven sixes—a world record for most sixes in a first-class innings at that point—much to the jubilation of the crowd, who poured in as the news spread like wildfire. When he fell, the English cricketers, and even the umpires, applauded his strokes.

That one innings changed Indian cricket like nothing before or after. 'His polished display of batsmanship was one of the best I have ever seen,' felt Gilligan.

At the same venue a few days later, the MCC made 362 and reduced the All-India XI to 180–5 when D.B. Deodhar, a professor of Sanskrit, drove and cut with panache to carve out 148 in four hours to put the home team in the lead. The ice to Nayudu's fire.

On the same tour, Gilligan spoke on the lawns of Roshanara Club, Delhi. His audience included the Maharaja of Patiala, captain of the 1911 side and the sponsor of the ongoing MCC trip; R.E. Grant Govan, a Delhi-based business owner and founder of the club; and Grant Govan's employee, Anthony de Mello.

Impressed by the performance of the Indian cricketers, Gilligan promised to speak to the MCC about a return tour. Following this, he requested the Indians to form their own cricket board.

In December 1928, the BCCI was founded at the Roshanara Club with Grant Govan as the first president and de Mello the first secretary. Five months later, the duo represented India at the ICC. They invited South Africa to tour India in 1929 and planned an England tour in 1931. The former was called off—South Africa refused to play non-White nations, and the ICC kept looking the other way—while the latter got pushed back by a year.

From there, it took the BCCI less than a century to establish itself as the most powerful cricket board in the world.

Chapter 31

'A MICROPHONE WILL BE INSTALLED IN THE PAVILION AT LEYTON.'

Radio Times (BBC), 14 May 1927.

In 1922, the New South Wales Cricket Association arranged a benefit for Charles Bannerman. During this match, they gave Len Watt, a grade cricketer and reporter, a microphone and asked him to 'go on talking' about the match at the Sydney Cricket Ground (SCG). Watt is usually accepted as the first cricket commentator.

The concept caught on. By 1924, a boot-polisher in Melbourne, equipped with 'a small headset for the benefit of his patrons' ran the advertisement: 'Shine, Sir? With the cricket result thrown in!'

Sydney radio station 2BL got Monty Noble and Watt for the 1924–25 Ashes. Clem Hill and Hyram Marks were subsequent additions. They narrated 'occasional passages of continuous play'. The reception—pun intended—was excellent.

The *County Life Stock and Station Journal* (Sydney) interviewed several people for opinions. One Mr McDonald of the Imperial Hotel provided some inputs about the frequency (yet again, pun intended) of the updates: 'He got the progressive results of the first and second Test cricket matches every half hour' on a 'five-valve set, single wire aerial, 50 ft high running N. E. and S. W'.

During a match between an Australian XI and The Rest in 1925–26 at the SCG, Watt commentated for the Sydney-based 2FC using, to quote Geoff Tibballs from *No-Balls and Googlies*, 'a microphone suspended from the boundary fence'. This was billed as 'unique ball-by-ball commentary'.

The BBC began their sports telecast on 15 January 1927, with a rugby match between England and Wales at Twickenham. This was covered by Captain Teddy Wakelam. Next was an Association Football match between Arsenal and Sheffield at Highbury a week later. On 25 March, they covered the Grand National from Aintree. On 2 April, the Varsity Boat Race. And on 23 April, the FA Cup final (Cardiff City versus Arsenal) from Wembley.

Amidst all this, on 1 April, the *Guardian* had reported that the BBC wanted to add cricket to their programme. The lukewarm interest did not discourage them. They got on board fifty-one-year-old Frank Gillingham, a temporary chaplain during the Great War, *still* an active Essex cricketer, and 'an after-dinner speaker with a wonderful sense of humour'.

Two days after the FA Cup final, the BBC announced that it would cover the match between Essex and the touring

New Zealanders at Leyton. Gillingham would be on air from 2.10 to 2.20 in the afternoon, followed by four other five-minute instalments, and a round-up at 6.45. The London Radio Dance Band would fill in the gaps, but Gillingham would interrupt them to break major updates 'at any period when play is especially interesting'.

Print media was apprehensive. The *Manchester Guardian* felt that it 'would be boring in the extreme'. The *Telegraph* found it 'difficult to see how else such a broadcast could be made thoroughly interesting'.

In a long piece, the *Radio Times*, the BBC's own publication, described what the listeners would expect, but even they assured that they 'will not have to sit through descriptions of maiden overs and wait while the batsman sends to the pavilion for his cap'. The *Daily Herald* went a step further by frivolously wondering whether chess and billiards would not be more exciting to broadcast on the wireless.

But Gillingham exceeded all expectations. On 11 June, Plum Warner covered a match between Middlesex and Nottinghamshire at Lord's from the top of the Clerk of Works office. Soon enough, Warner emerged as the first-choice commentator for matches at both London venues.

On 3 July, he covered the third day of the Oxford–Cambridge match at Lord's as a car waited outside. As soon as the match got over, he rushed to the Oval for Gentlemen versus Players. By the end of the summer, the BBC's local stations had also joined in.

By the time Don Bradman arrived in Australia in 1930, anyone with a headset could follow the cricket. By then the legendary Howard Marshall had arrived as commentator with his famous mantra ('Paint a picture and keep it the right way up').

Radio coverage reached unprecedented levels during the Bodyline series of 1932–33. The French station Poste Parisien put up Australian cricketer Alan Fairfax studio *in the Eiffel Tower.*

Match updates were cabled to him. Fairfax 'mounted a synthetic condensed "commentary" on the day's play, crammed in two hours', starting at 6 a.m.

Alan McGilvray, Vic Richardson, Hal Hooker and Noble improved on this from a Sydney studio when Australia toured England in 1938. Artificial crowd noises were played in the background, and a pencil was used to hit wood to imitate the sweet sound of a perfectly timed ball. The BBC broadcast England's 1938–39 South Africa tour in both nations with E.W. Swanton as commentator.

Over the years, Richardson and former England captain Arthur Gilligan formed a very popular on-air duo, Arthur and Vic.

When entertainment became expensive after the Second World War, fans often queued outside radio shops to catch live commentary. The BBC launched 'Test Match Special' in 1957.

In the same decade, All India Radio launched Hindi, Tamil and Bengali commentary depending on states, while continuing with English. They also tried Marathi for a while, but that did not work out. Radio Pakistan began Urdu commentary in 1978, while Sri Lanka launched Sinhalese in 1963.

One did not need to know English to listen to cricket anymore. Nor, as we will see, to play the game—despite the snobbish observations of Neville Cardus regarding the indispensability of the language.

Chapter 32

'I DID SOME HARD THINKING, AND NOT ONLY SOME THINKING, BUT SOME ACTING TOO. I SET TO WORK AT MY CRICKET.'

Learie Constantine, early 1928.

In the nineteenth century in the Caribbean, prestigious jobs remained beyond the scope of the non-White population, while the White minority occupied the high ranks at workplaces. The Whites often owned industries and fields, and until a time, *people*.

Then came cricket. The two classes combined to form representative cricket teams from the West Indies, though there was a well-defined division. The Whites were almost always batters, while the fast bowlers were invariably Black. And a Black captain was unthinkable.

An all–West Indies team did reasonably well on the England tour of 1900. They began with four defeats on the trot but lost only four more matches on the tour and won five. Lebrun Constantine, whose grandfather and father-in-law were slaves, made the first hundred by a West Indian on English soil. Charles Ollivierre got the most runs, and Tommie Burton and 'Float' Woods the most wickets. All four were Black.

On the next visit, in 1906, they won seven and lost ten—better than most South African and some Australian touring sides to England. It was on this tour that Burton 'was sent home after refusing to carry out menial duties for white members'. He could not find employment back home and had to emigrate to Panama.

The 1923 tour is considered 'the first great turning point of West Indian cricket'. The tourists won thirteen matches and lost seven. They found their first outstanding batter, George Challenor. Harold Austin, their captain on the tour, became the first president of the West Indies Cricket Board of Control in 1926, the year when they also became an ICC member.

The West Indians returned to England in 1928 to play Test cricket for the first time but were routed by an innings in all three games. 'The time is certainly not yet when the West Indies can hope to challenge England with a reasonable hope of success,' concluded *Wisden*.

But on this tour, something significant happened. Lebrun Constantine's son Learie had made little impact with the bat on the 1923 tour, but his 37 wickets had come at 22, and his fielding had drawn attention. For the tour, he had to quit his 30-shillings-a-week job at Llewellyn Roberts.

Broke by 1925, Learie Constantine had to move in with his parents. He married in 1927 and became a father soon afterwards. While working as a clerk for Trinidadian solicitors, he realized that his complexion would hamper his professional growth.

So, he decided to become a professional cricketer in England: 'I knew I could not keep up with both cricket and business, and I did not want to do as so many other West Indians had done—be forced into a position where I did neither thing to the best of my ability.'

'He revolted against the revolting contrast between his first-class status as a cricketer and his third-class status as a man,' explained C.L.R. James in *Beyond a Boundary*. In this, Constantine would surpass the stature of even Ollivierre, whose performance in England in 1900 had earned him a contract with Derbyshire.

At this point Constantine was at the peak of his career. He was gifted with skills that would, over the decades to follow, become the 'Caribbean flavour' cliché. He 'laid down the template for the Black West Indian cricketer—fast bowler, hard-hitting batsman and electric fielder'.

Constantine knew he had to impress at Lord's, the hub of English cricket. He did that in the Middlesex match, when he walked out at 79–5 after the hosts had declared on 352–6. He raced to 50 in eighteen minutes, and eventually made 86 in under an hour to avert the follow-on. He then destroyed Middlesex with 7–57.

But he was not done yet. The West Indians needed 259 to win. Constantine re-emerged at 121–5 and smashed a hundred in an hour. During this innings, he played two astonishing strokes. One broke Jack Hearne's finger and ruled him out of the rest of the season. Another, *off the back-foot*, 'flew over cover point and ricocheted off the Old Father Time vane on the roof of the North Stand'.

'His movement was so joyously fluid and, at need, acrobatic that he might have been made of springs and rubber,' noted the usually cautious *Wisden*.

The performance got Constantine the one thing he needed—a contract from Nelson in the Lancashire League. He played as a professional from 1929 to 1942. In his first nine seasons, Nelson won the League seven times and were runners-up twice.

Constantine took 884 wickets at under 10. In the League alone, his 799 wickets and 79 five-wicket hauls are records *to this day*. He remains the only one to take five-fors against every club. His 7111 runs came at 36. So attached did he become to Nelson that he did not return to the relative safety of Trinidad during the Second World War ('I would have felt like a rat deserting a ship').

He won personal battles on the way. He received mail that opened with 'Dear nigger'. On the field, he was called 'Black bugger'. When little boys shook hands with him, they were astonished to see that the colour of his skin had not come off on theirs.

'It will be a pity if Constantine allows his crowd to endow him with the irresponsibility of a "jazz" coon cricketer,' wrote Neville Cardus. The era *does not* justify the racism in the description. 'You can hardly credit that Cardus, an educated man, failed to comprehend the insult he was hurling; or how hurtful Constantine would find it,' Duncan Hamilton would later write.

Of course, this was hardly surprising of Cardus. 'In the day's warmth, the colour of the West Indians seemed as natural as that of the green grass,' he had written in his Manchester Guardian *report of the 1928 England–West Indies Lord's Test match. 'There are six of them black as ebony, and three with faces of chocolate brown. When they smile they are lovable, we see white teeth and we think of melons and the dear humorous friends of our nursery days in a hundred tales of the old plantations.' The era cannot be an excuse for these words.*

By 1943, Constantine was a British citizen working at the Ministry of Labour and National Service. That year, he was scheduled to play two wartime fundraising matches. He booked two rooms for four days at Imperial Hotel, Russell Square. He was denied entry: 'We are not going to have these niggers in our hotel.'

The American servicemen at the hotel had complained about the presence of Constantine and his family. It did not matter to the hotel management that Constantine was playing for *English* sides to raise funds for *England.*

Constantine checked in at the Bedford Hotel, sued the Imperial and won. Over the course of the legal battle, he found tremendous support from the government and his fans. The case, the first of its kind in England, triggered a chain of movements that led to the Race Relations Act being passed in Britain in 1965. It deemed discrimination on 'grounds of colour, race, or ethnic or national origins' as illegal.

He had been knighted three years before that. In 1969, he became the first Black peer of the UK.

There have been greater cricketers in the history of the West Indies, but no one put them on the cricket map as firmly.

Chapter 33

'HE AND HIS GENIUS CAME OUT WITH A STROKE WHICH WAS NEVER SEEN IN THE ANNALS OF INDIAN CRICKET.'

L.P. Jai, about an incident from 3 December 1928.

Richard Newland, who played most of his cricket around 1750, was the first left-handed batter of any repute. By 1790, however, there were enough of them—in both number and pedigree—to form an XI and beat a team of right-handers by 39 runs.

Despite that, batting left-handed was a novelty. Right-handers did reverse their stance in exhibition matches, but it was unthinkable in serious cricket. When they did, they drew attention.

The ambidextrous William Yardley was batting for Kent against Surrey at The Oval in 1870. Before Walter Anstead came to bowl, Yardley warned fielder James Southerton that he might bat left-handed without warning. Southerton 'merely laughed'.

When Anstead (right-arm fast) bowled, Yardley simply 'reversed his normal right-handed stance and leathered the ball, only narrowly missing the nearby fielder Southerton at point'. When he did an encore next ball, Southerton dropped spread-eagled on the ground. 'Not cricket! Not cricket!' yelled the Surrey supporters, but Anstead was taken off the attack (though he later bowled Yardley).

Yet another instance took place circa 1893 at Clifton. The Gloucestershire bowlers stuck to a negative line outside off-stump with a packed off-side field. The incessant sledging from the Grace brothers, E.M. and W.G., did little to improve the mood of Middlesex's Tim O'Brien. To the next wide ball, he 'turned and hit it left-handed past the heads of the waiting fieldsmen in the slips'.

W.G. wasn't amused: 'You mustn't do that, Tim, you'll kill my brother.'

'And a good thing too,' responded O'Brien, and repeated the shot. W.G. walked off with the team.

Percy Fender, the wonderful innovator, tried his hand at it during the Old Trafford Test match of the 1921 Ashes—again, as response to negative bowling. As Warwick Armstrong pitched his leg-breaks well outside the leg-stump, Fender 'once shifted hands on the handle of the bat and pulled him back-handed across the wicket to the place where cover-point generally stands'.

Ranjitsinhji never played in the Bombay Quadrangular, but Duleepsinhji did. When he turned up for the Hindus for the 1928–

29 edition, there was already anticipation about this man, one of their own, who had been in such dazzling form in a faraway land.

The Hindus needed an early declaration in the third innings. L.P. Jai, one of the finest Indian batters of the 1920s and 1930s, joined Duleep at 163–3. The two men treated the crowd to an exhibition of exquisite shots against the Parsees. Then it happened.

The moment left Jai awestruck: 'Without changing the grip of the bat, he tried to hit the wide ball backwards towards the third man with his bat turned around and facing the wicket-keeper.'

Jai had just witnessed Duleep play a reverse-sweep. The fielders appealed in confusion, for they had seen something inconceivable to them.

The shot, however, did not catch on—until Mushtaq Mohammad arrived in England. Sometime in the mid-1960s, he was playing for International Cavaliers against Middlesex. His team was chasing a big target, but Mushtaq found scoring difficult against the off-breaks of Fred Titmus.

'I looked around and realised that the only gap was at third man,' he recalled. 'My shot was pre-meditated, but it connected and went for four; but Titmus appealed! … He went wild and pulled his hair out.'

One can see why the fielding side was aghast at these strokes and sometimes even appealed. Not only was a batter changing their identity—everyone is classified as right- or left-handed but never both—but they were also going against cricket's basic characteristic of being a side-on game.

Mushtaq described his shot as a 'reverse hit'. It is not clear whether Yardley, O'Brien or Fender played reverse-sweeps or switch hits—in other words, whether they flipped the position of their hands (Duleep did not change his grip). However, there is little doubt that all of them—and Mushtaq—were right-handed batters who played left-handed strokes in competitive cricket.

Javed Miandad mastered the stroke, but coaches began to disapprove it in most corners after Mike Gatting's infamous failed attempt in the 1987 World Cup final. Warwickshire eventually made it popular in the 1990s, largely due to coach Bob Woolmer and captain Dermot Reeve.

Andy Flower played the stroke in Test cricket with élan against the Indian spinners in India. Jonty Rhodes played the *reverse-pull* against short-pitched bowling, fast or slow. Craig McMillan and Kevin Pietersen aced the switch hit—they brought their right arm above the left—forcing pundits to question the fairness when bowlers cannot switch arms without a warning.

That battle will continue for some time, but one thing cannot be doubted: the shot has helped cull negative bowling significantly.

Chapter 34

'HE'S A GREAT BOY, ISN'T HE?'

Dorothy Pickle, 19 August 1930.

Even after seven decades of his retirement, Don Bradman continues to remain a stumbling block for the staunchest believers of the numbers-do-not-mean-anything-in-cricket cult. Even in gully cricket it is difficult to ignore a batting average of 99.94 in a career spanning two decades.

Yet, the Bradman phenomenon, at least his early impact, transcended his near-absurd batting records.

The story should begin with the Wall Street Crash of 1929. Several Australian sectors had been hit by strikes even before that, when the nation was still recovering from the 60,000 deaths in the Great War. The economy plunged.

Strikes became common, particularly in the timber and mining sectors, where working conditions were unsatisfactory. The Australian GDP fell by 10 per cent between 1929 and 1931. Unemployment rates soared to 30 per cent by 1932. Recovery was slow, recovery began that year, but the average unemployment rate between 1930 and 1934 read 23.4 per cent. The usual symptoms of an economic crisis—mass poverty, serpentine queues for a handful of jobs, even an increase in suicide rates—were evident.

There was little to look forward to, but the great sporting nation found solace in sports. In this, they found two contrasting heroes.

The thoroughbred racehorse Phar Lap won thirty-seven of the fifty-one races he entered in, including fourteen in a row. He died under mysterious circumstances in California before turning five.

The other was a man whom Mark Gosling, chief secretary of New South Wales Ministry, called 'the Phar Lap of cricket'.

Bradman had an excellent (by anyone else's standards, that is) debut Test series in the 1928–29 home Ashes, but his 468 runs at 66.85 were drowned by Wally Hammond's 905 at 113.12. He dominated the domestic season with 1690 runs at 93.88. The next summer, he improved on even that, with 1586 runs at 113.28. This included a world-record unbeaten 452 against Queensland off just 465 balls.

At twenty-one, he visited England in 1930—and became the first overseas batter (and youngest ever) to amass 1000 runs by May. He finished the summer with an incredible 2960 runs at 98.66. No one else averaged even 65.

The Test series alone fetched Bradman 974—*still* a world record series aggregate—at 139.14. He made 131 at Trent Bridge,

254 at Lord's, 334 at Headingley (including 309 in a single day) and 232 at The Oval. He failed only at Old Trafford, the only venue he could never master.

Not even W.G. Grace in the mid-1870s had achieved something this extraordinary. English fans thronged to the grounds to watch him flog their own bowlers to every corner.

Trevor Wignall of the *Daily Express* hailed him as 'the greatest athlete or sporting figure in the wide world'. The *Daily Herald* called him superior to Jack Hobbs. 'You may talk of Alexander, Hercules, Trumper and Macartney,' noted Plum Warner, 'but this young Australian is a super-batsman and the equal of anyone.'

Having watched Bradman in 1928–29, Percy Fender had predicted that he would fail in England. He had to swallow his words: 'I do not think any of us realised that it was possible to be so really brilliant without taking risks.' Umpire Frank Chester was 'firmly convinced that he was the greatest batsman of all time'.

Back in Bowral, Bradman's hometown, one Dorothy Pickle had been glued to the wireless and keeping scores. When Bradman reached his hundred at The Oval, she swallowed her pen in excitement and had to be rushed to the hospital. On regaining consciousness, her first words were, 'He's a great boy, isn't he?'

Bradman got a hero's welcome back home when the Australians returned with the urn, but not all his colleagues were overtly happy at his enjoying the lion's share of attention. There was a feeling that his individual fame overshadowed the performance of the team and his teammates. 'Perhaps bolstered by the confidence of their home surroundings [they] were beginning to talk about Bradman,' theorized his biographer, Irving Rosenwater.

Having seen the Depression at close quarters, Bradman would set out to accumulate wealth as single-mindedly as he pursued runs. A teetotaller, he was never part of the post-match trips to the pub with the team. These would affect his popularity over the years as well.

But none of that mattered at that point. Throughout the England tour, as reports were cabled home, the average Australian found something to celebrate amidst the gloom. Bradman was no messiah. He would not solve the real problems. That would take years.

But he brought rare smiles on faces in destitute families that survived on soup kitchens. 'He was, for the army of the unemployed, their beacon of hope,' *The Times* would write in his obituary over seven decades later.

And even the greatest cynic will hesitate to argue with that 99.94.

Section 6

Cables and Televisions

Chapter 35

'I DO NOT WANT TO SEE YOU, MR WARNER. THERE ARE TWO TEAMS OUT THERE; ONE IS TRYING TO PLAY CRICKET; AND THE OTHER IS NOT.'

Bill Woodfull to Plum Warner, 14 January 1933.

As we have seen, Don Bradman demolished attacks and enthralled fans on the 1930 tour of England. However, during the 232 at The Oval, his final innings of the Test series, the pitch 'livened up almost supernaturally'.

A Nottinghamshire fast bowler called Harold Larwood hit Bradman on the chest so hard that play had to be held up for five minutes. Encouraged, Larwood peppered Bradman with bouncers, at times hurrying him, and hitting him on the wrist once.

Noting all this was Percy Fender, a former cricketer renowned for strategic brilliance. Now a journalist, he stayed in touch with his Australian counterparts. He tracked Bradman's progress at the Sheffield Shield and passed on the information to Douglas Jardine, Fender's successor as Surrey captain.

Jardine was the kind of man who would not let *anything* come between him and his goal. He realized what Fender had been trying to say. When he saw a clip of Bradman's discomfort at The Oval, Jardine famously yelled, 'I've got it! He's yellow!'

When he set out for Australia, in 1932–33, Jardine—by then the captain of England—had a blueprint ready for Bradman. Balls would be hurled at the batter's *body* with an arc of six to eight fielders on the leg-side, mostly behind square.

For that, Jardine needed bowlers of genuine pace. He had Larwood, Bill Voce and 'Gubby' Allen. Hedley Verity, the all-time great left-arm spinner, was underused in the series. Maurice Tate, the champion medium-pacer, did not get a single Test. Bill Bowes, somewhere between medium and fast-medium, played only once (though his only wicket was a famous scalp). They did not fit into Jardine's plan.

The tactic was first deployed at a first-class game at Melbourne, by stand-in captain Bob Wyatt against an Australian XI featuring Bradman. Larwood hit Australian Test captain Bill Woodfull on the chest, holding up play for ten minutes.

Allen resisted the plan throughout the tour. He bowled to a 'normal' field. But Allen was an amateur of Eton and Cambridge background, and the protégé of Plum Warner, an important establishment figure and the MCC manager on the tour. That granted Allen immunity. He also did not have problems fielding in the leg-trap. In fact, he held six catches there.

The 'conscientious objector' I.A.K. Pataudi, however, refused to stand in a Bodyline field and was dropped during the series. Though he did subsequently field in the leg-trap, Pataudi's initial refusal is remembered more.

However, Larwood and Voce bounced without inhibition as the leg-trap stayed put. In his letters back home, Allen referred to the Nottinghamshire pair as 'swollen headed gutless uneducated miners'.

Bradman was particularly ruffled. He hopped around the crease, trying to evade the bouncers. He was hit on the shoulder. He hit some cracking shots off the back-foot (he was Bradman, after all!), but they looked more desperate than measured, especially the tennis-forehand shot that soared over the empty, wide mid-on area for an all-run five.

In the second innings of the Melbourne game, Bradman exposed all three stumps, trying to cut. Larwood knocked the off-stump out. Wyatt duly submitted his reports to Jardine, who had been away fishing in the Bogong Valley, more than 300 kilometres away, with his friends.

Bradman missed the first Test, at Sydney, because of a dispute with the board over his contract with the *Sun* (Sydney). Some, including Jardine, suggested that he might have been shaken by the previous match. England used the tactic anyway and won by 10 wickets.

Bradman returned for the second Test, at Melbourne. Walking out to a standing ovation, Bradman took a long, semicircular route to the middle to get his eye in. He then tried to pull the first delivery he faced, a good-length ball from Bowes, and inside-edged on to the wicket. However, he made a second-innings hundred to help Australia level the series.

So far, so good ... but now came Adelaide.

Woodfull refused to give England a dose of their own medicine. Australia did not pick express bowlers like Eddie Gilbert and Laurie Nash. Gilbert had dished out a painful blow to Jardine in a tour match, but as an Aboriginal cricketer, he was unlikely to play. Tim Wall, the only Australian bowler of pace in the Test match, used the bouncer generously en route to 5–72. England made 341.

Bradman arrived after Allen snared Jack Fingleton. The fifth ball of Larwood's second over missed Woodfull's head by a whisker. The sixth hit him just over his heart. Woodfull dropped his bat and doubled over in pain. The English fielders gathered around him. Allen rushed to fetch a glass of water.

Woodfull collapsed and died before he turned sixty-eight. His wife, Gwen, always maintained that he had never completely recovered from the blow.

But Jardine yelled, in a voice audible enough for both Woodfull and Bradman: 'Well bowled, Harold!'

When play resumed, Bradman faced the next over, from Allen. For Larwood, the fielders *now* switched to the leg-trap.

The Adelaide Oval crowd, usually quieter than their counterparts in other Australian venues back then, had grumbled when Larwood hit him. At least the field had been conventional. But trying to hit an injured person was crossing a limit in their book. They barracked Larwood after every ball.

Dick Whitington noticed 'Adelaide's octogenarians in the members' enclosure rise to their feet, flush scarlet of face, and with their Adam's apples throbbing, count Jardine and his team out'.

Larwood did not pay heed. He knocked the bat out of Woodfull's hand, had Bradman caught at short-leg, and McCabe at mid-wicket off a mistimed hook. Allen got Woodfull for 22.

Soon afterwards, MCC managers Warner and Dick Palairet went to the Australian dressing-room to express sympathies.

But Woodfull was curt in greeting them, uttering words that form the quote of this chapter, and would be echoed almost verbatim by Anil Kumble seventy-five years later. Warner left (in tears, according to some sources). He confided in Jardine, who had little sympathy for such conversations.

The conversation was leaked. Newspapers ran the exchange the next morning (the rest day). The versions predictably differed. The question of who leaked the conversation also loomed large. Warner blamed Fingleton, the only active journalist at the spot. Fingleton would later accuse Bradman. In his seminal *Bodyline Autopsy*, David Frith mentioned accounts that corroborated with Fingleton's allegations.

When the cricket resumed, Bill Ponsford 'showed he could take a hiding' by accepting blows on the body. Then, at 218–7, Larwood bowled short. Bert Oldfield, aiming to cut, changed it to a pull at the last moment.

The ball took the top edge and hit him on the temple, and Oldfield dropped his bat and staggered towards point, clutching his head. As the fielders and umpire George Hele rushed at him, Oldfield assured: 'It wasn't your fault, Harold.'

Woodfull strode out in a suit (he and Bradman were guests at the governor's box). With Oldfield's bat held firmly in one hand, he guided his wicketkeeper back to the pavilion. As the crowd threatened to explode, the South Australia Cricket Association called the Angus Street Police Headquarters. A force arrived on motorbikes.

Ironically, Larwood had hit both Woodfull and Oldfield while bowling to conventional fields.

The Australians were bowled out for 222. 'Hit him on the bloody head,' someone yelled as Jardine came to bat in a multicoloured Harlequin cap.

England won by 338 runs. As the triumphant English cricketers returned to the pavilion, shrieks of 'Go home, you Pommie bastards' filled the air.

By then, Jardine's strategy was being referred to as Bodyline. Some credit journalist Hugh Buggy for coining the term, but no conclusive evidence to this has been found.

Chapter 36

'IN OUR OPINION IT IS UNSPORTSMANLIKE.'

Cable from the Australian Board of Control (ABC) to the Marylebone Cricket Club, 18 January 1933.

We have seen the events of the Australian first innings of the Adelaide Test of the 1932–33 Ashes.

The controversy spilled over outside the confines of the ground, into the dressing-room, in the stands, all over the newspapers … and threatened to put Anglo-Australian diplomatic relations at risk.

The fifth day of the timeless Test had ended with Australia on the verge of defeat. Four days had elapsed since Harold Larwood had hit Bill Woodfull, who then refused to speak to Plum Warner.

Over this period, the ABC had made up its mind to write to the MCC. Of the thirteen ABC delegates, four drafted the contents and wired them to ABC chair A.W.D. Robertson in Melbourne. Four others supported them.

The other five opposed it for obvious reasons. They represented Queensland and New South Wales, the state associations scheduled to host the remaining Tests, at Brisbane and Sydney. The motion was passed with an 8:5 majority. The ABC also tried to convince Woodfull and Don Bradman, but neither agreed.

The Australian cricketers voiced their support—except Vic Richardson, who was sure that the MCC would back *their* cricketers, especially after the 'unsportsmanlike' accusation. His suggestion of a secret end-of-series report without press involvement fell on deaf ears.

Bill Jeanes of the South Australian Cricket Association copied out the final contents *inside the Australian dressing-room at the Adelaide Oval* and read it out at an SOS press conference: 'Bodyline bowling assumed such proportions as to menace best interests of game, making protection of body by batsmen the main consideration. Causing intensely bitter feeling between players as well as injury. In our opinion it is unsportsmanlike. Unless stopped at once likely to upset friendly relations existing between Australia and England.'

Surprisingly, parts of the *Australian* media criticized the ABC. The *Herald* (Melbourne) went to the extent of blaming them for holding a pistol to the MCC's head. ABC delegate W.L. Kelly denied this.

Back in England, few were aware of these proceedings. News took time to travel in those days. Radio coverage was sketchy. Print reporting was limited.

Reuters had sent Gilbert Mant, an Australian who used to work for them in London, to cover the tour. Mant (whose accounts are in the wonderfully titled *Cuckoo in the Bodyline Nest*) promptly sent the contents of this cable to England. The media called MCC president Heneage Legge (Viscount Lewisham) at half past two in the morning. The MCC were ready by the time the actual cable arrived.

Meanwhile, in Australia, England captain Douglas Jardine asked fellow amateur 'Gubby' Allen about his reactions. Allen had refused to bowl Bodyline, but he had retained his place in the eleven: being an amateur cricketer had its privileges. Jardine was apprehensive that the MCC might not have his back.

'No, Douglas, you're wrong. No one can call an Englishman unsporting and get away with it,' assured Allen. 'They've lost the battle with the first shot they've fired.' The words turned out to be prophetic.

The MCC did not mince words: 'We, Marylebone Cricket Club, deplore your cable. We deprecate your opinion that there has been unsportsmanlike play. We have fullest confidence in captain, team and managers, and are convinced that they would do nothing to infringe either the Laws of Cricket or the spirit of the game. We have no evidence that our confidence has been misplaced. Much as we regret accidents to Woodfull and Oldfield, we understand that in neither case was the bowler to blame. If the Australian Board of Control wish to propose a new law or rule it shall receive our careful consideration in due course.

'We hope the situation is not now as serious as your cable would seem to indicate, but if it is such as to jeopardise the good relations between English and Australian cricketers, and you consider it desirable to cancel remainder of programme, we would consent with great reluctance.'

This was a major threat. Cancelling the rest of the tour would mean serious financial repercussions for the ABC.

Amidst all this, the English cricketers drew against Victoria XIII at Ballarat, beat New South Wales at Sydney, and travelled to Queensland.

In their response, the ABC appreciated the MCC's 'difficulty in dealing with matter raised in our cable without having seen the actual play', but they also called Bodyline 'opposed to the spirit of cricket and unnecessarily dangerous to cricketers'; and vowed to form a committee to obliterate bowling of similar nature from cricket in Australia and send relevant reports to the MCC.

But the most relevant words were at the end: 'We do not consider it necessary to cancel remainder of programme.'

The tourists meanwhile played a Queensland Country XII at Toowoomba. Wally Hammond and Les Ames got hundreds. Despite bowling at a reduced pace, Larwood bowled seven batters to finish with 8–28.

The MCC response arrived the day this match got over: 'May we accept this as a clear indication that the good sportsmanship of our team is not in question? We are sure you will appreciate how impossible it would be to play any Test match in the spirit we all desire unless both sides were satisfied there was no reflection upon their sportsmanship.'

The ABC had little option but to swallow their pride and concede defeat.

Warner admitted that the MCC 'are pretty good at drafting telegrams'.

To drive the message further, Larwood took 2–24 and 6–38 *without a Bodyline field* to inflict an innings defeat on Queensland at Brisbane.

England regained the Ashes in the same city a fortnight later. They claimed the series 4–1.

Chapter 37

'WHAT MATTER WE LOST, MERE NERVY MEN/SINCE ENGLAND'S WOMEN NOW PLAY ENGLAND'S GAME/ WHEREFORE IMMORTAL WISDEN, TAKE YOUR PEN/AND WRITE MACLAGAN ON THE SCROLL OF FAME.'

Morning Post, December 1934.

We have discussed the early days of women's cricket and the abrupt rise and fall of the Original England Lady Cricketers in the 1890s. The disdain towards women's sports continued for years. In 1895, *Physical Culture* wrote that 'girls … can sit on coaches to watch us play cricket … but girls cannot run, jump or climb trees'.

The twentieth century saw a gradual rise in the popularity of women's sports, especially after the First World War. On 4 October 1926, the Women's Cricket Association (WCA) was founded in Victoria, London, and continued as a separate body until its affiliation with the ECB in 1999.

In 1927, it launched a Cricket Week at Colwall Cricket Club, Malvern, where teams participated in 'tunics of a sort most suitable to the game'. It continues to this day. By 1929 it had thirty-seven affiliated clubs, thirty-two schools and several colleges. It organized a match that year between London & District and Rest of England.

Women's Cricket, edited by Marjorie Pollard, was launched in 1930, with a circulation of over 500. Pollard wrote instructions, match reports, summaries and historical pieces. She hunted down news and scorecards—often illegible or unintelligible—and typed them herself. There were some contributors, but it was largely a solo show.

Women's cricket was shaping up, but not all was smooth. 'The game was still expensive for those taking part. It was not wired enough to attract big, curious crowds, nor well enough established to count as a major sport and so attract sponsors,' pointed out Tessa McLaren in the 1992 *Wisden*.

Despite support from the likes of C.B. Fry and Frank Chester, women's cricket remained 'a minor sport, with few women knowing anything about it, still less how to play it', noted Roy Case in *The Pebble in My Shoe*, though it 'never quite experienced the negative attention as women's football'.

There was even no uniformly accepted attire. In 1930 alone, the female cricketers wore 'black shoes, brown shoes, shoes with coloured saddles ... coloured woolly coats, striped woolly coats ... silk frocks, pique frocks, all sorts of frocks—with sleeves, without sleeves, and some with nearly sleeves'.

In 1931, the WCA formalized the Laws of Women's Cricket. In the same year, the Lancashire and Durham County Associations were formed, and Durham took on a combined team of Lancashire and Cheshire.

In 1932, the WCA organized an 'international' between 'England' and 'Scotland' at New Road. England won by 91 runs, but three Scots went on to become luminaries of the sport. Off-spin bowling all-rounder Myrtle Maclagan had 50 and 41, and 3–42 and 4–35; wicketkeeper Betty Snowball 9 and 14, and two dismissals; and Betty Archdale 15 not out and 13.

In 1933, Mabel Bryant scored 106 at Aigburth—the first hundred in a WCA-recognized match. That year, an England team played The Rest at Leicester. In 1934, Yorkshire and Lancashire combined to form the English Women's Cricket Federation.

The WCA planned an international tour of Australia and New Zealand for that winter. A one-day trial was played at Old Trafford on 14 July, where the WCA enforced a ban on 'bare legs', making stockings compulsory. After bowling out The Rest for 93, England Women had made 219–1 when time ran out. Maclagan (100*) and Snowball (77) added 140 for the first wicket. Like Archdale, they were eligible to play for England.

The squad set sail for Australia and New Zealand in October, shortly after England had conceded the Men's Ashes at home. There were embargoes on smoking, drinking, gambling and male company.

Archdale led the side. Her mother, Helen, had been a renowned suffragette, feminist and journalist who had served a sentence for breaking a window at Whitehall. *Wisden* noted that the toddler Betty had collected some of these stones for her mother ...

Archdale had not been a unanimous choice as captain. She herself felt that her appointment 'was not based upon her experience or cricketing ability, but that her law degree would be beneficial when called upon to prepare or deliver speeches'.

Other stars included Molly Hide, Maclagan and vice-captain Snowball. Barring the twenty-seven-year-old Archdale, every member was below twenty-five. The squad featured, to quote Maclagan, seven teachers or future teachers; two secretaries; an art student, a lawyer, a nurse and three 'ladies of leisure'.

Unfortunately, the hosts did not bear the travel expenses. The WCA announced that an £80 tour fee had to be borne by each player, ruling out the underprivileged cricketers, irrespective of talent.

'It is against our policy to play for cups. We play only for the love of the game,' said Archdale at a mayoral reception in Fremantle upon arrival. 'The trouble with Australians as a whole is that you take the game too seriously.' Sledging? Perhaps. The tourists played splendid cricket amidst the odd surprised stare, the 'you ought to be at home looking after your children' comments, and the Mayor of Goulburn's request to 'marry the local men and breed good Australian cricketers'.

The Australians did not have a structure robust enough to produce a team that would compete with England, who comfortably won the first-ever women's Test match, at Brisbane. Maclagan claimed 7–10 and broke Hilda Hills's nose to end her Test career (though some reports suggest she missed the rest of the Test due to influenza). After bowling out Australia for 47, Maclagan (72) outscored them on her own. England won by 9 wickets. As cricket fans back home finally found something to rejoice, the *Morning Post* printed a plea for *Wisden.*

England won the second Test by 8 wickets. Maclagan made 119 (the first hundred in women's Test cricket) and claimed 6 wickets. Snowball had 71 runs, 5 dismissals and a run-out.

Maclagan finished the series with the most runs and wickets. Snowball, second on the runs chart, had the most dismissals. And

Archdale's 'forthright yet engaging personality made her a popular figure to whom the sizable Australian crowds responded warmly'.

England (503–5) then thrashed New Zealand (44 and 122) well inside two days en route home. Women's Test cricket had taken off, somewhat against Archdale's request ('We do not want the words "Test cricket" to be introduced into the tour').

Chapter 38

'IF WITH ANY PART OF HIS PERSON (EXCEPT HIS HAND) WHICH IS BETWEEN WICKET AND WICKET HE INTERCEPT A BALL, WHICH IN THE OPINION OF THE UMPIRE AT THE BOWLER'S WICKET SHALL HAVE BEEN PITCHED IN A STRAIGHT LINE FROM THE BOWLER'S WICKET TO THE STRIKER'S WICKET OR SHALL HAVE BEEN PITCHED ON THE OFF-SIDE OF THE STRIKER'S WICKET AND WOULD HAVE HIT IT: LEG BEFORE WICKET.'

Law 24 of Cricket, 1937.

Until high-quality coverage came along, the LBW remained one of the most difficult concepts of cricket. Indeed, street cricket—where the batting side often provides the umpire—sometimes does away with it altogether.

As we have seen, the 1744 Laws did not mention LBW at all, because on those undulating surfaces, batters seldom stuck their legs out. But John Small's straight bat and the subsequent pad-play forced the authorities to introduce a new dismissal in 1774. In 1788, they added 'the ball must pitch straight' to the law. In 1823, they changed that to 'the ball must be delivered in a straight line to the wicket'.

This was ambiguous. James Dark and Will Caldecourt, eminent umpires of the 1830s, failed to agree over the interpretations. While Dark 'considered that the ball must be delivered from a spot which was on the line of wicket and wicket', Caldecourt 'said that it was equally correct for the ball to travel straight from hand to wicket'.

To avoid the confusion, there was another change in 1839. A batter would now be ruled out 'if with any part of his person he stop the ball, which in the opinion of the umpire at the bowler's wicket shall have been delivered in a straight line from it to the striker's wicket and would have hit it'.

This stayed for some time, much to the chagrin of bowlers who brought the ball into the right-hander. Over time, the batters simply began to pad away everything not in line. This overdose of pad-play—a defensive ploy—did not make for great viewership.

Batters often went back to anything pitched outside off irrespective of the length, for they knew they were safe even if they missed the ball. Sometimes they simply thrust their front foot forward. Lesser batters managed to thwart excellent incoming deliveries using this method.

Bob Thoms, who had umpired in the first two Tests on English soil, summed up in 1888: 'This very unsightly play cannot be termed batting; 'tis simply scientific legging, and ought to be stopped.'

Indeed, pitches had improved, pads had been in vogue, so why not update the archaic law?

The MCC responded by branding pad-play as 'contrary to the spirit of the game and inconsistent with strict fairness'. Since they did not impose any actual penalty, this artificially concocted sense of morality predictably failed to influence anyone.

Over time, several cricketers insisted on a reform, but nothing came of that. In a monograph in the 1924 *Wisden*, Alfred Lyttelton demonstrated the decrease in LBWs over time. While one out of forty dismissals used to be LBW in 1770, the count rose to one in seventeen in 1890, one in fourteen in 1900, and one in eight in 1923.

This may seem counterintuitive. If LBWs were more difficult, how did they become *more frequent*? Pad-play had actually become so common that the mediocre batters often preferred it to the bat. The rate of LBWs had shot up as a result.

Finally, the MCC introduced two changes in 1929. In English domestic cricket, batters would be given out if all other conditions of the LBW held and *even if they edged*. This was in practice until 1933. And in 1931, they increased the dimensions of the wicket by 17 per cent—from 27' x 8' to 28' x 9'. This was implemented globally.

Obviously, neither change addressed pad-play. The batters moved their stance slightly towards off and watched out for that extra movement that might have induced an edge, but that was it.

So, they had to amend the law again, in 1935. This time they got the desired result. The batter could now be given out, all other conditions remaining the same, *even if the ball pitched outside the off-stump*.

This, too, was implemented only in first-class cricket in England, including the home Test matches against South Africa. Australia were reluctant to embrace this.

The MCC took measures to test the efficiency. The umpires made separate signals for LBWs according to the new law.

The scorers noted these as 'LBW (n)'. The scoresheets were sent for analysis.

This changed things drastically. Of the 1560 LBWs in 1935, 483 were 'LBW (n)'—a whopping 31 per cent. It was a success. New Zealand had accepted the law earlier. Australia now agreed to implement it for the 1936–37 Ashes.

The method also ensured the best batters finished at the top. Wally Hammond scored the most runs that season, followed by Herbert Sutcliffe. The usual suspects, in other words. 'Class told,' concluded *Wisden*.

Law 24 was amended for all countries in 1937. Pad-play to anything pitched outside off was no longer foolproof. Batting became aggressive. As batters took risks, wickets fell too. Cricket became brighter.

One problem remained. The batters still offered their pads if they felt the impact would be outside off. In 1969–70, Australia and the West Indies experimented by giving LBWs even if the point of impact was outside off, provided no stroke had been offered. England adopted this in 1970.

In 1980, the new law (now 36) had a section titled 'Striker Making No Attempt to Play the Ball'. The point of impact did not matter if that happened. That is roughly the law as we know it today.

Chapter 39

'IT WAS ONE OF THOSE REMARKABLE PIECES OF JUDGEMENT UPON WHICH I BASE MY OPINION THAT CHESTER WAS THE GREATEST OF ALL UMPIRES.'

Don Bradman, about a 1938 incident, in *A Farewell to Cricket.*

Frank Chester played three seasons before the Great War and earned his Worcestershire cap at sixteen. Some, including Jack Hobbs, considered him as an England probable.

In the First World War, Chester was hit by shrapnel in Salonika in Greece. The gangrenous right arm had to be amputated from the elbow. He was only twenty-four when cricket resumed, but his playing days were over. Plum Warner advised him to take up umpiring.

Three years later, Chester picked up six small pebbles from his mother's garden at Bushey and made his way to Leyton for his umpiring first-class debut. Throughout his career, he used them to count the balls of overs for bowlers spanning generations.

On debut, Chester gave close calls against both captains, Johnny Douglas leg-before and John Daniell stumped. His colleague Harry Butt, former Test cricketer and thirty years his senior, was worried: 'Boy, you won't last long as an umpire … If you give skippers out, you sign your death warrant.' Chester refused to budge.

'You've made a mistake. This is a first-class match,' they said at Northampton when they saw this fresh-faced youth arrive for a County Championship match. Two years later, he walked out for his Test debut at Lord's in a trilby hat, the wooden stump of his hand covered in a dark leather glove.

At twenty-nine, he was the youngest to officiate in Test cricket since 1896; he would remain the same until 1965. In all, he stood in forty-eight Tests between 1924 and 1955—a world record that was intact until 1992. His 774 first-class matches remain the most by some distance.

Chester used to be trusted by everyone. 'There never should be any doubt,' he used to explain when asked about the benefit of doubt going to the batter. The confidence was visible in his promptness with decision-making.

To improve precision, he became the first major umpire to stoop very low behind the stumps as the bowler ran in. The practice was subsequently followed across the world.

It is impossible to tell how Chester would have fared in the DRS era, but there is little doubt that he would have adapted.

There is no technology to validate his accuracy, for television coverage was still in its nascent days. But we have contemporary accounts.

'As an umpire, he was right on top,' felt Hobbs. Joe Hardstaff Sr hailed Chester as 'one of the outstanding Test umpires of all time'. E.W. Swanton praised him 'as nearly infallible as a man could be in his profession'.

'His eyes are his most striking feature, quick, alive, ever ready to pounce on the unusual. In another sphere he might have made his mark in the C.I.D.,' wrote Viv Jenkins of Glamorgan, who felt that Chester's lapses 'have been remarkably few, and have served to accentuate, not minimise, his virtues'.

The most celebrated moment came in the 1938 Trent Bridge Test. A ball 'very faintly touched the inside edge' of Bradman's bat and hit his pad. As Bradman lost his balance, wicketkeeper Les Ames whipped the bails off and appealed. When the leg-umpire ruled not out, Ames appealed to the bowler's end.

'Very calmly, as though it was obvious to all, Chester simply said "Out, caught," and turned his back on the scene.' That act won Chester a new fan—Bradman.

Chester's mannerisms made excellent stories, some perhaps exaggerated. Legend goes that he once silenced 'a very famous bowler' in a Lord's Test with 'not out, and that was a very bad appeal'.

But the same man put youngsters to ease with a kind word, maintaining impartiality at the same time. Like Bird after him, visiting teams felt reassured when they knew Chester would officiate. 'You never umpire for this team or that; you just umpire,' he would say.

That arm was a subject of his dry humour. 'When the stump begins to ache, rain is almost invariably on the way,' he let people know. This often led to cricketers asking: 'Is the arm aching today, Frank?'

But it never became a hindrance. If anything, it added to his charm, though there were woes. At Hove in 1932, a hard-hit shot knocked the stump off the arm socket and carried it some distance towards the boundary. Poor Chester had to leave the ground to reattach it.

Age changed Chester. Stomach ulcers left him perennially irritable. The new-age excessive appealing irked him. He thought Bradman's Invincibles of 1948 'went too far in their appealing, which often they accompanied by excited leaping and gesticulating'. Ian Johnson, member of that side, said that 'the feeling was fully reciprocated'.

He turned obstinate, often irrationally. Sonny Ramadhin bowled Doug Insole off his pads at Trent Bridge in 1950, but Chester was adamant on leg-before, as he had ruled Insole out in the brief period between the ball hitting the pad and the stumps. That, along with the dismissal of Gilbert Parkhouse in Wellington in 1950–51, prompted the MCC to change the laws: bowled would overrule leg-before irrespective of when the umpire declared out.

Still, it was not until he started turning down appeals in a sarcastic voice during the 1953 Ashes that Australian captain Lindsay Hassett raised the matter to the MCC. He missed the final Test, and never stood in the Ashes again.

Yet, there was a moment during that tour, one final hurrah for the legend. A young leg-spinner called Richie Benaud appealed for leg-before against an Oxford undergraduate called Colin Cowdrey. Not out, ruled Chester. Benaud 'wasn't certain how umpire Chester could possibly have given it not out', until wicketkeeper Gill Langley explained to him: 'Just the faintest inside edge.'

Chapter 40

'IT IS A VERY HAPPY THING TO BE ONE WITH THE TEST CROWD IN YOUR OWN HOME, AND TO SEE THE BATSMEN SENDING THE BALL TO THE BOUNDARY AND TO HEAR THE ROAR OF THE CROWD. AT TIMES THE VIEWER MUST HAVE FELT HIMSELF ON THE PITCH.'

The Times, 1938.

John Logie Baird gave his first public demonstration of televised silhouette motion pictures in 1925. In 1929, he combined with Bernard Natan of Pathé to found Télévision-Baird-Natan. They made the first-ever outdoor remote broadcast in 1931, of the Epsom Derby, and repeated it in 1932.

In 1930, the BBC ran experimental television broadcasts. This became regular in 1934. In 1936, they set up the world's first regular public television service in Alexandra Palace. The range of coverage was a 40-kilometre radius of the transmitter. In 1937, they telecast the coronation of George VI and Queen Elizabeth *live*.

Soon, they began to cover live sporting action from London and its vicinity—an England–Scotland football match from Wembley, the Varsity Boat Race, Wimbledon …

A brochure called *On Television* mentioned about 1,00,000 people watching the Derby. Michael John Law felt that the count '… is probably correct if families and friends sitting around this unusual new attraction were taken into account'.

It was only a matter of time before the BBC added cricket to its itinerary. That happened for the Lord's Test of the 1938 Ashes. Obtaining permission was not difficult. In fact, the MCC were keen to have an 'omnibus agreement' with the BBC that included both radio and television.

For the match, producer Orr Ewing had two cameras placed on a platform at the Nursery End, one focusing on the bowler and the other on the batter. A third was placed at the Tavern, near the pavilion. Commentator Teddy Wakelam sat in a stand at the Nursery End, between the Free Seats and the Old Mound Stand. There was no scorer: Wakelam had only the ground scoreboard.

The Test match was telecast from 11.30 to 12.30; 2.30 to 3.30; and 3.50 to 5. If the match continued after 6.15, there was transmission until stumps. There was a reason behind these hours: the Test ran from 24–28 June, whereas Wimbledon started 20 June.

Telecast was archaic. The coverage was from one end, which meant that every alternate over had to be viewed from behind the batter. There was obviously no action replay. Richard Haynes pointed out that 'the three Emitron cameras gave a poor and oblique view of play, mainly because the *BBC* was unable to position its cameras directly down the wicket'.

But there were unprecedented experiences as well. The cameras included telephoto lenses for close-ups. As *Radio Times* pointed out, these would 'show things as intimate as the expression on a bowler's face when Bradman is missed in the field'. That put the television viewers at an advantage over the fans in the stands.

Most were impressed. *The Times* called it 'a delight of viewers'. 'The TV cameras were swung smoothly about the field so that every detail of the play could be followed,' reported the *Telegraph*. 'A striking example of the advance in television and the improvement in the receiving apparatus.'

The coverage of the Lord's Test must have been a success, for the final game of the series, a timeless Test at The Oval, was a late addition to the BBC schedule. 'It will be possible to televise the whole of the Oval Test match, however long it lasts,' announced the *Radio Times*.

This was where Len Hutton famously scored 364 and England 903–7, both world records. Since Wimbledon was over, the fans got to see a significant part of these runs.

For the two Tests, the BBC paid the MCC a combined amount of 100 guineas as 'facilities fee'. As per Haynes, this 'covered the estimated loss of revenue caused by use of seating and other facilities'.

The 1939 Tests at the same two venues, against West Indies, were telecast as well. Once the Second World War was over, services resumed during the India series of 1946. Live cricket on television became popular.

A delightful anecdote about Lindsay Hassett, vice-captain of Bradman's Invincibles of 1948, is worth a mention. After being bowled by England captain Norman Yardley first ball in the Lord's Test, Hassett blamed the television set in the dressing-room. Watching sport on television with one eye and the ground with the other, he had apparently turned cross-eyed …

The BBC added Edgbaston to the live coverage list in 1950, Old Trafford in 1951 and Headingley in 1952. Television coverage arrived in Australia in 1956 for the Melbourne Olympics. In 1968, the BBC televised a cricket match in colour for the first time. Australia took to coloured coverage shortly after that.

Before that, in 1966–67, a match between the touring West Indians and the Indian Prime Minister's XI at Feroz Shah Kotla was telecast in Delhi. Over the following decades, revenue from television coverage would play a significant part in the BCCI emerging as the most powerful cricket board.

But that is another story.

Chapter 41

'"SEE YOU TOMORROW" WAS THE POPULAR FAREWELL PARTING.'

Louis Duffus on the 1938–39 Durban Test match.

For decades, Test cricket could be played over a varying number of days. In England, matches against Australia would run for five days, but it was usually three days against other teams. However, if the last Test of a rubber was a decider, the Test match would be played to a finish.

South Africa and the West Indies adopted the same policy. With the series drawn 1–1, England made 849 at Kingston in 1929–30, took a lead of 563, batted again and set a target of 836. The hosts finished *the seventh day* on 408–5. Then it rained for two days, and the sides had to agree to a draw because the tourists had to catch the *Changuinola* back home.

In Australia, every Test used to be 'timeless'. Tours lasted for months, so there was adequate time.

South Africa's transition to turf wickets had almost been complete when England toured in 1938–39. The tourists encountered matting wickets at only Bulawayo and Salisbury. But there was a problem: 'Excess of zeal, in the desire to prevent grass not fully ripe for hard wear from crumbling, influenced some groundsmen to water the pitch in the morning before the resumption of play'.

This effort to prevent wear often resulted in featherbeds. In that series, only one of the first four Tests reached the fourth innings. With England 1–0 up, the last Test at Durban was scheduled to be a timeless affair.

South Africa won the toss, batted first and crawled to 423–6 after two days of cricket. They did not hit a single boundary in the first session. After taking forty-five minutes to get off the mark, Pieter van der Bijl slept his way to a hundred. This was followed by the *first rest day*.

Dudley Nourse completed his hundred on the third day ('It was a timeless Test, with no need to get on with the scoring'). Alan Melville had no reason to declare. South Africa made 530 and, by the third evening, took a wicket.

England reached 268–7 on the fourth day before being bowled out for 316 on the fifth. Of course, there was no question of a follow-on. This time the openers added 191. Van der Bijl missed out on a second century by 3 runs. Melville himself made 103. Ken Viljoen, who had *two haircuts during the Test*, got 74.

The dwindling ticket sales had forced the organizers to offer discounts. Despite that, the first five days had yielded £3640—the highest in the history of Kingsmead.

England needed 696 when they began on day seven. Len Hutton fell for 55, but Bill Edrich played his shots as Paul Gibb was resolute in defence despite batting in a drizzle with glasses. They were 253–1 at stumps.

All this left little time before their last match, against Western Province. Hugh Bartlett, Tom Goddard and Len Wilkinson of the English touring party were not part of this Test. They had gone ahead to Cape Town for the tour game, but that obviously had to be cancelled.

Rain washed out the eighth day of the Test. The *second rest day* followed (why did they not reschedule the eighth day as the rest day?). Melville got fully dressed for the Test match, only for a hotel waiter to convince him that he had miscalculated the days.

England opted for the heavy roller on the ninth morning. South African wicketkeeper Ronnie Grieveson felt that the pitch 'looked as good as it had on the first day'. As England reached 333–1 by lunch, legendary scorer Bill Ferguson feared running out of pages in his scorebook. Hammond agreed that he had never seen Ferguson more agitated.

Eric Dalton knocked out the middle-stump to send Gibb back for 120. It must have come as a relief, for Dalton would later get nightmares from bowling on the unyielding pitch. He would appeal for leg-before in his sleep.

Edrich reached his double ton before tea but fell for 219 after adding 89 with Hammond. England finished the day on 496–3. The target was only 200 now. 'The whole team was saying "we can win this match",' their wicketkeeper Les Ames recalled.

England began rapidly on the tenth day before Dalton got Hammond for 140 and Eddie Paynter for 75. At tea, they needed only 42 with five men standing. But the skies opened, and no more cricket was possible that day.

This posed a problem, for the Englishmen were scheduled to catch the 8.05 train to Cape Town, where they would board the *Athlone Castle* back home.

The South African board wanted an eleventh day. One can see their point. They were losing the series anyway, but they had an outside chance on an uncovered wicket on a fresh day …

But the MCC declined the offer. The South Africans offered to fly the two unbeaten men and the four batters yet to bat in a chartered aircraft to Cape Town to join their teammates. The MCC declined again.

The longest Test in history, thus, ended in a draw. 'Another half-hour or so would have won the match,' sighed Edrich. 'The weather had the last say, but we were then in with a good chance,' added Ames.

One man who was happy with the result was England manager A.J. Holmes. 'I'm glad there was no result. It showed that the game was more than victory or defeat,' he told journalist Louis Duffus.

The ten-day exercise in futility hastened the demise of timeless Tests. In *Wisden*, Norman Preston criticized 'over-prepared wickets'. Such contests were 'null and void of all the elements which go to make cricket the enchanting game it naturally is,' felt *The Times*. 'Even chess has its limits,' pointed out the *Guardian*.

Timeless Tests faded out after the Second World War. Australia insisted on them if the final match of the series was 'live'. While in place for the 1946–47 and 1948 Ashes, it was not required. By 1950 they were more or less a thing of the past.

Chapter 42

'I CAN UNDERSTAND MATCHES BETWEEN COLLEGES AND INSTITUTIONS, BUT I NEVER UNDERSTOOD REASONS FOR HAVING HINDU, PARSI, MUSLIM AND OTHER COMMUNAL ELEVENS.'

Mahatma Gandhi, 6 December 1940, to Bombay Gymkhana representatives at his Wardha ashram.

The Parsis of Bombay were the first Indians to play cricket. In 1892–93, the Zoroastrian Gymkhana challenged the Bombay

Gymkhana to a two-match contest. The first match, at Bombay, was washed out after the first day, but the Parsis won the return match, at Poona, by 3 wickets. This Parsees versus Europeans fixture became the annual Bombay Presidency Match.

By the early twentieth century, the Hindu and Mohammedan Gymkhanas prepared strong teams as well. They joined in 1907–08 and 1912–13 respectively to help form the Bombay Quadrangular. There have been cricket competitions around the world over years, but nothing this big based solely on religion.

Qualification for the teams could be stringent. In 1924, the Hindus tried to recruit P.A. Kanickam of Bangalore but withdrew the offer once they found out he was a Christian. Being an Indian, Kanickam could not play for the Europeans either. Over time, the authorities became lenient. Yadavindra Singh and Lall Singh, both Sikh Test cricketers, played for the Hindus in 1934–35.

Rain forced the Quadrangular to be shifted from September to December from 1917–18. Around this time, the organizers also drafted neutral umpires. The Quadrangular inspired replica tournaments in various Indian cities, but the Bombay version remained the most prestigious and boasted of the biggest names.

All but one of the five teams of the tournament were defined by religion. The British did not mind sharing a team with fellow Europeans. Throughout the Raj, most signs and notices in areas reserved for the British, after all, were marked 'Europeans only', not 'British only'. On the other hand, naming their team 'Christians' would mean the British extending the camaraderie to the native Indians of that religion.

A fifth team, The Rest, was added in 1937–38, to accommodate non-European Christians (the most famous being Vijay Hazare), Sikhs and other communities. Over time they recruited Ceylonese players including the redoubtable Mahadevan Sathasivam. This was also the season when the larger Brabourne Stadium replaced the Bombay Gymkhana as the venue for the tournament.

Despite being formed largely on religious lines, the Pentangular never witnessed serious communal violence. There was the odd 'down with the Hindus' or 'down with the Mussalmans' or '*har har Mahadev*' chant, but that was about it. If anything, performances by the opposition cricketers were cheered.

Cricket, however, was hardly the most important thing going on in India at that point. In 1930, the Indian National Congress declared their demand for Purna Swaraj on 26 January, and Mahatma Gandhi began his Dandi Satyagraha on 12 March.

The Bombay Quadrangular was not contested from 1930–31 to 1933–34, though inter-religion cricket continued in other parts of India. When Gandhi was arrested, the Hindu Gymkhana boycotted India's 1932 tour of England. India toured without three certainties—L.P. Jai, Vijay Merchant and Champak Mehta.

The tournament returned in 1934–35, and the Hindu–Muslim final attracted a massive crowd: 'Thousands were turned away, and all vantage-points were taken … Outside, late-comers or paupers sat atop buses, trees, poles and apartment buildings,' described Ramachandra Guha in *A Corner of a Foreign Field*. The Ranji Trophy 'debuted' that season, but it was a distant second in popularity.

The same teams met in next season's final. Fans across Bombay gathered in public places equipped with radio receivers. The Hindu–Muslim clash was, after all, the crème de la crème of the tournament. It 'had the intensity of an Ashes Test match', recalled future PCB chair Shaharyar Khan.

A faction felt that religion-based cricket should be abolished in a nation that needed to be united in its quest for independence. Duleepsinhji requested the fans to focus on the Ranji Trophy, named after his uncle. 'Bobby' Talyarkhan, India's first great commentator, adopted the opposite stance: 'I ask you now, is or is not the Pentangular, far from being a snag, a solution to communal unity in India?'

One can see Talyarkhan's point. After not being allotted enough seats at the Brabourne Stadium in the 1937–38 semi-final against the Europeans, the Hindus boycotted the match and the Europeans got a walkover. In the final, the Muslims crushed the Europeans by an innings inside two days amidst loud cheer from fans of all religions. Nationality trumped religious differences.

But the debate continued. When the British included India as a participant nation in the Second World War (without consulting a single Indian, of course), many Congress members across India resigned in protest. Hindu Gymkhana president S.A. Shete, vice-president M.M. Amersey and member of managing committee Jamnadas Pitambar met the most important Indian of the time.

Gandhi made it abundantly clear that he wanted the Pentangular to be scrapped. The representatives returned. Five days later, they wired again, asking whether Gandhi wanted *only the Hindus* to boycott the Pentangular. 'All who hold my opinion must refrain whether few or many,' came the response.

That season, only four teams took part. The Hindus returned, but it was evident that the Pentangular could not continue, though as late as in 1943–44, the *Times of India* noted how it was 'nothing more than clean, healthy rivalry between the various communities'.

The scenario had turned murky by 1946. Religious riots had broken out all over India. The Pentangular had never been marred by crowd violence, but it could not be ruled out anymore. The BCCI replaced it with the Zonal Quadrangular Tournament, predecessor of the Duleep Trophy. J.C. Maitra, sports editor of the *Bombay Chronicle* and a firm believer that cricket should be played 'without any communal colour or bias', had suggested the idea in an article on 28 February 1937.

This new tournament featured most major stars, but the crowd response was lukewarm at best. However, the Pentangular was never played again. Fittingly, it ended just before India gained Independence.

Chapter 43

'AUSTRALIANS WILL ALWAYS FIGHT FOR THOSE TWENTY-TWO YARDS. LORD'S AND ITS TRADITIONS BELONG TO AUSTRALIA JUST AS MUCH AS ENGLAND.'

John Curtin in May 1944.

On 1 September 1939, German battleship *Schleswig-Holstein* opened fire on a Polish military transit depot. The UK issued an ultimatum to Germany to withdraw forces. Two days later, the UK, France,

Australia and New Zealand declared war on Germany. And just like a quarter of a century ago, Europe was ripped apart.

Cricket came to a halt. The West Indian cricketers, in England to play a Test series, had to leave English shores without playing the last seven matches of their 1939 tour. Instead of boarding the *Athenia* on 3 September, they left by the *Montrose* on 26 August. The *Athenia* was torpedoed en route.

The County Championship was called off, as was England's twenty-six-match tour to India (including three Tests). Of the tour members, Roger Human visited India—but as a member of the Oxfordshire and Buckinghamshire Light Infantry. He died in service in Bangalore in 1942.

'England has now begun the grim Test match against Germany,' wrote Home Gordon in the September 1939 issue of *The Cricketer*. The Oval, venue of the last Test before the War, was converted into a Prisoner-of-War camp.

Not Lord's. The government and the army felt that 'cricket provided a healthy and restful antidote to war strain,' though 'there were sandbags everywhere, and the Long Room was stripped and bare, with its treasures safely stored beneath ground'.

The major domestic tournaments were immediately stopped in South Africa and the West Indies. In New Zealand and Australia, it lasted the 1939–40 season. But as with the First World War, cricket continued in India. Posted in the country on military duty, English cricketers played for the Europeans in the Bombay Pentangular. Denis Compton also played for Holkar and Reg Simpson for Sind in the Ranji Trophy.

Not all were fortunate. While commanding B Company on 19 July 1943, legendary left-arm spinner Hedley Verity was hit on the chest by shrapnel and captured by the Germans. Being moved around from one packed hospital to the next, he passed away on 31 July, at thirty-eight.

Pilot officer Ken Farnes, an England fast bowler, was thirty when he succumbed to a crash near Chipping Warden,

Oxfordshire. Sergeant-Observer Ross Gregory of Australia was killed in combat near Gafargaon (now in Bangladesh). He was twenty-six. In the Melbourne Test of the 1936–37 Ashes, Farnes had caught Gregory off Verity.

A Lockheed B34 Ventura flown by South African 'Chud' Langton crashed in Nigeria. His compatriot Dooley Briscoe was killed in combat in Ethiopia. Geoffrey Legge of England died in a plane crash in Devon, Sony Moloney of New Zealand, in Egypt. Maurice Turnbull of England, who had also played rugby for Wales, was killed by a sniper's bullet near Montchamp after the 1944 Normandy Landings.

Len Hutton fractured his left forearm and dislocated his ulna during a commando-training exercise. Several surgeries later, his left arm was reduced to a length 2 inches shorter than his right arm. That could not prevent him from becoming the legendary batter or the first professional to lead England.

Captured when Tobruk fell in 1942, Bill Bowes served three years as a Prisoner of War in Italian and German camps. Despite losing about 25 kilograms, he played Test cricket after the war. Bob Crisp of South Africa commanded an M3 Stuart Light Tank to charge at a German army *all on his own* and triumphed.

Keith Miller's oft-quoted line 'pressure is a Messerschmitt up your arse, playing cricket is not', on the other hand, does not count for much. He spent most of the war in training and went on two missions, including a 'spoof patrol'. No part of his anatomy was at the receiving end of any sort of ammunition.

E.W. Swanton had a copy of the 1939 *Wisden* when he was captured by the Japanese after the Battle of Singapore. There used to be a perennial queue for the dog-eared copy, 'thumbed by thousands in twelve different camps'. The twenty-odd bookbinders in these camps put it together with rice-paste glue. It had to be booked in advance, and no one was allowed to borrow it for more than twelve hours. The Japanese got suspicious, but their censors eventually classified it as 'not subversive'.

Lord's kept hosting cricket, at times to raise funds, or merely to boost morale. They featured first-class cricketers, even Test players, who were now part of the armed forces. In one of these matches in 1944, Flight Officer Bob Wyatt ran to bowl at Lieutenant Jack Robertson when the players heard a German doodlebug. The cricketers flung themselves on to the ground and the crowd tried their best to hide behind the seats. Sources vary on exactly where it landed, but Lord's was spared.

The bombings impacted the attendance at Lord's for the year, but the crowd only increased—from 53,330 in 1940 to 2,32,390 in 1943. The Australian Prime Minister visited the venue twice in May 1944. Cricket kept a war-ravaged nation going.

Cricket kept being referred to throughout the war. At Ruweisat Ridge in 1943, Bernard Montgomery famously addressed the Eighth Army with 'we ourselves will start a great offensive; it will be the beginning of a campaign which will hit [Erwin] Rommel for six right out of Africa'. The 1906 *Wisden* mentions Montgomery being part of a last-wicket century partnership for St Paul's School.

And when Benito Mussolini fell, leaving Hitler the last man standing, the British intelligence agencies used a cryptic message: 'McCabe is out, but Bradman is still batting.'

Not for long, though.

Chapter 44

'A DRAW WOULD HAVE BEEN SOMETHING OF AN ANTI-CLIMAX AND PRAISE IN WHICH THE AUSTRALIANS WERE UNSTINTED IS DUE TO HAMMOND AND HIS MEN FOR NEVER WASTING A SECOND.'

The Cricketer, Vol. 3, 1945.

Germany surrendered on 9 May 1945. Shortly after V-E Day, with Japan still at war, Australian Prime Minister John Curtin pushed for resumption of Test cricket. Pressure came from Winston Churchill as well, on Plum Warner, who had tirelessly organized wartime cricket matches at Lord's. The war was as good as over, so why wait?

And who better for resumption of cricket than England and Australia?

The Australian team was created from members of the Royal Australian Air Force (RAAF) and the Australian Imperial Force who were in Europe at that point. RAAF squadron leader Stan Sismey, a former New South Wales wicketkeeper, was put in charge.

Sismey had been the co-pilot of a Consolidated Catalina that was gunned down in the Mediterranean Sea in 1942. The plane sank, but the crew stayed on the sea for eight hours before being rescued. Sismey, his body punctured all over by shrapnel, stayed unconscious for eight hours—but survived.

He played the matches, but on field the Australians were led by Lindsay Hassett, the only one in the squad with Test cricket experience. Hassett would succeed Don Bradman as Australian Test captain. There was also a St Kilda footballer called Keith Miller, who used to bat but rarely bowl for Victoria. This series marked his first steps towards becoming one of the greatest all-rounders of all time.

The team also included, at various points depending on health and discharge date, Dick Whitington, Cec Pepper, Keith Carmody, Jack Pettiford, Dick Whitington and Bob Cristofani, all first-class players or umpires or both at some point.

They played five unofficial 'Tests'—three at Lord's, one at Bramall Lane, one at Old Trafford—against an English side led by Wally Hammond and consisting of Len Hutton, Bill Edrich, Les Ames, Alf Gover, Cyril Washbrook, Dick Pollard, Doug Wright, Walter Robins, Laurie Fishlock and George Pope.

Curtin could not attend the series due to poor health, but he sent his 'warmest good wishes' to MCC president Stanley Christopherson, who reciprocated Curtin's wish of 'never again will the matches be interrupted'. Curtin passed away between the second and third 'Tests'.

For the first 'Test', at Lord's from 19 May, the crowd queued up from the night before. They included soldiers of the Allied forces, many of them in uniforms. The gates opened at ten but had to be closed by eleven: it was a full house.

After England made 267, Miller slammed 105 in 186 balls as the Australians secured a lead of 188 at stumps on the second day, which also marked the end of the war in the Netherlands. Australia won by 6 wickets with 2 balls to spare.

A poignant moment came when South Australian seamer Graham Williams joined Miller. Williams had been shot and taken prisoner during the Libyan War. Despite losing 31 kilograms at the camp, he had worked closely with blind prisoners. He had become so weak that they had to periodically administer glucose water, but he refused to stop bowling. A packed Lord's cheered him to the wicket as he walked out.

At Bramall Lane, Hammond scored 100 out of 286 before Pope (5–58) bowled out the Australians for 147. This time the tourists had to chase 320 on the last day. Whitington and James Workman added 108 for the opening wicket but Pollard (5–76) bowled England to a 41-run win roughly around when the United Nations Charter was being signed in San Francisco.

The third 'Test' began at Lord's on the day Italy declared war on Japan. Hutton made 104 before Miller sent his stump cartwheeling. By now a new-ball bowler, Miller took 3–44 and Cristofani 4–43 in a total of 254. Pollard (6–75) got England a 60-run lead. Sismey (54) held the fort in a chase of 225 before Miller finished the match with an unbeaten 71. Meanwhile at

Potsdam, Churchill, Stalin and Truman decided to insist on Japan's unconditional surrender.

The fourth 'Test' began on the day of the Hiroshima bombing. The Australians batted first for the first time. This time Miller scored 118 out of 388 as Pope and Pollard took 4 wickets apiece. Washbrook then scored a hundred and the match ended in a draw. About 93,000 watched the match, a record for a three-day match at Lord's.

The Old Trafford 'Test' began five days after Japan's surrender. Yet again, Australia batted and Miller top-scored, this time with 77 not out in an innings of 173. England responded with 243 against Cristofani (5–55) before Lancashire seamer Eddie Phillipson (6–58) reduced the Australians to 105–8. Cristofani now hit 110 in 120 balls to lift Australia to 210, but England won by 4 wickets to level the series.

In all, the Australians played twenty-one matches in England. Of these, the five 'Tests' and the Scarborough Festival match got first-class status. En route home, the Australian Services played nine matches in India—including three against all-India sides at Bombay, Calcutta and Madras—and one in Ceylon.

Denis Compton, posted in India, played at Calcutta against East Zone. During the game, a group of rioters approached him at the crease with 'Mr Compton, you very good player but you must stop.' Compton pointed at Hassett as the man in charge. The unruffled Hassett addressed the leader: 'You wouldn't happen to have a cigarette, would you, old boy?' The match resumed.

But there was no respite for the war veterans even after they returned to Australia. They now had to play all six Australian states before they were free to go home. By the time they were done, the players—to quote Hassett—were 'absolutely fed up with cricket'.

Test cricket resumed next summer.

Section 7

The Times, They Are a-Changin'

Chapter 45

'GIRLS DON'T PLAY CRICKET.'

Wolverhampton policeman to Rachael Heyhoe, circa 1947.

In the early post-war years, a group of boys was playing cricket on a street in the old Midlands city of Wolverhampton. A policeman caught them in the act and took their names down. The only person who got away was a girl who had been batting as proficiently as the boys.

'Girls don't play cricket,' came the explanation, a dozen years after England Women had won Test series in both Australia and New Zealand. Rachael Heyhoe (later Heyhoe Flint) later described it as 'about as devastating a blow to my pride as anyone could have delivered'.

She had a remarkable *cricket* career. The italicization of 'cricket' is deliberate here, because she also played hockey for England as a goalkeeper, had a single-figure handicap in golf, played squash for Staffordshire, and became director of the Wolverhampton Wanderers Football Club.

In the Oval Test of 1963 against Australia, she hit the first six in women's Test cricket. On captaincy debut, in 1966, she made 113 and 59 not out. Her series tally read 356 at 71.20, at that point a world record for a three-Test contest. She retired with 22 Tests, 1594 runs, three hundreds and thirteen fifties—world records at that time. Her ODI average of 58.45 is *still* the best with a 500-run cut-off. As captain, she never lost a Test, and was the first to win a World Cup across genders.

Yet, none of that matches her contributions off the field. In an era when women's cricket was in the doldrums, she turned things around with an ally, her friend 'Union Jack' Hayward, benefactor of Wolverhampton Wanderers and chief patron of women's cricket in the England of that era.

They obtained the sanction from WCA president Sylvia Swinburne. Hayward put in some money, as did Prudential. Heyhoe Flint set out to organize the first multinational cricket competition since the Triangular Test Tournament of 1912. England won that first World Cup.

That done, Heyhoe Flint set out to achieve the unthinkable, of arranging a women's match at Lord's, the hallowed abode of chauvinism of the time. When the MCC were reluctant, she responded: 'There are a lot of sex discrimination cases in the news these days—I think I'll take Lord's to the Equal Opportunities Commission.'

Of course, she had said it 'half-jokingly', as Heyhoe Flint admitted to in her autobiography: 'Deep down, I knew that I never had the slightest intention of carrying out the threat, or indeed the capability.' But the media ensured her words became big news over the next two days. They also approached Lord's and the WCA for reactions.

At this point, it transpired that the WCA had been negotiating with Lord's 'in a quiet and correct manner' with the same goal in mind. It is not clear why they had kept Heyhoe Flint, 'in charge of WCA promotions for the summer', oblivious to these updates. Now they were livid, for her words might have sabotaged their cause.

Thankfully, no damage was done, and the MCC agreed: Lord's would host the second ODI of the 1976 series against Australia.

Ten days before that, at The Oval, Heyhoe Flint had batted for a day and a half to save a Test against Australia. She was received in the pavilion by her husband, former Warwickshire leg-spinner Derrick Flint, with 'a kiss and a glass of cold beer'. This had not gone down very well with the authorities. Not 'appropriate behaviour for an England captain', they had said.

At Lord's, she was chastised for posing with her child, for players' children were not allowed at the venue. It did not matter that she had led England two months after giving birth, and 'would pack the car with a play pen, potty, clothes, toys, pram, food and her baby boy in a carrycot, as well as all her cricket kit' on most Saturdays.

They dropped her from the 1978 World Cup squad 'with youth in mind for the future'. It was a ridiculous reason: Heyhoe Flint might have been thirty-eight, but she was six months younger than Mary Pilling, who led the side. A furious Hayward withdrew his sponsorship at his friend's ignominy. In one sweep, England lost their captain, main batter, the face of women's cricket in the country, and financer. To add to the irony, England recalled a forty-three-year-old Heyhoe Flint for the 1982 World Cup.

Amidst all this, Heyhoe Flint voiced her discomfort on the boycott of apartheid in South Africa—a reminder of no human being perfect. She tried her best to organize fixtures against South Africa throughout her career. She was unhappy when Jamaica and Trinidad & Tobago's protests forced South Africa out of the 1973 World Cup.

At the same time, her continued fight for equal rights for women cannot be denied. In 1998, more than two centuries after its existence, the MCC relented by allowing their women as members for the first time. In 1999, Heyhoe Flint was among their first ten female members. In 2004, she became the first woman to be elected to the MCC full committee.

Upon being appointed to the House of Lords in 2010, she famously said 'I will certainly look forward to the commute from one Lord's to another Lords.'

The following year she became a life peer. Even there, she decided to not adhere to norms. Peerage titles had to be of one word; and unlike Baron Lloyd-Webber and Viscount Alanbrooke, among others, Baroness Heyhoe Flint would not hyphenate her two surnames.

Chapter 46

'BROWN LEARNS THE HARD WAY; RUN OUT AGAIN.'

Ray Robinson, the *Sun* (Sydney), 14 December 1947.

Thomas Barker ran out the non-strikers who had left the crease before he released the ball, in 1835, 1836, 1837, 1842 and 1843—the first recorded instances of such dismissals in first-class cricket. There had been no uproar.

James Pycroft, who did his bit towards mythologizing cricket as a noble sport, described Barker in his *Cricketana* (1854) as 'an old player quite unequalled in his experience as an umpire' before chronicling Barker's commentary on the Laws of Cricket. The run-outs had not blotted Barker's image.

William Hendley created some confusion when he did an encore at Christchurch in 1864–65 and at Dunedin in 1865–66. Newspapers reported the dismissals as 'st and b Hendley', though these were subsequently changed to run-out.

At Lord's in 1870, Eton captain George Harris (later Lord Harris) ran out Conrad Wallroth of Harrow. Spencer Gore, the first man to win Wimbledon, noted in the 1898 anthology *Harrow School* that Harris 'put himself on to bowl (quite rightly, to my mind), and, pretending to bowl, caught Wallroth tripping, and he paid the penalty'.

There were other instances too, but no one cast any aspersion on the bowler. In fact, Nicholas Felix warned non-strikers 'too anxious to obtain a run' in *Felix on the Bat* (1845): 'It is dangerous to leave your ground before you are well convinced that the bowler is not watching your over anxiety [*sic*].'

By the time India toured Australia in 1947–48, such dismissals had taken place seventeen times in first-class cricket. This is a conservative estimate, for scorecards merely recorded them as run-outs. Only the most diligent scorers mentioned additional information in their footnotes.

Now, in a tour match in Sydney, Bill Brown stepped out of the crease before Vinoo Mankad released the ball. Mankad warned him. When Brown erred again, Mankad ran him out. Bill O'Reilly summed up with characteristic clarity: 'There is nothing in the laws of the game to say that the bowler shall even warn the batsman of his unfair play. Mankad subscribed to the ethical rule … Brown was at fault.'

Brown did not learn his lesson. He left the crease again at Brisbane during another tour match. Mankad warned him, and that was that. Perhaps emboldened by that, Brown was at it again, in the Sydney *Test match*.

There was obviously no warning this time: Mankad simply took the bails off. Brown threw his bat in anguish but had to pick it up and walk back. The venerable Ray Robinson came out in Mankad's support. The title quote of this chapter was, in fact, the headline of his column.

Australian captain Don Bradman made his team's stance clear: 'There was absolutely no feeling in the matter as far as we were concerned, for we considered it quite a legitimate part of the game.'

The Australian public generally sided with Mankad as well. The *Sydney Morning Herald* invited reactions from readers. 'If a schoolboy was dismissed in this way, the sports master would probably stand him down for a couple of matches,' wrote one I.W.M. 'Did Brown do this sort of thing against the Englishmen? I'll guarantee he didn't, because he knew he wouldn't have got away with it.'

'If Brown does not know the rules or will not accept decisions in a sporting manner, he is not a proper person to play for Australia,' added one A.W. Richards.

Mankad received near-unanimous support (exceptions included Jack Fingleton and Duleepsinhji). Brown himself got over it quickly. Later that season, he tried to do it himself, albeit as a joke. Australian newspapers reported that he was 'doing a Mankad'.

Looking back at the incident all these years later, one cannot help but admire Mankad. India, a new country, were playing against one of the greatest sides of all time at their den. None of that prevented him from doing the right thing.

Over time, however, cricket's attitude changed, towards both the dismissal and the bowler.

When Charlie Griffith ran out Ian Redpath without a warning at Adelaide in 1968–69, the *Age* reported that he 'pulled a "Vinoo Mankad"'. When Greg Chappell warned and ran out Brian Luckhurst at Melbourne in 1974–75, Percy Beames incorrectly mentioned that 'Mankad started the fad'. In the *Sydney Morning Herald* in 1978–79, Kersi Meherhomji noted that the word 'Mankaded' had already been coined.

The narrative changed over the next few decades. The bowlers were blamed instead of the errant non-striker. Courtney Walsh was praised when he spared Saleem Jaffar at the 1987 World Cup. After running out Peter Kirsten, Kapil Dev drew the wrath of opposition captain Kepler Wessels when India toured South Africa in 1991–92.

What Kapil did was right, for Kirsten was the one at fault, said Ravichandran of Chennai to his son, Ashwin. He reminded the boy that Walsh's act had knocked the West Indies out of the World Cup. His words—'Do not let the batters get away with it'—left a lasting impression.

When a twelve-year-old Ashwin was bowling in a club match, Ravichandran gestured from behind the striker that the non-striker had been leaving the crease prematurely. Ashwin ran him out. His coach did not speak to Ravichandran for a week. Decades later, R. Ashwin would run out Jos Buttler in similar fashion.

During the Australia–India Boxing Day Test match of the 2011–12 tour, Paul Sheahan, former Test cricketer and president of the Melbourne Cricket Club, introduced Rahul Mankad, the youngest son of Vinoo, as 'son of the notorious Mankad'. Rahul voiced his discomfort about his father's name entering the cricketing lexicon, for he had realized it was being used in a derogatory way.

This form of dismissal saw a revival in the late 2010s. Keemo Paul did it at the 2016 Under-19 World Cup. Ashwin at the IPL.

In 2021, Cameroonian Maeva Douma ran out *four Ugandans in the same innings* ('Why shouldn't I use this opportunity to get the players out?').

Finally, after Deepti Sharma ran out Charlie Dean at Lord's in 2022, things escalated enough for the MCC to issue a statement: 'MCC's message to non-strikers continues to be to remain in their ground until they have seen the ball leave the bowler's hand.'

There is still an illogical stigma associated with the dismissal in some quarters, but the misplaced sense of moral superiority is disappearing rapidly.

Chapter 47

'LADIES AND GENTLEMEN, THERE IS A CORRECTION TO YOUR SCORECARDS. FOR F.J. TITMUS, READ TITMUS, F.J.'

The Lord's PA system, 3 May 1950.

For their match against Surrey, the MCC had included a teenage off-spinner called Fred Titmus. The announcement blared across the ancient venue even as the spectators were settling down with the blank scorecards in their hands.

The placement of the initials on the scorecards indicated whether the cricketer *officially* made money out of cricket. The rich amateurs (Gentlemen) did not: their initials preceded their names. For professionals (Players), it was the other way round. This preposterous ritual was among the least repulsive aspects of the amateur–professional divide, a salient feature of English cricket for centuries.

The British nobility used to own cricket teams from at least the early eighteenth century. Many of them were inept cricketers, but they hired the best professionals in the country. Not only did they pay them to play cricket, but they often kept them on their payroll as gardeners, gamekeepers or similar—'retainer' jobs to prevent them from playing for rival teams.

The MCC, the headquarters of cricket, allowed only amateurs as members, but also employed and contracted professionals. While this often caused some resentment from the members, there was little doubt that the latter—being superior cricketers—drew more crowds.

This social divide in English cricket became more prominent over time. The amateurs, who obviously came from the upper social strata, enjoyed separate dressing-rooms and used different gates to enter the playing ground. On tours, they were entitled to superior travel and boarding facilities.

Few represented the era more than Bladen Hawke and George Harris, almost invariably referred to as 'Lord'. Both men were incompetent with the bat, and neither bowled nor kept wicket. Being born into nobility, however, enabled both to lead not only their counties but also England at Test cricket. They also enjoyed important positions in the cricket establishment.

The professionals, who hailed mostly from the working class, were the second-class citizens of the sport. They were not even allowed to address the amateurs by first names. In the 1930s, amateur Errol Holmes even considered reporting Wally Hammond, the greatest English professional batter of the time, for addressing him by the Christian name.

What made the system more hypocritical was that the amateurs often made more money from cricket by holding on to token jobs (a secretary's, for example) at the clubs. The Australian media did not think much of this practice; by the late 1880s, they began to refer to them as 'shamateurs'.

The first Gentlemen versus Players match was played in 1806. It became a regular fixture from 1819, and remained the most important match in England until the County Championship began in 1890. The Players won 125 and the Gentlemen 68 despite the blip during the W.G. Grace era (Gentlemen 27, Players 4).

So lopsided was the contest that the matches used 'odds' at times. Sometimes the Gentlemen played with more than eleven players. In 1831, the Players had only nine. In 1832, the wicket was 22" x 6" when the Gentlemen batted but 36" x 12" for the Players. And so on.

The mindset did not improve significantly in the new century. In 1912, C.B. Fry wrote that amateur cricketers 'enjoyed good cricket' while professional teams could not provide 'the combination of skill and moral prestige which constitute good cricket'. The next year, Home Gordon insisted that every county side included at least six amateurs.

The age-old taboo on making money out of cricket was voiced by the upper echelons, most of whom were born into wealth. 'When cricket is played for profit and for profit only, the end of cricket—of good cricket—is at hand and Lord's and The Oval may as well be delivered to the builders,' felt Plum Warner. He acknowledged that the professional was 'loyal and reliable', but at the same time he insisted that 'the amateur element should predominate'.

Surrey captain Percy Fender did not care much for such traditions. In 1924, he led out his entire team through the same gate at The Oval, leaving A.G. Gardiner aghast: 'It was a painful sight, and many of us closed our eyes rather than look upon it. We felt that Bolshevism had invaded our sanctuary at last.'

But society changed rapidly after the Second World War as many professionals 'who had fought the Germans and the Japanese, survived death marches and POW camps' returned to cricket. They were unlikely to put up with the nonsense for long.

Before the war, a cricketer of Hammond's stature had not been allowed to lead England while he was a Gloucestershire professional. To become captain, he had to declare himself an amateur. For that, he had to join Marsham Tyres as a director.

But now, the professional Len Hutton emerged as a candidate. As a cricketer, he was far superior to his amateur (and even professional) teammates. The MCC could not delay the inevitable. To the disgruntlement of some (still!), Hutton became England's first full-time professional captain in 1952. He silenced the outcry by regaining the Ashes after two decades, in 1953, and retaining it in Australia in 1954–55.

Lord Hawke, who had once said, 'Pray God, no professional will ever captain England,' was not alive at this time, but many had imbibed his mindset. Their resentment could not change the tide.

By the early 1960s, English cricket was on the verge of turning fully professional. By 1962, there were only fifty amateurs across the seventeen counties—but they included twelve of the captains. But even the latter was about to change.

The last Gentlemen versus Players fixture—the final bastion of the social divide—was played that summer. Players captain Fred Trueman was happy that the 'ludicrous business' was 'thankfully abolished'.

On 31 January 1963, the MCC finally abolished amateur status. All cricketers became professional. It did not make traditionalists happy. 'By doing away with the amateur, cricket is in danger of losing the spirit of freedom and gaiety which the best amateur players brought to the game,' lamented *Wisden*.

Jack Hobbs, arguably the greatest English professional batter until that point, felt: 'It is sad to see the passing of the amateurs because it signals the end of an era in cricket. They were a great asset to the game, much appreciated by all of us because they were able to come in and play freely, whereas many professionals did not feel they could take chances.'

However, it was a landmark moment in cricket upgrading itself to the professional sport we know today.

Chapter 48

'WITH THOSE TWO LITTLE PALS OF MINE, RAMADHIN AND VALENTINE.'

Egbert Moore aka Lord Beginner, 1950.

Across their first three tours of England—all between the wars—the West Indies lost six Test matches and drew three. They did beat England over this period, but those were the times when

England seldom sent first-string sides to anywhere other than Australia.

The squad that toured England in 1950, however, was significantly stronger. For the first time, they had two solid openers, in Allan Rae and Jeffrey Stollmeyer. The three men in the middle order—the majestic Frank Worrell, the relentless Everton Weekes and the powerful Clyde Walcott—would, over time, be referred to as the 'three Ws'.

Yet, when the tour got underway, none of them became the biggest talking point. The honours were shared by two young spinners, both of whom had played exactly two first-class matches on matting wickets before embarking on the tour.

Left-arm spinner Alf Valentine was *literally* short-sighted. Halfway through the tour, when a teammate asked him the score, he could not read the 'large and clear' figures on the scoreboard. It was then that they diagnosed his problems and prescribed him glasses.

Off-spinner Ramadhin, the first cricketer of Indian ancestry to play for the West Indies, did not have a first name. It was only when he toured England that he was told that 'nobody could go through life without initials'. The newspapers arbitrarily began to use K.T. Ramadhin. He eventually began to use 'Sonny', a name he had been assigned at school, as his first name.

On that tour, captain John Goddard deployed Ramadhin and Valentine in tandem, and they wheeled away, hour after hour, taking out the English batters one by one. Ramadhin (135) and Valentine (123) shared nearly half West Indies's tally of wickets (518). They also did 43 per cent of the bowling.

Their contributions went up in the Test series, where they accounted for 69 per cent of the overs. Across four Tests, Valentine claimed 33 wickets at 20.42 and Ramadhin 26 at 23.23: their teammates shared only 18 scalps.

Both youngsters debuted in the first Test match, at Old Trafford: Valentine claimed 11 wickets and Ramadhin 4, but they were outdone by the home spinners—Jim Laker, Eric Hollies and Bob Berry. England won by 202 runs.

But at Lord's, after Rae's masterful hundred took the tourists to 326, none of the England batters 'showed evidence of having mastered the problems of deciding which way Ramadhin (5–66) would spin' as Valentine (4–48) kept the pressure on at the other end. Walcott's ferocious 168 then helped Goddard set England an improbable 601—against Ramadhin and Valentine.

England began the final day on 218–4 in front of a small crowd dominated by Caribbean expatriates. Whatever they lacked in numbers, they more than made up in decibels. They arrived with 'guitar-like' instruments but also anything that could pass as an instrument, even metal dustbin lids. One of them even 'scraped away on a cheesegrater with a carving knife'.

Their 'loud commentary' became more intense as the day went on and the English wickets fell. This did not go well with some MCC members, of course. Some felt it was 'unnecessary'. England went to lunch 9 wickets down—Ramadhin 6, Valentine 3.

When Worrell finally got the last wicket, the crowd invaded the field, and, as the *Jamaica Gleaner* reported, 'bottles of rum were produced as if by magic and toasts were drunk to Goddard'. The celebrations spilled over outside the ground. They sang the lines Lord Kitchener (Aldwyn Robert) had written that day. The calypso would begin with '*Walcott, Weekes, and Worrell held up their name*' and end in '*With the spin bowling of Ramadhin and Valentine.*'

The words inspired Lord Beginner's (Egbert Moore) more famous *Cricket, Lovely Cricket*, where four of the five stanzas would end with the same two-line ode to the spin twins. The fans drank and danced in London, and the celebrations reverberated back home.

The West Indies won by 10 wickets at Trent Bridge (Ramadhin 7 wickets, Valentine 5). At The Oval, England made eight changes and Len Hutton made a magnificent double hundred, but the tourists won again, this time by an innings (Ramadhin 4, Valentine 10), to clinch the series 3–1.

'In the summer of 1950 West Indies cricket firmly established itself,' summed up *Wisden.* But the triumph transcended beyond the 22 yards.

'True West Indian independence and the national consciousness it required would be impossible until the West Indies had taken on the colonisers at their sacred game and mastered it sufficiently to defeat them at home,' C.L.R. James had predicted.

The seeds of that had been sown.

Chapter 49

'SOME HAD BIRTH RIGHT TO THE MEMBERSHIP: WE HAVE WON IT.'

Abdul Hafeez Kardar to *The Times* (published 13 February 1952).

As a nation, Pakistan was only four and a half years old when Abdul Hafeez Kardar wrote the letter. Born in Lahore, he had played all three Test matches for India on their 1946 tour of England but had stayed back in Pakistan after the Partition of 1947, as had former Indian Test cricketers Amir Elahi and Gul Mohammad.

The Partition of India had ripped the Indian subcontinent apart. The death toll was almost certainly around a million, while somewhere between 10–20 million were displaced.

The extent of the tragedy did not have an impact on Lord Mountbatten, the last Viceroy of India. In the 1968 Nehru Memorial Lecture at Cambridge, he (then Earl of Burma) proudly claimed: 'What I did in India in 1947 was one of the three most important events in the world in this century., equalled in significance only by the Russian revolution of 1917 and the Chinese Communist takeover of 1949.'

Of course, the cricketers were affected as well. India had picked young fast bowler Fazal Mahmood for their first-ever tour of Australia, in 1947–48. While travelling on a train from Poona to Bombay, Fazal was attacked by religious rioters. Had it not been for the timely intervention of C.K. Nayudu, armed with a bat, Fazal might have been lynched.

Fazal left for Pakistan and became the first spearhead of their attack, inspiring the next generation. Without a fast-bowling role model and with an excellent group of spinners, India resorted to spin. The bowling attacks of the neighbours followed different trajectories.

From Junagadh, Gujarat, went the Mohammad brothers—Wazir, Hanif, Mushtaq and Sadiq, all of whom played Test cricket, while a fifth brother, Raees, was the twelfth man in a Test match. Pananmal Punjabi, born in Karachi, opened the batting for India, while Comilla-born (Comilla was in East Pakistan, now Bangladesh) Probir Sen kept wicket. The list of cricketers born on one side of the future border and playing for the other is long.

Meanwhile, there was some deliberation over India entering the Commonwealth. Had they refused at this point, they would have had to relinquish their ICC Full Membership and Test status.

India's Test status was reinstated only after they agreed to enter the Commonwealth.

South Africa should have lost their status when they left the Commonwealth in 1961. The South African Cricket Association requested a change, and the votes were split by colour: India, Pakistan and the West Indies opposed them, while England, Australia, and New Zealand supported South Africa's inclusion. South Africa stayed put. Their games in the 1960s should not have Test match status, but they do.

India were not scheduled to play England for some time. To fill this gap, two Commonwealth teams toured India, in 1949–50 (featuring Frank Worrell, George Tribe, et al.) and 1950–51 (Worrell, Sonny Ramadhin, Jim Laker). Both teams also played in Ceylon, while the first tour also included Pakistan. On both tours, the visitors played combined XIs of India, Pakistan and Ceylon in Colombo.

But that was not all. An MCC side toured India, Pakistan and Ceylon, the next winter, in 1951–52. They played five Test matches in India. England then hosted India in the summer of 1952—pushing the Ashes by a year!

Pakistan were not a Test-playing nation when the MCC came over in 1951–52. The tourists played two unofficial 'Tests' against All-Pakistan XIs led by Kardar. Pakistan declared with a 174-run lead at Lahore, but the match fizzled out to a draw. Then they created history in Karachi.

Bowling first-change, Fazal claimed 6–40 to skittle out the MCC for 123. Pakistan managed a slender lead of 7 runs before Tom Graveney's 123 helped the visitors set a target of 285. The chase was led by Hanif, the diminutive teenager who held the fort for over four hours for his 64, but Pakistan still slipped to 178–5.

Kardar himself then held the fort with an unbeaten 50 ('I did not play a single aggressive shot for 165 minutes') and saw his team home with Fazal for company in front of 20,000 jubilant fans. Prime Minister Khawaja Nazimuddin himself greeted Kardar and Fazal as they left the ground.

The ICC had been founded by England, Australia and South Africa in 1909. India, New Zealand and the West Indies were invited in 1926. Two years before the 'Test' between Pakistan and the MCC, the ICC had announced that they would accept new members 'provided their cricket attained a high standard'—though the extent of this standard was not defined. Like many things in cricket back then, it was left to a few privileged old men who used to control cricket from Lord's.

The triumph against the MCC should have made a strong case for Pakistan, but sections of the media raised concerns over the standard of umpiring in the match. 'Pakistan's right to the membership of the ICC cannot be challenged,' Kardar affirmed.

At the ICC meeting on 28 July 1952, India proposed Pakistan's name for membership. England seconded it. That winter, Pakistan toured India for their first-ever Test series. For the first time, a team travelled to play a Test series by land—a two-hour bus journey from Lahore to Amritsar.

For some Pakistani cricketers, it was a homecoming. It was just as emotional for their former neighbours who greeted them.

And amidst all this, one of international cricket's greatest rivalries was born.

Chapter 50

'KEEP YOUR EYE ON THE BALL. WHEN YOU SEE IT COMING, KEEP LOW. THE BATSMEN WILL TRY TO KEEP IT DOWN, BUT THEY CAN'T PROMISE.'

Arsenal Stadium, Highbury PA system, 11 August 1952.

Surrey needed 25 to win at stumps on the second day at The Oval in 1889. They were 8 down, but Maurice Read would not bat—so all Yorkshire needed was 1 wicket. It was already a quarter past six. The light was as good as gone. The gas-lamps in the pavilion were lit. The streetlights were on. Yet, both sides agreed to do away with the match on that day.

Surrey eventually won this 'Gas-lamp game' by 2 wickets after forty-five minutes of play in the dark, but for years, cricket under lights was not considered seriously.

Then, in the 1930s, Alf Stone, a war veteran and tram dispatcher in Cowandilla (an Adelaide suburb), rolled a part of his back lawn and invited the local young fellows ('most of them unemployed') to play cricket after sunset. For illumination, he 'rigged up an overhead light, using most of the house light globes'.

As Electric Light Cricket (also known as Diggers' Game) grew in popularity, Stone patented it. Test cricketers like Lindsay Hassett, Garry Sobers and Ian Chappell played the sport. The games were played under varying rules, the most common of which featured an enclosed area about 'three quarters the size of a tennis court', eighteen-a-side teams, two or four runs (sixes came later), and innings of 36 overs of 12 underarm balls each. Three-over individual hundreds and four-digit team scores were not uncommon.

In 1938, there was even an 'Electric Light Cricket Test match' in St Kilda—an attempt to expand the sport to Melbourne—but it largely remained within South Australia. By the time the Second World War broke out, Adelaide the metropolitan area had twelve associations. By 1949, 7000 were playing it. But while floodlit, it was not quite bona-fide cricket.

The story for that began with Arsenal manager Herbert Chapman, who had a vision in the early 1930s. It did not materialize immediately: Chapman died in 1934, and the Second World War broke out. It was not before 1951 that floodlights were set up in the Arsenal Stadium of Highbury. That year, Arsenal hosted Rangers in the evening in front of 62,000 fans.

But that was football. Surely cricket, with the smaller, darker ball, white clothing, could not be played after sundown? This was, after all, a sport where they called for bad light, and everyone went off the ground when the umpires agreed …

But that was precisely what happened. A left-arm spinner, Jack Young of Middlesex played eight Tests between 1947 and 1949; he is best known for bowling 11 consecutive maiden overs in the Trent Bridge Test of the 1948 Ashes with Don Bradman at the crease. Young's benefit match was an exhibition cricket game between the Middlesex County Cricket Club and the Arsenal Football Club at Highbury—*under lights.*

The Compton brothers both played football for Arsenal and cricket for Middlesex at various points of their careers. In this novel game, Leslie led Arsenal and Denis captained Middlesex.

It was obviously not going to be a serious affair, but 8000 turned up. Millions tuned in to the live coverage of the concluding parts of the match on television. The ball and the stumps were painted white. They had to keep replacing the ball as the paint kept chipping off!

The white ball is not a recent phenomenon. In fact, the Laws of Cricket do not mention a colour for the ball at all. The first known mention of a colour was as late as in 1753: 'The crimson ball attack the destin'd mark/ The Youth's disastrous, short-liv'd, luckless chance.' In a letter to his brother George and George's wife, Georgiana, John Keats wrote about getting a black eye from a white cricket ball the first time he 'took a Cricket Bat', on 19 February 1819. Gerald Brodribb mentions an 'unsuccessful experiment' with the white ball in the 1930s.[*]

The ground was obviously rectangular, with short boundaries on the sides but very long ones for the straight hits. The centre-circle was partially covered by a black matting wicket. The goal posts were replaced by sight screens. The Bedser twins of Surrey, Alec and Eric, stood as umpires.

It was not easy for the Middlesex cricketers. They were already playing a three-day match against Surrey at the Oval and had to

---

[*] Sevenoke, 'Poem, Humbly Inscribed to His Grace the Duke of Dorset'.

rush to Highbury after stumps on the second day. Perhaps that was why this had to be a thirteen-a-side match.

Leslie Compton won the toss and opted to bat. The Middlesex fielders emerged from the tunnel—in a cricket match!—*kicking footballs*. Colin Grimshaw hit seven fours and four sixes in his 65 as the Arsenal batters hit their way to 189 all out (thirteen players, so 12 wickets, one must remember) in 21 overs.

Off-spinner Alexander Thompson claimed 5–9 for Middlesex, while Young, the beneficiary of the match, had 1–27. An unusual moment came when Bill Edrich ran to field a ball and Leslie Compton sprinted for a single. Footballer's instinct kicked in, and Compton shoulder-charged Edrich!

The lights came on between the innings amidst loud cheers, but that was drowned by an announcement on the PA system. The words, almost certainly unheard of in cricket, form the title of this chapter.

Edrich hit four fours and five sixes in his 70, but from 118–2, Middlesex collapsed to 187–9—though they still had 3 wickets in hand. Young walked out at this point wearing a miner's helmet and a lamp. They got the runs, but there was still time, so they batted on until they were bowled out for 237.

The media generally praised the concept, though in a half-amused way. 'What is to prevent non-stop Test matches where the last wicket falls as the milkman arrives?' asked *The Times*. 'At least there will be no appealing against the light.'

As with many things in cricket, Kerry Packer was the first to make floodlit cricket popular, in the late 1970s. Australia embraced the concept, as did South Africa behind the apartheid curtains. In 1980, Stamford Bridge (Essex against the West Indies) and Ashton Gate (World XI versus Rest of the World) hosted two day-night cricket matches.

But the concept really took off after the 1992 World Cup. Today, the shorter formats are almost always played under lights in major cricketing nations.

Chapter 51

'C'MON SON, THIS IS NO PLACE FOR YOU. LET'S SWING THE BAT AT THE BALL AND GET OUT OF HERE.'

Bert Sutcliffe to Bob Blair, Ellis Park, Johannesburg, 26 December 1953.

It was a day with no parallel in Test cricket. New Zealand lost by plenty, but Dick Brittenden still called it 'a great and glorious victory, a story every New Zealand boy should learn at his mother's knee'.

The South African attack had already consisted of the prodigious swing bowler David Ironside; the inexhaustible Anton Murray; and the parsimonious Hugh Tayfield, who still holds the world record for the most consecutive dot balls in Test cricket. And for the first Test, at Durban, they bolstered that attack even more by bringing in Neil Adcock, one of the deadliest fast bowlers in their history.

They won by an innings. In the second Test, at Johannesburg, South Africa were 259–8 at stumps on day one. In that era of archaic communication, the New Zealand cricketers had little idea of the disaster that had been unfolding back home.

An express train was travelling from Wellington to Auckland, but the bridge they had to cross on the Whangaehu River had lost a pier. The train crew was unaware. A last-ditch effort from driver Charles Parker and fireperson Lance Redman saved some lives; but the locomotive, the tender and five second-class carriages plunged into the river.

With a death toll of 151, the Tangiwai disaster is the worst-ever rail accident in New Zealand. It was 10.21 p.m. at Tangiwai when it happened; 12.21 p.m. in Johannesburg.

The next day, the rest day of the game, the anxious cricketers spent their Christmas by tuning in to the radio and reading the newspapers. Fast bowler Bob Blair's fiancée Nerissa Love was among the deceased. Blair stayed back at the hotel as his teammates left for the venue the next day. Manager John Kerr kept him company. The Ellis Park PA announced that Blair would not return that day.

Flags were lowered to half-mast as South Africa resumed their innings. They were bowled out for 271. Then they unleashed Adcock on what Bert Sutcliffe, New Zealand's best batter, called one of the fastest pitches he had batted on.

Adcock hit both openers with balls that kicked off a length. A short-pitched ball brushed Murray Chapple's glove, hit him on the chest and fell on the stumps.

'I had played only two balls from him when another flew at my head,' recalled next man Sutcliffe. 'I tried desperately to hook but was hit on the side of the head and went out like a light.' Blood trickled down a visible gash in his ears.

New Zealand captain Geoff Rabone rushed with two men and a stretcher. Sutcliffe recovered to his feet, refused the stretcher, and even shook home captain Jack Cheetham's hands on his way out, but the blow affected him for the rest of his life.

But Adcock had only begun. He hit John R. Reid all over the body before dismissing him. He rammed a ball into Lawrie Miller's chest: Miller coughed blood and joined Sutcliffe at the hospital with 'rattled ribs'. A ball ricocheted off Matt Poore's chest on to the stumps.

New Zealand were 35–4. They needed another 86 to avoid the follow-on with two men in the hospital and one in the hotel.

Adcock then hit John Beck on the groin so hard that the box *inverted* on impact. Jackie McGlew, fielding close-in, repaired it with Beck's bat handle. And when Beck eventually fell, Miller stunned the 23,000-strong crowd by walking out: he had left the hospital against the doctor's advice. He resisted for a while, but when he fell, the follow-on mark was still 40 away.

Meanwhile, back at the hospital, the doctors could not detect a fracture when they x-rayed Sutcliffe's 'fist-sized lump'. But when a doctor poked at the lump while dressing it up, Sutcliffe fell, unconscious. His left ear had been split, behind which there was a ghastly gash. He somehow recovered, fortified himself with 'a generous helping of Scotland's chief product', and returned to the venue.

When Rabone tried to stop him, Sutcliffe quipped, 'Have a look at the scoreboard, we're too many gone, for not enough,' and walked out. Blood oozed out of his ears. Visible streaks of red appeared on his bandage as he strode in.

He was obviously not going to hang around. He hooked a bouncer from Ironside for a six and cleared the fence twice off Tayfield; by the time he lost Frank Mooney, the follow-on had been averted. Tony McGibbon and Guy Overton fell quickly. As the players walked back, the crowd cheered Ironside for his five-wicket haul—before being stunned into silence.

Back at the hotel, Blair had been following the proceedings on radio. He had requested Kerr to call a taxi and proceeded to the ground. As he walked out to bat, tears rolling down his cheeks, 'the New Zealanders wept openly and without shame; the South Africans were in little better state'.

Sutcliffe, obviously distressed, put an arm around Blair. He then tore into Tayfield, one of the most parsimonious bowlers of all time. He deposited the first, second and fourth balls into the stands before running a single. Blair 'passed his glove across his eyes in the heart-wringing gesture of any small boy anywhere in trouble but defiant'; smashed the next ball for six over mid-wicket; and played out the rest of the 8-ball over. They set a world record for most runs in an over in Test cricket.

Blair did not add to his score. Sutcliffe remained unbeaten on a 112-minute 80 with four fours and seven sixes. They added 33 in ten minutes before walking back. 'Through they went, arms about each other, into the darkness of the tunnel, but behind them they left a light and an inspiration which several thousand lectures on how to play a forward defensive stroke will never kindle,' wrote Brittenden in *Silver Fern on the Veld.*

The fielders and crowd who were left were reduced to tears that day, as most of our species would have been. Yet, it was a study in cruel contrast. As Arunabha Sengupta observed in *Apartheid: A Point to Cover*, the same people had been 'largely apathetic and often condoning towards apartheid, to the evils of subjugation and discrimination, to the violation of the most basic human rights; not unsupportive of the ridiculously brutal and barbaric legislations handed out to the vast majority of their people'.

It was not that the White South Africans were incapable of empathy; they were simply selective about it.

Set to chase 233 in the fourth innings, New Zealand reached 75–3 before collapsing to 100, but none of that mattered. 'It is not the result of the match that will be best remembered when men come together to talk about cricket. They will speak of a match that was as much worth watching as it was worth playing, a match the New Zealanders decided must go on,' summed up the *Rand Daily Mail.*

From 2024, New Zealand and South Africa play bilateral Test series for the Tangiwai Shield.

Chapter 52

'IF IT WASN'T FOR NASSER AND MONROE, I'D BE ON THE FRONT PAGES EVERY DAY.'

Bert Flack, curator, Old Trafford, end-July 1956.

Jim Laker was used to freakish bowling figures. He took 6 wickets without conceding a run when Salts High School bowled out a team for a solitary run. In a Test match trial in 1948, he took 8 wickets for 2 runs from 14 overs.

But he saved his best for Australia. If his career record of 193 Test wickets at 21.24 sounds astonishing, it pales in comparison when pitted against his 79 wickets from 15 Ashes Tests at 18.27.

It began early. Posted as a corporal at Cairo during the Second World War, he claimed 6–10 against the Australian Servicemen. 'Laker Skittles Australians', ran the *Egyptian Gazette* headline.

Over a decade later, he was taking Australian wickets to win a contest. Brylcreem had announced £100 and a silver cup for the best bowling figures in the summer of 1956. Playing for Surrey, Laker claimed 10–88 *against the Australians*. Ken Smales of Gloucestershire trumped this with 10–66. Laker's Surrey teammate Tony Lock then got 10–54. But Laker's best was yet to come.

England won the third Test, at Headingley, to level the series 1–1. With 11–113, Laker was at the thick of things, while Lock played his part with 7–81. The teams then arrived at Old Trafford.

Seven years after the Test, pitch curator Bert Flack admitted to Ian Chappell that the ''eadqua'ters' had ordered him t' prepare a bleedin' turner'. England left out Fred Trueman and opened the bowling with Brian Statham and all-rounder Trevor Bailey, who described the 'dry and white' surface as a 'beach'.

Peter Richardson (104), Colin Cowdrey (80) and David Sheppard (113) took England to 459 as the spinners, captain Ian Johnson and Richie Benaud, shared 94 of the 158.3 overs and claimed 6 wickets.

Statham and Bailey bowled only until the ball had some shine. Then Lock and Laker took over. McDonald and Jim Burke still took Australia to 48–0 before Peter May got Statham to bowl an over to switch Laker to the Stretford End.

Laker had McDonald caught at short-leg. Two balls later, he produced 'the ball that won the Test': an off-break that pitched on the left-handed Neil Harvey's leg-stump, turned past the bat and hit the off-stump. 'The only ball I've seen similar was the ball that Warne got Gatting with,' recalled Harvey.

Lock got Burke soon after tea, the only Australian wicket Laker would not take in the match. Thirty-five minutes later, Australia folded for 84. Laker took 7–8 in 3.4 overs to finish with 9–37, but his job was only half done.

Ian Craig, one of Laker's victims, summed up the spell: 'Jim bowled well, and we batted very badly. We were all pissed off, felt we'd been dudded, and we dropped our bundle a bit.'

As it often happens, the touring side were not impressed by the pitch. 'If a team is invited to a series of five-day Tests, then the pitches should be prepared accordingly,' criticized Jack Fingleton. Bill O'Reilly called it 'a complete disgrace'.

Johnson overheard Flack thanking the Suez Crisis and Marilyn Monroe's wedding for taking the media attention off him. When Flack asked him about the choice of rollers, Johnson responded with, 'Please your f**king self.'

By stumps, Australia were 53–1 in the second innings. Harvey hit the first ball he faced—a knee-level full toss from Laker—to short mid-on. Rain washed out the next two days, on either side of the rest day, restricting cricket to 32.2 overs. Laker struck once, but when play resumed at 84–2 on the final day, a draw was not impossible.

Laker reduced Australia to 130–6 before McDonald and Benaud took them to 181–6 by tea, then to 198–6, but the resistance did not last. Once Laker had McDonald caught at backward square-leg, Australia caved in. After making 32 out of 84 in the first innings, McDonald made 89 in the second, but this was not his day.

'England cheated: if by cheating you include the practice of preparing wickets to suit your own purposes … The Test pitch was like Bondi Beach when it was dry and a mud-heap when it was wet,' he reminisced, before adding: 'They bowled well. We batted very badly.'

Benaud's 105-minute vigil included taking guard every over and walking out to tap the pitch 'after every ball'. Laker eventually got him, followed by Ray Lindwall. And at 5.27, he trapped wicketkeeper Len Maddocks leg-before to round things off. Australia made 205.

Laker finished with 10–53, still the best innings figures in Test cricket, and a match haul of 19–90. He remains the only bowler to take 19 wickets in a *first-class match*. He left the ground at eight and drove back to London. En route, he had a beer and a sandwich in a pub in Lichfield while watching his spell on television. No one recognized him.

There was no break for the new world-record holder. Despite reaching home late in the night, he had to show up at The Oval next morning to play for Surrey *against the Australians*. He rounded off the summer by taking 7 of the 15 Australian wickets in the fifth Test match, at The Oval.

Chapter 53

'I WANT TO SAY CLEARLY THAT THE IDEA OF ALEXANDER CAPTAINING A SIDE ON WHICH FRANK WORRELL IS PLAYING IS TO ME QUITE REVOLTING.'

C.L.R. James to the *Nation* (Trinidad), January 1960.

For decades, every person to lead the West Indies—in Test cricket or representative teams—had been a White man. Now, as the islands underwent significant sociopolitical change after the Second World War, there began calls for a Black captain.

Not everyone in the board agreed, and a compromise was reached. George Headley would become West Indies' first Black captain, but only for the first and fourth Tests of the 1947–48 home series against England: Gerry Gomez and John Goddard, both White, would lead in the other two.

When a back injury ruled Headley out of the fourth match, Goddard stayed on. He led the West Indies to a 2–0 win, then series wins in India and England. Jeffrey Stollmeyer succeeded him. For the 1954–55 home series against Australia, Denis Atkinson—with only twelve Test caps under his belt—was named Stollmeyer's vice-captain. When Stollmeyer missed three Tests of the series, Atkinson stepped in.

For the 1957 tour of England, the selectors recalled Goddard out of retirement and appointed him captain. After the dismal campaign, they replaced Goddard with Gerry Alexander. Stollmeyer, Atkinson and Alexander were all White, like Gomez and Goddard and unlike Worrell.

Worrell missed the first two years of Alexander's tenure—he was studying for his degree at the University of Manchester—but returned for the 1959–60 home series against England. In the first Test, Alexander declared with Worrell on 197. There was some merit in it, for Worrell had made only 20 in 130 minutes on the final morning, but it did cause a stir.

Two days after the Test, the *Nation* ran an article by political activist and Marxist writer C.L.R. James, with the headline 'Alexander Must Go, Make Worrell Captain': 'It is bad captaincy that is causing us to be scrambled, everybody is whispering and shrugging shoulders … This fooling with the West Indies captaincy has gone on too long. It has to stop and the time to stop is now.' That edition of the newspaper sold out at a rapid rate.

James's words during a Test series did not sit well with Alan Ross, who had been covering the tour. Calling James a 'malicious xenophobe' and an 'irresponsible agitator', he added: 'Worrell's great gifts as a player, his intelligence and charm, and no doubt his capacity for leadership, cannot benefit from such advocacy.'

But James had only begun. A man on a mission, he would not give up until he succeeded. He addressed a subsequent article to the West Indian players: 'Enlighten the public. They are deeply concerned, worried and angry at what they consider the deliberate rejection and humiliation of Frank Worrell.'

A more strongly worded article followed: 'Whatever the result of this series I shall mobilise everything I can so that Frank should captain the team to Australia … If he [Alexander] is selected, I shall do my damnedest to see that Alexander is stood down for captaincy for the first Test … The Board should know that the eyes of the world are upon them … Not to select Worrell would be an act of war.'

He felt that the selectors sent 'populations of white people, black or brown men under a white captain. The more brilliantly the black men played, the more it would emphasise to millions of English people: "Yes, they are fine players, but, funny, isn't it, they cannot be responsible for themselves—they must always have a white man to lead them".'

That was what James had set out to change. He had been fighting for the right cause, but his attacks centred around Alexander the individual, a fine batter and an excellent wicketkeeper who had built a strong team over two years 'after the shambles of the 1957 tour of England'. With seven wins and four defeats from eighteen Tests, Alexander was the most successful West Indies captain until Worrell.

It is worth a mention that despite being light-skinned, Alexander was of mixed race. 'His mother was brown,' Simon Lister quotes Jackie Hendriks (Alexander's successor as the West Indian Test wicketkeeper) in his excellent biography of Worrell. 'And I knew his sisters of course, and one of the girls was dark-skinned.' If James was aware of this—it is difficult to believe that he was not—his stance seems even more surprising.

'I put my scruples aside and I think that for the first, and I hope the last, time in reporting cricket I was not fair,' James later admitted, 'but I was determined to rub in the faces of everybody that Frank Worrell … was being discriminated against.'

The end perhaps justified the means.

The 'Alexander must go' campaign predictably succeeded. 'Only a man with the stature and reach of James could have effectively launched and won the struggle,' admitted Weekes in *Mastering the Craft: Ten Years of Weekes.*

James's other great initiative had been unsuccessful. He wanted a Black West Indian side under Worrell to tour apartheid-era South Africa in 1959. Mixed-race cricket was out of the question there, but a non-White South African team had been selected with Basil D'Oliveira as captain. An itinerary had been drawn. However, the tour did not go through largely due to a campaign led by anti-apartheid educator and poet Dennis Brutus, who believed that organizing cricket between non-White teams in South Africa would be 'following the dictum of the apartheid regime'. It is difficult to disagree with Brutus.

In his first series as captain, in Australia in 1960–61, Worrell became the first Black man to lead the West Indies on a full tour. Named vice-captain, Alexander 'accepted Worrell as his leader and publicly extolled his virtues' and provided consistent support.

The new era in West Indies cricket would begin with the greatest Test series of all time.

Chapter 54

'WHATEVER YOU DO, DON'T BOWL A NO-BALL. THEY WILL NEVER LET YOU BACK IN BARBADOS.'

Frank Worrell to Wes Hall, Brisbane, 14 December 1960.

It began at Brisbane, with the greatest Test of all time. Garry Sobers set the tone with 132, and Norm O'Neill responded with 181. After Alan Davidson claimed 11 wickets to go with his first innings 44, Wes Hall (9 wickets in the game) reduced Australia to 109–6 by tea on the final day.

With 124 left in 120 minutes, chair of selectors Don Bradman approached captain Richie Benaud at the break: 'What is it going to be?'

'Well, we're going for a win.'

'I'm very pleased to hear it.'

Davidson and Benaud, the unbeaten batters, adopted a touch-and-run strategy. Loose balls were few, but they ran the short runs frantically to bring the target down to 7. It was Australia's match to lose, but Benaud pushed the penultimate ball of what seemed like the penultimate over to the leg-side and set off. Joe Solomon, 25 yards away, had only one stump to aim at—but still ran out Davidson.

The match changed its course again. Wally Grout had been chain-smoking for two hours. So anxious was he that he lost his gloves as he walked out, and finally recovered them from inside his pads.

Australia needed 6 in the final 8-ball over. Hall's first ball hit Grout on the solar plexus. Gasping for air, Grout noticed Benaud tearing down the pitch, and he somehow scrambled to the other end. An annoyed Hall now ignored Worrell's advice and banged the ball short. Benaud hooked but could only top-edge it to wicketkeeper Gerry Alexander.

Ian Meckiff played out the next ball. With 5 to score off 5, Grout set off as soon as Hall released the ball and made it to the other end by the time the ball sped past Grout's swinging bat and reached Alexander. Hall gathered Alexander's throw but missed running out Meckiff at the non-striker's end; in fact, he was fortunate to not concede overthrows.

A fuming Hall pitched up. Grout's hoick descended at square-leg. As Rohan Kanhai waited for the easy catch, Hall went for it too. A serious collision was averted—as was the near-certain dismissal. Amidst the pandemonium, they ran a single.

Three in three. Meckiff swung towards leg. The ground staff had left the clovers at that part unmown in the morning. That slowed the ball down enough for Conrad Hunte to cover acres of land, swoop down and throw the ball to Alexander in one swift motion. Alexander's dive beat Grout's, but not before the batters had run two to level the scores.

Last man Lindsay Kline could not find his gloves either: he had been sitting on them. As he took guard, Worrell had a word of caution for his pace spearhead.

Hall did not overstep. Kline flicked. Meckiff set off. Peter Lashley sprinted in from mid-wicket. Then Solomon, yelling, 'Move, move, move', emerged out of nowhere, and for the second time in less than ten minutes, broke the stumps from an absurd angle and found the batter short of his ground.

The West Indians celebrated as the dejected Australians walked back. Everyone thought the tourists had won. To add to the confusion, the ground scoreboard had stopped moving for a while during the last over, while the radio announced a West Indian victory.

In the commentary box, Johnny Moyes was the first to figure out that it was a tie. Bradman broke the news to the Australian cricketers, who showed up at the West Indies dressing-room, and there was champagne for everyone.

The second and third Tests featured 'normal' wins—for Australia in Melbourne, the West Indies in Sydney. In the fourth, at Adelaide, Australia were 9 down with an hour and fifty minutes to play. Ken Mackay and Kline played out time.

Chasing 258 in the decider in Melbourne, Australia were 254–7 when Grout late-cut Alf Valentine and ran 2. A bail lay on the ground, but Grout was ruled not out. Nevertheless, he soon fell, but Johnny Martin was dropped, and Australia won by 2 wickets to clinch this incredible series 2–1.

The stars lit up the contest. Lance Gibbs took 19 wickets in three Tests, including a hat-trick. Ten Australians and nine West Indians made fifties. Alexander scored a fifty in each of the Tests and held 16 catches, while Grout effected 23 dismissals. Benaud finished with 23 wickets and Hall 21. Kanhai made two hundreds, Bob Simpson four fifties. And, of course, there were Sobers (430 runs, 15 wickets, 12 catches) and Davidson (212 runs, 33 wickets).

But it was not merely about the results or performances either.

Post-war cricket had been 'a dull, lifeless pastime', dominated by flat wickets and slow run-making. With a run rate of 2.30, the 1950s are still the slowest-scoring decade in Test cricket. Bowlers struck every 79 balls, a drop from 76 from between the wars.

That was when this remarkable Test series took place. Worrell kept his promise of re-instilling 'some lost adventure into cricket', the Australians responded, and the crowds swelled. The gate receipts for the last match were at that point a record for a Test in Australia. The crowd celebrated the visitors as the tour went on. During the second Test, Benaud appealed for hit wicket when Solomon's cap fell on the stumps. When the umpire ruled out, the Melbourne crowd booed Benaud.

After the Brisbane tie, the Australian board had commissioned former-Test-cricketer-turned-jeweller Ernie McCormick to design a trophy. Bradman himself bore the request to his former colleague. Ahead of the final Test match of the series, they announced that it would be named after Worrell.

After the series, a smiling Worrell gave a final polish to the trophy with his coat sleeve in front of 40,000 people. Then he himself presented it to Benaud. The West Indians got 'a send-off the like of which is normally reserved for Royalty and national heroes … Open cars paraded the happy players from the Caribbean among hundreds of thousands of Australians who had been sentimentalised through the media of cricket as it should be played.'

But even that was not all. Until this point, England used to be the centre of cricket, a predominantly British colonial sport. The focus of the sport was invariably around how the other teams, especially Australia, played against them. Now, for the first time, a Test series not involving England became the centre of attention.

Chapter 55

'PERHAPS IT WAS NOT, STRICTLY SPEAKING, FIRST-CLASS CRICKET BUT AS ENTERTAINMENT IT IS WITH US FOR THE FORESEEABLE FUTURE. LET US BE GRATEFUL FOR IT.'

John Arlott, the Observer, 1963.

As we have seen, the popularity of cricket took a nosedive after the Wars. As many as 2.2 million had paid to watch the County

Championship in 1946. By 1962, the count had dropped to 7,00,000. Something needed to be done.

The solution lay in plain sight. For decades, league cricket—especially in the Lancashire League—used to be played over a day. While there was no restriction on overs per innings, both sides would get to bat once each.

Limited-overs cricket, meanwhile, had been showing up around the world. In January 1944, the Madras Cricket Association had launched the 55-overs-a-side B. Subramaniam Memorial Tournament. The All-India Pooja Cricket Tournament and the Talim Shield had followed suit, though none of these was a national contest.

The seeds of a national competition were sown in 1962. Leicestershire secretary Mike Turner noticed that four Midlands counties—Nottinghamshire, Northamptonshire, Derbyshire and his own team—did not have any Championship matches scheduled on the first two Wednesdays of the summer.

So, he sent out a proposal to the other three teams: would they be interested in a 65-overs knockout competition—two semi-finals on 2 May and the final on 9 May? All four clubs came on board. Leicestershire beat Derbyshire and Northamptonshire prevailed over Nottinghamshire in the semi-finals and Leicestershire in the final to win a trophy that Turner had acquired from a second-hand shop and got polished.

The result was of little consequence. The feedback was largely, though not unanimously, positive. One semi-final was telecast live. Ticket sales were not great, but that was largely due to the gloomy weather. The cricketers themselves were 'won over by the enjoyment'. Turner had managed to create a buzz.

'I was left wondering why the same approach could not go into three-day county cricket,' wrote Leslie Smith in *The Cricketer*. 'I am sure that the players and the public would enjoy

themselves far more than they do now.' He was talking about the knockout format.

The MCC had attempted the knockout format before. In 1873—seventeen years before the County Championship began—they had envisioned a knockout 'Champion County Cup' where 'the matches will be arranged by lot'. The MCC offered a silver cup for the tournament, which was supposed to be played at Lord's in its entirety. It is not clear whether the idea was inspired by the FA Cup, which had started in 1871–72.

Six counties had accepted the proposal, but following some withdrawals, the tournament was left with hosts Middlesex and two others. It stopped after one match, between Kent and Sussex on a 'dangerously bad' pitch that the former won by 52 runs. 'What became of the Cup seems an unsolved mystery,' concluded *Wisden*.

Ninety years later, they relaunched their idea of a knockout competition where matches would be 65 overs an innings and no bowler would be able to bowl more than 15 overs. Gillette stepped in as sponsor.

Lots were drawn in the Lord's Long Room in front of television cameras to determine the fixtures. Since seventeen counties played in the Championship, there had to be a lone preliminary match before the first round of sixteen teams. The Lancashire versus Leicestershire match at Old Trafford on 1 May 1963 was the first-ever List A game.

A first-round match at Tunbridge Wells drew some attention. Derek Underwood of Kent went for runs, but his captain Colin Cowdrey insisted he attack the batters. Underwood finished with 11–0–87–0 and Sussex with 314–7.

In response, Kent became 19–2 before Peter Richardson and Cowdrey added 80. While Richardson looked dangerous, Cowdrey was not scoring as quickly. Sussex captain Ted Dexter now pushed the field back (there was no restriction) for Richardson and brought them closer for Cowdrey. In other words, he did what every captain would have done today.

But these were different times. The Kent committee wrote a letter about such 'unsporting tactics'. The crowd booed Dexter as well, for they had not seen anything like this before. Dexter did not care: 'Everyone thought it was a rotten thing to do, but there it was. I had shown people what they could be let in for!'

In the first-ever Gillette Cup final, Sussex made 168 in front of a Lord's crowd of at least 20,000. Worcestershire crawled to 133–9 before Roy Booth and Bob Carter added 21 for the last wicket. As the asking rate mounted, Dexter put all nine fielders on the ropes. The last wicket was a run-out.

Sussex won the cup and £6500, but Dexter took flak. 'The wrong team won ... Dexter's tactics, successful as they were, could eventually kill a great idea,' wrote Brian Chapman in the *Daily Mirror*. Richie Benaud felt 'it would be a pity if every team did this next year and brought about the demise of what could be a fine competition'. *The Times* called it 'a perversion of positive cricket'.

Dexter's criticism notwithstanding, the Gillette Cup managed to breathe life into English cricket. The idea caught on around the world. Australia played a 50-over 'international' on their South Africa tour of 1966–67, though this did not get ODI status. Two years later, Australia had their own domestic one-day cup—where New Zealand were one of the teams. South Africa had their own Gillette Cup from 1969–70.

Gordon Ross wrote in the 1974 *Wisden* that 'the need was felt to place restrictions on the fielding side' when the Gillette Cup was launched in South Africa. For the first 8 overs, there had to be at least two fielders in 'slip and/or gully', and at least seven fielders inside a 30-yard circle—the powerplay's truncated predecessor. At any point there could not be more than five fielders outside the circle or on the leg-side, and so on. One can perhaps attribute field restriction in limited-overs cricket to South Africa.

When rain washed out a significant part of the Melbourne Test match of the 1970–71 Ashes, Australia hosted England for a 40-over (8-ball) match on the scheduled fifth day. This became the first-ever ODI. By the next five years, the women and the men had a World Cup each.

By the early 1980s, the West Indies, India, New Zealand and Pakistan had all launched their own domestic limited-overs competitions.

Chapter 56

'IF YOU WANT TO BOWL UNDERARM, THAT'S OKAY.'

Richie Benaud to Ian Meckiff, Brisbane, 9 December 1963.

In 1885, over two decades after overarm bowling had been legalized, umpire Jack Platts deemed Lancashire fast bowler George Jowett's action as illegal and ruled a no-ball. Later that summer, Kent captain Lord Harris wrote to the Lancashire committee, expressing concerns over the actions of fast bowler Jack Crossland and left-arm spinner George Nash. Kent even cancelled their match against Lancashire at Tonbridge.

Over the years, pacers figured out that bending elbows enabled them to bowl quicker. Finger-spinners, too, could turn the ball more. Some bowlers bent their elbows due to physiological constraints. The umpires called the bowlers sporadically in first-class cricket.

During the 1897–98 Ashes, Australian fast bowler Ernie Jones became the first to be no-balled for throwing in Test cricket. It was not until 1953–54 at Kingston that another bowler, Tony Lock of England, was called in Test cricket.

To be fair to Lock, he did not understand where he was going wrong. It was only when England were touring New Zealand in 1958–59 that home captain John R. Reid showed the tourists a film of the Lord's Test match between the two nations. The 'pronounced bending and straightening' of Lock's arm was evident.

There was an 'absolute roar of mirth' from the teammates of Lock, who had destroyed New Zealand with 5–17 and 4–12 in that Test. 'Had I known I was throwing I wouldn't have bowled that way,' admitted a horrified Lock. He later remodelled his action.

In 1958–59, Charlie Stayers of Guyana and Geoff Griffin of Natal were called for throwing in first-class cricket, but it was the Ashes in Australia that hit the headlines. Ian Meckiff, Keith Slater, Jim Burke and Gordon Rorke were all accused of throwing; Rorke was also guilty of 'dragging' his front foot too much.

Ahead of the 1959 English summer, the MCC cricket subcommittee asked the umpires to prepare a list of bowlers with suspect actions. That season, the umpires no-balled Lock, Derek Pearson (twice) and John Aldridge. It was evident that they were going to be stricter than ever.

South Africa still included Griffin in their squad for their 1960 tour of England. There had been some buzz around him even before the tour. In England, he was called eight times against Nottinghamshire.

This was unfortunate, for a childhood accident had prevented Griffin from straightening his bowling arm completely. However, he set about to correct his action. A three-day session at Alf Gover's school in London seemed to have sorted it out. Bowling at a reduced pace on Test debut, at Edgbaston, he took 4 wickets. He was then called six more times against Hampshire.

Then, in the Lord's Test, Griffin returned to full pace. He became the first South African to do the hat-trick in Test cricket. Yet, there was little reason to celebrate, for the additional pace had come at a cost: his old action had returned.

The umpires called him eleven times in the first innings. Desperate, Griffin switched to underarm, but Frank Lee called no-ball again—for he had forgotten to inform his change of action. His Test career was over.

The Law was changed that summer. 'The bowling arm having been bent at the elbow, whether the wrist is backward of the elbow or not, is suddenly straightened immediately prior to the instant of delivery' amounted to no-balls now. Australia wisely left Meckiff, Slater and Rorke, all active cricketers, out of the 1961 Ashes squad.

Born with a semi-disjointed shoulder, Meckiff was yet to be called in first-class cricket, but there had been buzz around him. Jim Laker compared him to a dart thrower, while Fred Trueman deemed his action 'totally illegal'. All that, and more, earned him the nickname of 'Chucker'. As the relentless pressure took a toll, his son Wayne was bullied at school. Meckiff's own health deteriorated.

But Meckiff rallied on. He changed his action once, in 1959–60. The touring West Indians of 1960–61 felt he had been doing fine. After Alan Davidson's retirement, he was the best left-arm fast bowler in Australia.

The blow came when Bill Priem no-balled him in a Sheffield Shield match in 1962–63. Later that summer, he was selected for the first Test against South Africa, at Brisbane. After Australia made 435 and Graham McKenzie was done with the first over, captain Richie Benaud summoned Meckiff.

As Meckiff released the second ball of his 8-ball over, square-leg umpire Col Egar signalled no-ball. Meckiff bowled again. Egar called again. In his effort to keep the arm straight, Meckiff bowled a full toss that Trevor Goddard put away for four. Benaud offered him a chance to switch to underarm, but Meckiff declined. It took him 12 balls to complete the over.

The crowd, meanwhile, got behind Meckiff and booed Egar incessantly. Despite the incessant 'We want Meckiff' chants, Benaud did not recall him, not even from the other end. After stumps, a section of the crowd carried Meckiff 'shoulder high' off the ground.

'I think the best thing you can do, Mecky, is retire,' Don Bradman, one of the selectors, told him over a two-hour chat the next day, the rest day of the Test. Sensing the finality, Meckiff retired from first-class cricket.

But the Test was not over yet. When play resumed at Brisbane, there was extra police 'because of fears that the umpires, selectors and Benaud might be molested'. An anonymous caller warned the police that Egar would get the 'Kennedy treatment' at Melbourne. On ABC, Vic Richardson called the entire saga 'a very noisy execution'.

Conspiracy theories ran wild. Some accused Benaud of deliberately bringing on Meckiff when Egar was the leg-umpire. Some accused Bradman of suggesting the idea to Benaud or to Egar (the latter being fuelled by the fact that Bradman and Egar had taken the same train to Brisbane). Everything added fuel to the conspiracy fire. None of these theories bore evidence.

However, it cannot be denied that the Australian board did not bother to warn Meckiff when they could have. They did not invest in him for long enough for him to change his action. They found it easier to end his career.

The spectacle of a gifted cricketer bowing out in front of a packed crowd during a Test match remains one of cricket's saddest stories.

Chapter 57

'THAT, MR ALLEN, IS £500, AND WE'RE SKINT.'

Bernie Coleman to 'Gubby' Allen, The Oval, 22 August 1968.

Cricketers had been endorsing sporting equipment for years, but W.G. Grace was probably the first to endorse a non-cricketing product. Sometime around 1900, a print advertisement featured an image of Grace—in complete cricketing gear—with the text 'Colman's Mustard: like Grace, heads the field'.

But Grace was an individual. Over the years, cricketers have endorsed products, but it was not as easy for establishments.

Part of the reason was the 'very toffee-nosed' club committees, who were not keen on caving in to sponsors.

Gillette had been sponsoring the domestic limited-overs tournament in England between 1963 and 1980. As the competition grew in popularity, people began to associate their name more with cricket than with razor blades. But that had been about it.

Then, in the late 1960s, Bernie Coleman, a South London publican who had recently joined the Surrey County Cricket Club committee, stepped in.

As we have discussed, the amateur–professional divide had been eradicated from English cricket earlier that decade. The amateurs' dressing-room at The Oval lay unused. Coleman gave it 'a fresh coat of paint', turned it into a hospitality tent, and sold it to XS Insurance as a box for £500.

The 1968 Ashes was still live when the two teams arrived at The Oval for the final Test. 'Gubby' Allen, the supremo of English cricket of the time and the epitome of everything old-school, walked into the dressing-room with his cigarette holder, and noticed the XS advertisement board.

He was horrified at this intrusion: 'What's that sign? We can't have that.'

Coleman revealed the amount and reminded Allen of Surrey's financial position (as detailed in the quote). The next day, the MCC—run by 'mostly Old Etonians and public schoolboys'—sent Coleman a letter, asking him to remove the sign. He did not bother.

By the next summer, every Test venue in England had advertisement hoardings. They soon became a common feature around the world.

It was not Coleman's last legacy at The Oval. Through two Australians—former Test cricketer Bob Cowper and business owner John Elliott—he struck a deal with Foster's. Elliott wanted to launch Foster's beer in London. Coleman offered him the naming rights of the venue for £1 million.

Elliott agreed. When the Surrey committee did not, Coleman reminded them that Thomas Lord, who had lent his name to the more famous cricketing venue in the city, used to be a wine merchant. Surrey eventually got £4 million from Foster's.

Coleman did not stop there. In 1981, he found out that Gillette had been offering only £30,000 to renew their contract for the one-day tournament—significantly lower than the NatWest Bank's £1,00,000. Coleman replaced Gillette with NatWest.

By then, cricket had found other patrons, particularly in the tobacco sector. Banned from advertising cigarettes on television since 1965, John Player stepped in as sponsors for the 40-over Sunday League. They paid £65,000 annually and gave out free cigarettes to fans during the matches.

From 1972, Benson & Hedges joined the bandwagon with £80,000 a year. Over time, they became synonymous with ODI tournaments in Australia. Rothmans were another sponsor of ODI tournaments, especially in Sharjah, while Wills sponsored the 1996 World Cup.

Tobacco brands continued to put in money until cricketers stopped endorsing the products, while some grounds ran anti-tobacco campaigns. The latter caused some hilarity at The Oval in 2007 when a man, dressed as a cigarette to raise awareness, caused some disturbance in front of the sight screen, forcing the PA to announce, 'Would the cigarette please sit down?'

Other sectors saw cricket as a market as well. Prudential sponsored bilateral ODIs and the early World Cups in England. Reliance stepped in when India and Pakistan co-hosted the tournament in 1987. The next two decades or thereabouts were marked by an increasing number of brands associating themselves with cricketers, teams and tournaments.

Now, in franchise-run T20 leagues, commentators name the sponsor before nearly everything, from 'maximums' to 'game-changing moments'.

Overkill, perhaps, but then, the sponsors foot the bills …

Chapter 58

'OH CHRIST, YOU'VE PUT THE CAT AMONG THE PIGEONS NOW.'

Charlie Elliott to Basil D'Oliveira, The Oval, 23 August 1968.

In 1948, the South African National Party won the elections and made apartheid a government policy. An already racist society took a deeper plunge towards abnormality.

Cricket continued at all levels in a way befitting of the detestable policies. White and non-White players were barred from playing together. Facilities for the non-White cricketers were sparse. The non-White fans were confined to a tiny section of the stands, colloquially referred to as 'The Cage'. Nelson Mandela and Basil D'Oliveira watched Test cricket from there.

The White-only South African Cricket Association was, as we have seen, an ICC member. The South African Cricket Board of Control, representing the substantially larger non-White section of the South African population, applied for affiliation as well, but the ICC predictably turned down the proposal.

The White South Africans played only the White nations—England, Australia, New Zealand—but the ICC had no problem in calling them Test matches. The South African non-Whites, on the other hand, had to remain content with playing among themselves. They went on the occasional tour, but their matches did not get Test status. Test cricket survived this blatant encouragement of racism.

The immensely talented but Cape Coloured (a South African ethnic classification consisting of people of mixed African, Asian and European descent) D'Oliveira led non-White South African sides to wins against the Kenyan Asians and East Africa, but he knew he had little hope of playing Test cricket. So, he reached out to John Arlott.

D'Oliveira could hardly have chosen a better person to write to. Not only was Arlott influential as a legendary commentator but he was also a prominent voice against the apartheid policies. He had once written 'Human' in the entry next to 'Race' in a South African immigration form. Arlott arranged a contract with Middleton in the Central Lancashire League.

D'Oliveira left South Africa at twenty-nine. He played for Worcestershire at thirty-one and for England at thirty-four—numbers that were, by his own admission, three years less than his actual age. His best days were past him, but three series into his Test career, he had 572 runs at an average of 52 along with 13 wickets.

But he lost form completely on the West Indies tour of 1967–68, managing only 137 runs from five Test matches at 22.83. There were reasons: a hero to the locals, he had his share of invites on tour and accompanied by Rohan Kanhai, he probably indulged in the bottle more than he should have.

Tracking his progress were the MCC as well as South African Prime Minister B.J. Vorster and his government, for England's next tour would be *in South Africa* a year later. D'Oliveira had a chance of making the cut. Before that, however, England hosted Australia—his last chance to prove himself.

England lost the first match of that home Ashes, at Old Trafford. Coming in at 105–5, D'Oliveira made an unbeaten 87 in England's fourth-innings total of 253.

This was not good news for Vorster or the MCC, both of whom probably expected D'Oliveira to lose form and not return to contention. In March 1968, Vorster had told former MCC president Lord Cobham that the tour would be cancelled if England picked D'Oliveira. It was not an empty threat. The New Zealand rugby union team was scheduled to visit South Africa the year before, but the tour had to be called off because of the apartheid issues around the former's Māori members.

On the eve of the second Test, at Lord's, MCC secretary Billy Griffith requested D'Oliveira to withdraw from the XI and make himself available for the *South African* Test side instead. E.W. Swanton put forward a similar proposition. D'Oliveira obviously turned down these laughable proposals. The next morning, England captain Colin Cowdrey told D'Oliveira that he had been relegated to twelfth player: England would be playing an extra seamer.

Soon after this, Tienie Oosthuizen of the British branch of Carreras Tobacco offered D'Oliveira a coaching contract of £4000 plus expenses in South Africa. All he had to do was pull out of the tour. D'Oliveira refused the bribe.

All Vorster could do at this point was hope for the MCC to not select D'Oliveira. A dry run in the County Championship kept him out of the Test side until Roger Prideaux went down with pleurisy just ahead of the fifth Test. This opened a spot in the XI. England recalled D'Oliveira.

Walking out at 238–4, he gave a chance on 31, but wicketkeeper Barry Jarman dropped it. There was no further lapse. As is evident from the quote of this chapter, umpire Charlie Elliott realized the enormity of the hundred. 'It'll be interesting to see what happens,' quipped John Gleeson of the Australian side. D'Oliveira finished on 158 and left amidst a standing ovation.

Oosthuizen called the MCC *from Vorster's office*. When Griffith was unavailable, he left a message: 'If today's centurion is picked, the tour will be off.' Unaware of this, D'Oliveira confirmed his availability for the South African tour to Doug Insole, the chair of selectors.

Derek Underwood then spun England to a famous win with minutes to spare: a cloudburst had almost saved the Australians, but the spectators had come down with whatever they could grab to help the ground-staff get the flooded ground in condition for play. But the result faded into insignificance the next day, when England named their squad for the South Africa tour after a six-hour selectors' meeting that went up to two in the morning. There was no D'Oliveira.

Worcestershire were playing Essex at Chelmsford when the news broke. D'Oliveira was glued to teammate Brian Brain's transistor radio set. He wept when Brian Johnston finished reading out the squad.

Louwrens Muller, Vorster's newly appointed minister of police, had been addressing a Nationalist rally in Potchefstroom when the news arrived. Muller interrupted his speech to announce that D'Oliveira had not been chosen. His words were greeted by 'loud and jingoistic cheering'.

The British media tore into the MCC selection committee. There were protests in the parliament. Former England captain David Shepherd insisted the tour be cancelled. The MCC was swarmed by letters. Several members resigned. 'If he doesn't go, I'm not going,' announced D'Oliveira's friend and teammate Tom Graveney.

'To say he is not in the best 16 cricketers of England is nonsense,' asserted Learie Constantine, who—as we have seen—had himself faced racism in England. 'I am convinced that if Dolly [D'Oliveira's nickname] was White he would be packing his bags.'

Amidst all this, Vorster threatened that he would not allow D'Oliveira in South Africa even as a journalist covering the tour.

As the protests intensified, Warwickshire seamer Tom Cartwright withdrew from the tour citing a shoulder injury—though he later admitted to two other reasons. He did not want to spend an entire winter away from the family; and he was at unease over the entire D'Oliveira saga.

The MCC had little option but to name D'Oliveira as Cartwright's replacement. 'We are not prepared to receive a team thrust upon us by people whose interests are not in the game but to gain certain political objectives which they do not even attempt to hide,' responded Vorster. 'The MCC team is not the team of the MCC but of the anti-apartheid movement.'

The tour was cancelled. The MCC's keenness in hosting South Africa for the summer of 1970 led to a chain of nationwide protests, the Stop the Seventy Tour movement. This had to be called off as well. Protests led to Australia calling off their 1971–72 home series against South Africa as well.

The New Zealand Women's tour in 1971–72 marked the end of international cricket in South Africa for nearly two decades. The Gleneagles Agreement of 1977 put the official stamp of South Africa's exile from international sport by the Commonwealth nations.

For his adopted country, D'Oliveira continued to play international cricket until 1972—till the age of forty-four, if we go by his words. His forty-four Tests fetched him 2484 runs at 40.06 along with 47 wickets—terrific numbers for someone who debuted at thirty-eight. He also played four ODIs (including the first in the history of the format).

How would he have fared had he debuted at his peak? How would the other non-White South Africans have fared had they lived in a normal society?

Chapter 59

'THE WORLD RECORD COULD NOT HAVE BEEN DONE WITHOUT ME.'

Malcolm Nash to Garry Sobers, Swansea, 31 August 1968.

Over centuries, cricket coaches have conditioned the batters to protect the wicket. The urge to hit a six involves overcoming this ingrained instinct. Perhaps that is what makes the six exhilarating. There is also the fact that a ball landing in the stands is the closest the crowd can get to the cricketers during a match—in John Arlott's words, 'the most companionable act in cricket'.

Until 1910, batters needed to hit the ball out of the stadium (not the boundary) to get six runs, though the likes of C.I. Thornton or Gilbert Jessop did that often. Once the law was changed, sixes became more common. Since matches in England were 6 balls an over, six sixes became a Holy Grail for batters.

During his famous onslaught of 1911, Ted Alletson of Nottinghamshire took 34 in an over off Ernest Killick of Sussex, but 2 no-balls made it an 8-ball over, and Alletson hit only three sixes.

Arthur Wellard, the famous Somerset big hitter, was the first to hit five sixes in an over, in 1936. After not scoring off the first ball from Derbyshire's Tommy Armstrong, he hit each of the next five for six. Two summers later, against Frank Woolley of Kent, Wellard began with five sixes but managed only a single off the last ball.

Denis Lindsay (off Bill Greensmith, 1961) and Majid Khan (off Roger Davis, 1967) also hit five sixes in an over. Between them, in 1965, Clive Inman hit Noman Hill for 32, but there were only four sixes. The Perfect Six remained elusive until 1968. It took a special cricketer to get there.

Brian Bolus (140) gave Nottinghamshire a brisk start that day at Swansea. Captain Garry Sobers walked out at 308–5 and began to play his shots from the onset. He wanted quick runs before he could declare.

Earlier in the day, Glamorgan captain Tony Lewis had asked left-arm seamer Malcolm Nash to switch to finger-spin. It worked for a while: Nash claimed four of the five wickets to fall, including Bolus's. By the time Nash began the fateful over from round the wicket, Sobers had raced to 40 and Notts were on 358–5.

Nash had never faced Sobers in first-class cricket until that game. Neither of his first two balls of this over was particularly bad; but Sobers sent both flying over the mid-wicket boundary.

The second, the more violent of the two, 'was still going up when it hit the building'.

Nash altered his line by bowling outside off-stump, but Sobers's brute force comfortably cleared the straight boundary. Nash responded by bowling shorter: this time Sobers hit over square-leg so hard that it ricocheted off an adjacent building and returned to the square-leg umpire.

The crowd cheered to celebrate … and in anticipation. It did not matter that the home side was getting hammered.

A concerned Lewis now stepped in. Would Nash prefer to revert to bowling seam? But Nash backed himself. To beat Sobers in flight, he gave the ball more air. It worked … almost. Roger Davis caught the ball at long-off but fell on his back, on the line.

The umpires conferred before ruling six. Had it been a year ago, Sobers would have been out, but they had changed the law before that summer. The crowd cheered, as did (much to Nash's dismay) Tony Cordle, one of the fielders.

Sobers had equalled the world record of five sixes in an over. Could he complete the full set?

Lewis sent everyone to the boundary. Nash decided to bowl seam … but off his spinner's run-up. It turned out to be 'an absolute disaster'—a rank long hop. Sobers hit it to a bus stop and declared immediately. He finished on 76 and Nash with 4–100.

At the end-of-day interview, Nash reminded the great man of his role in the world record. A schoolboy found the ball and brought it to Sobers the next day. That one over inspired Grahame Lloyd to pen *Six of the Best: Cricket's Most Famous Over*—one of the shortest spans of cricket with a book on the subject.

Starting that summer, every county had been allowed one overseas professional (earlier, cricketers needed a mandatory residence qualification). Sobers was obviously the star attraction. Nottinghamshire's offer was, to quote Jon Hotten, 'burnished by the same glamour as the IPL auction': £7000 a year along with an apartment and a car in 'a Britain that smouldered with post-war austerity'. Sobers had 1590 runs and 84 wickets in first-class cricket that summer. The crème de la crème was Nash's over.

There is a two-part postscript to the story. In 1977, Frank Hayes of Lancashire hit five sixes and a four in an over, in Swansea. The bowler was … Nash.

The following year, Dennis Breakwell of Somerset conceded four sixes in an over. For once, Nash was happy—for he was wielding the bat.

Chapter 60

'ZAHEER, THE NEXT TIME I COME TO PAKISTAN, I MIGHT HAVE TO COME WITH A NEW PASSPORT.'

Raqibul Hasan to Zaheer Abbas, Dacca (now Dhaka), 1 March 1971.

In November 1970, East Pakistan was ravaged by Cyclone Bhola, the deadliest tropical cyclone of all time. At least 3,00,000 (half a million, as per some estimates) were killed. As East Pakistan was devastated by famine, cholera, typhoid and dysentery, the

Pakistan government was blamed for 'inadequate response' and 'waste or misuse of the international aid'.

President Yahya Khan turned up inebriated for an official visit in the cyclone-ripped regions of East Pakistan. On 24 November 1970, the *New York Times* reported how, in a strongly worded telegram sent to Yahya Khan, eleven East Pakistani politicians wrote about 'sinister attempts to play down news coverage' of the havoc: 'Not one single minister is here. You yourself left the province after a cursory glance at the first flush of news of the tragedy.'

East Pakistan responded by voting overwhelmingly in favour of Sheikh Mujibur Rahman's Awami League in the subsequent national general elections. They won 167 out of 169 seats in East Pakistan, which also gave them a majority in the 313-seat assembly. Zulfikar Ali Bhutto's Pakistan People's Party (PPP) managed eighty-six seats.

Mujib should have formed the government, but Yahya blocked that. 'Captain Mujib had won the toss,' wrote the brilliant Syed Mujtaba Ali. 'An opening bat, he was padding up when he was given out "leg-before wicket, in the pavilion" even before he stepped out to bat.' (Syed Mujtaba Ali's words in the essay *Mujib Out!* were in Bengali. My translation to English has predictably resulted in a substantial loss of flavour.)

Cricket continued amidst turmoil. The Board of Control for Cricket in Pakistan (BCCP) Trophy, the domestic first-class tournament, featured two teams from East Pakistan. The BCCP also hosted a thirteen-team Under-19s competition. East Pakistan had three teams here. None of the teams, however, had to play outside Dacca.

Raqibul (also spelled Roqibul, Raquibul and Roquibul) Hasan, barely past his eighteenth birthday, played in both tournaments. The previous year, he had been twelfth player in a Test match against New Zealand in Karachi. There, he got his cap from his idol Hanif Mohammad. Now, however, a greater call beckoned Raqibul as he joined the Awami League.

Raqibul's selection was a rare moment. Only one East Pakistani cricketer (Niaz Ahmed, two Tests) had played for the national side until then. 'No effort was made by the governments of Pakistan or by the cricket boards to promote cricket in East Pakistan,' Shahryar Khan later admitted.

An International XI toured Pakistan that winter. Led by Micky Stewart, the side featured, among other international cricketers, Younis Ahmed. The Pakistan team, playing under the name BCCP XI, won the Karachi 'Test'. The BCCP scheduled the second 'Test' at Dacca and added Raqibul to the squad. The local hero was a 'poster boy', theorized Peter Oborne.

The BCCP gave every member of the team a bat with the symbol of the PPP. Raqibul was obviously not going to have any of it. That night, he sneaked out of Hotel Purbani, where the cricketers had been put up. He met his friend Sheikh Kamal. A decision was made. Raqibul would cover the PPP logo with a sticker bearing the message *Joy Bangla* (Long live Bengal), the war cry of the Mukti Bahini that would become popular at the Bangladesh Liberation War later that year.

Intikhab Alam won the toss and opted to bat. Raqibul picked up his bat—it might well have been a bayonet that day—and stepped out with Azmat Rana. Chants of *Joy Bangla* reverberated across the venue.

The above facts vary slightly between versions. Some suggest that Kamal visited Raqibul in his room. Sarfraz Nawaz and Aftab Baloch, Raqibul's teammates that day, told Oborne that Raqibul had covered the PPP symbol with a map of East Pakistan. However, it must be mentioned that the major incidents match in every version.

Raqibul made one run in each innings, but that was of little consequence: he had sent the message he wanted to. Overnight, he became international news.

Riots had meanwhile broken across Dacca. The marquees in the stadium were set on fire. A group of students asked the cricketers to stop playing ('There's no danger to you or your players, but we wish the game to be abandoned'). Unable to grasp the gravity of the situation, Stewart requested them to wait until the match got over. He was probably fortunate to escape alive.

Sarfraz was at the crease during this pitch invasion. He urged a soldier, posted on security duty, to fire at the crowd before they could attack. The soldier aimed at Sarfraz instead.

The match was obviously called off. The International XI made it safely outside East Pakistan. The BCCP XI was not as lucky. A military truck took them to the Purbani, where they waited for hours until frantic efforts from Intikhab and timely intervention from Brigadier Haider (former manager of Pakistan) helped them escape. Even then, the charred trees on the road meant they needed three hours to cover the fifteen-minute journey to the airport in military jeeps.

They eventually made it in time for the next 'Test', but the BCCP had an alternate XI ready. Just in case.

Raqibul stayed back, of course. Before parting ways, teammate Zaheer Abbas assured him they would meet again, in Karachi. Raqibul's response—the quote of this chapter—turned out to be prophetic.

Six days after the match, Mujib delivered his iconic speech and declared Civil Disobedience, calling for 'every house to be turned into a fortress'. Raqibul, a first-year student of political science, took active part in the movement. On 25 March, Yahya initiated the notorious Operation Searchlight. The subsequent atrocities are accepted as a genocide.

A shoot-at-sight order was issued on Raqibul. The family escaped to Gopalganj, but Raqibul and his brother acquired their father's service revolver and joined the revolution. He lost six family members, his cricket mentor Mushtaq and his friend, opening partner and roommate on tours, Abdul Halim Chowdhury Jewel. But he survived.

Bangladesh became independent that year. Raqibul and 'Shaheed' (martyr) Jewel were celebrated as national heroes.

Five years after the Dacca match, another International XI toured Pakistan. Raqibul was part of the visiting side. He kept his word: now a Bangladesh citizen, Raqibul played against Zaheer at Karachi.

In 1976–77, he became the first to lead in a cricket match against an international cricket team (MCC) in Bangladesh. He led the national side against the touring Sri Lankans and later, in the ICC Trophy. He also played in Bangladesh's first two ODIs, in the 1986 Asia Cup.

Section 8

The Game Goes Places

Chapter 61

'WHY COULDN'T WE BRING EVERY NATIONAL WOMEN'S TEAM TO ENGLAND FOR A WORLD CUP COMPETITION?'

'Union Jack' Hayward to Rachael Heyhoe Flint, circa 1971.

We briefly touched upon the first-ever World Cup of cricket—in 1973. The idea was first proposed by the Australians, in 1966, but the Women's Cricket Association in England raised a valid concern: money. It did not go ahead.

Five years later, Rachael Heyhoe Flint was staying with her friend, the millionaire business owner Jack Hayward, at Eastbourne. It was here that Hayward floated the idea of having a women's cricket World Cup.

It would be expensive, pointed out Heyhoe Flint. Hayward assured £40,000. Another £1,00,000 came from Prudential Assurance. This did the trick with the WCA. The World Cup was on. The next step was finding the grounds and getting the teams.

Of the six Test grounds in England, only Edgbaston was available. It hosted the last game (there was no final: the entire tournament was played in a round-robin league). The only other county venue, at Hove, got another England game, but the rest of the World Cup was played over unusual venues like Tring Park in Hertfordshire and Kirby Muxloe in Leicestershire.

What about Lord's? The WCA did try, but the MCC secretary 'politely but firmly refused them'. That bridge would soon be crossed.

Of course, England were one of the teams. Australia and New Zealand came on board as well. The West Indies Women would not have an association until 1976, but Jamaica and Trinidad & Tobago sent teams. Along with England, the WCA also picked a Young England team.

The Women's Cricket Association of India (WCAI) had been formed the same year. India would be admitted to the International Women's Cricket Council less than a month after the tournament, but there was no team at this point. For the last match, the WCAI sent Neeta Telang, who had to convince the organizers that Indian cricketers did not play in sarees!

There was also a seventh team, the International XI. The idea of selecting a team from the rest of the cricketers—from the participating nations or elsewhere—seemed nice on paper, until it got out that five *South Africans* had been invited. The two teams from the Caribbean threatened to withdraw, and the team had to be selected from the five existing nations.

'Unhappily, politics won again,' lamented Heyhoe Flint. She was not without her flaws.

The tournament opener, Jamaica versus New Zealand at Kew Green, London, was washed out without a toss. Australia cruised past Young England in the second game—the first women's ODI in history.

New Zealand were the only team to beat England. After the match was reduced to 35 overs, New Zealand made 105–7. England were on track at 34–1 after 15 overs before rain washed out the rest of the match, leaving England short of the adjusted target of 46.

As the tournament progressed, it became evident that England and Australia were the teams to beat. The last match, between the two sides, predictably turned out to be a virtual final. The home cricketers had a rough night after a fire alarm set off, forcing them to evacuate the hotel. Despite that, they made 279–3, the highest total of the World Cup.

Having top-scored with 118, vice-captain Enid Bakewell now took 2–28 from 12 overs, held a catch and ran out Tina MacPherson. With the match all but dusted, Heyhoe Flint decided to bowl the final over ('Every one of my England team had placed themselves at least 70 yards out on the boundary's edge … such was their confidence in my bowling talent!'). England won by 92 runs.

Throughout the World Cup, Heyhoe Flint had been the unofficial brand ambassador of the tournament. She used to play the ukulele outside Lord's and distribute leaflets to raise awareness. She now collected the trophy from Princess Anne.

The WCA made a profit of only £1000. Ticket sales amounted to only £747. The numbers were far from impressive. There was no prize money (though the first prize of WCA's fundraising raffle was a colour television).

But it was the first of its kind, and it took the men two years to follow suit. Half a century later, the ODI World Cup remains the most coveted trophy for cricketers around the globe.

Chapter 62

'PERHAPS THE BOLDEST AND MOST AMBITIOUS INNOVATION THE GAME HAS KNOWN SINCE THE LEGISLATION OF OVERARM BOWLING.'

Tony Cozier, 1975.

Somerset captain Ben Brocklehurst was inside a train when he came up with the idea of a global cricket tournament. That was in 1969. The Cricketer World Cup, he decided to name it, after *The Cricketer*, the magazine he had recently acquired.

Not only did Brocklehurst seal a £50,000 sponsorship from Wills Cigarettes but he also found support from E.W. Swanton, 'Gubby' Allen and … Don Bradman. They must have been stumped by the response from the Test and County Cricket Board (TCCB, the predecessor of the England and Wales Cricket Board [ECB]): 'We did not feel that such a prestigious event should be subject to commercial sponsorship in the direct sense.'

Once again cricket demonstrated its rigidity. Football had its first World Cup in 1930. By the early 1970s, most major sports had joined in, but cricket continued to resist. One-day cricket, the new format, was still trying to make a mark outside England, but it did address the inherent impracticality of a World Cup of five-day matches.

England had continued to stay away from the FIFA World Cup until 1950. This included the 1938 edition, where FIFA had offered them a spot after Germany occupied Austria, who had qualified. England had turned the offer down. The delay of a global tournament in cricket—a Commonwealth sport for decades—was inevitable.

In 1972, a year and a half after the first ODI, Prudential Assurance stepped in as the sponsors of limited-overs cricket on English soil. After chipping in with £1,00,000 for the Women's World Cup, they matched that amount for the men's edition. When TCCB public relations officer Raman Subba Row got a matching bid from Castrol Oil, Prudential raised their sum to £1,55,000. They also insured every cricketer for £50,000, covering 'death or total disablement' as well as 'loss of limbs, eyes, fingers, toes and baggage'.

Most counties had incurred a financial loss in 1974. The TCCB could not afford to let Prudential's offer slip. Just like the women's event, the matches would be 60 overs a side. However, unlike the women's event, there would be eight teams, split into two groups, followed by the semi-finals and a final.

There were six ICC Full Member sides back then. Sri Lanka were invited, as were East Africa, a team composed of cricketers from Kenya, Tanzania, Uganda and Zambia. As hosts, the TCCB kept 10 per cent of the profit, while the other seven boards got 7.5 per cent each. The remaining 37.5 per cent went towards the development of cricket in the Associate Nations and an international coaching fund.

Unlike the women's edition, the major Test grounds—including Lord's—were all available. With four simultaneous matches a day, the league stage got over in three playing days. The ICC tweaked some rules. Every ball passing over the batter's head would be called a wide, while bowlers should not bowl bouncers at 'non-recognised batsmen'. As is often the case, the bowler was at the receiving end for both changes.

The first day witnessed a curious batting performance. After England amassed 334–4, Sunil Gavaskar batted through the Indian innings for an unbeaten 174-ball 36 with only two boundary hits. Manager G.S. Ramchand did not mince his words: 'It was the most disgraceful and selfish performance I have ever seen … Our national pride is too important to be thrown away like this.'

On the second day, Sri Lanka put up a much more spirited show to finish on 276–4 in pursuit of 329 against Australia. They might have pulled it off, but Jeff Thomson hit Sunil Wettimuny on the toe (after peppering him with bouncers) and Duleep Mendis on the head, forcing both to retire hurt. A police officer later asked Mendis whether he wanted to press charges for 'assault and battery'.

While all this was happening, the West Indian last pair of Deryck Murray and Andy Roberts added 64—the odds read 66:1—to beat Pakistan in the absence of Imran Khan, who was appearing for his university tests.

In the first semi-final, at Headingley, Gary Gilmour swung the ball prodigiously to take 6–14 to reduce England to 36–6. They recovered to 93 and had Australia at 39–6, but Gilmour now strode out to make a run-a-ball 28 not out, the highest score of the match, to pull off one of the greatest all-round displays in ODI cricket history. At The Oval, the West Indies cruised past New Zealand on the same day.

The final at Lord's, sold out three days in advance, was played in front of a capacity crowd of 26,765. The West Indies slumped to 50–3 before Clive Lloyd hit an 85-ball 102 to lift them to 291–8. Viv Richards then ran out Alan Turner and the Chappell brothers to reduce Australia to 233–9.

But Dennis Lillee and Thomson continued to score on either side of a crowd invasion, taking Australia to the brink of a win. They added 41 before Murray ran out the latter. The match, in its entirety of 118.4 overs, was played in one day: it went on until 8.41 p.m. Thankfully, it was played on the Summer Solstice.

Despite being played on only five different days across a fortnight, the World Cup 'exceeded the expectations of even the most cock-eyed optimist'. The fifteen matches got an attendance of 1,58,000 and gate money of around £2,00,000, of which £66,000 came from the final alone. Each defeated semi-finalist side won £1000, the runners-up £2000 and the world champions £4000.

'The initial reaction on looking back at my original assessment of the inaugural World Cup was to cringe at its hyperbole,' admitted Tony Cozier, one of the pre–World Cup cynics.

Chapter 63

'GENTLEMEN, I GAVE YOU 400 RUNS TO BOWL AT; AND YOU FAILED TO BOWL OUT THE OPPOSITION. HOW MANY RUNS MUST I GIVE YOU IN FUTURE TO MAKE SURE YOU GET THE WICKETS?'

Clive Lloyd to Raphick Jumadeen, Imtiaz Ali and Albert Padmore, 12 April 1976.

Clive Lloyd's West Indies had been thrashed 1–5 in Australia. The scars of that defeat had barely healed by the time their home series against India went underway. They still went 1–0 up, but India chased an improbable 403 at Port of Spain to level the series with one match to go.

Lloyd was criticized. 'A captain of a losing side is always made the scapegoat, and Lloyd will have his share,' warned Nari Contractor, whose Test career had ended in a violent brutal head injury in the Caribbean more than a decade ago. 'It was 1–1 in the series and, after Australia, we were under extreme public pressure to win,' Michael Holding would later admit in *Whispering Death*.

Lloyd had backed three spinners in the fourth innings on a pitch with a reputation of assisting spin. That needed to change. A solution was suggested by, among others, former Indian cricketer Rusi Modi to the *Times of India*: 'Perhaps a third medium-pacer might have made the difference.'

Lloyd went a step further. He had a firm word with his three spinners, Albert Padmore, Imtiaz Ali and Raphick Jumadeen. Then he set his new plan in motion, for the time had come for drastic measures.

The West Indies retained Jumadeen for the decider, but as the lone spinner. There was no Andy Roberts, but Holding led a pack of four fast bowlers. Debutant Wayne Daniel was very fast. Vanburn Holder and Bernard Julien were not express, but they helped form an extremely potent quartet.

The change would not have been as apparent had it happened gradually; but going from three spinners to four fast bowlers over the span of one game made everyone notice. The writing was on the wall.

The Kingston pitch was new, hard, shiny, untested. There were uneven spots around the good length. Lloyd did not hesitate to put India in and toss the new ball to Holding and Daniel. Sunil Gavaskar and Anshuman Gaekwad, the Indian openers, negotiated them well to remain undefeated until lunch.

The tactics changed completely after that. Holding began the next over with three bouncers at Gaekwad. Gavaskar received four bouncers and a beamer. Holding apologized for the beamer, but Gavaskar felt that he had 'pretended'.

Holding and Daniel unleashed fast bowling of a nature the Indians had not faced on that tour. Neither umpire made any effort to restrain them. 'In truth we bowled an awful lot of short balls,' Holding later admitted to Simon Lister, the author of *Fire in Babylon.* It was difficult for gloveman Deryck Murray, who stood far, far behind the wicket but the ball would still 'go over him and bounce into the sight screen'.

Backing them was a partisan crowd, with cries of 'kill him, *maan*', 'hit him, *maan*', 'knock his head off'. Gavaskar later referred to the fans as 'barbarian' and 'positively inhuman'. Daniel explained it away as their 'thrill to see the fear of God put into the batsman'.

Holding eventually yorked Gavaskar for 66, but Gaekwad and Mohinder Amarnath took India to 178–1 before bad light stopped play. Next morning, Lloyd claimed the second new ball. Holding dismissed Amarnath with a vicious bouncer five balls later.

The first ball Viswanath faced was 'one of the wickedest bouncers of the series': it whooshed to the boundary off his glove. Holding hit Viswanath on the glove again; this time the ball broke a finger and went for a catch.

Gaekwad (81) was then hit on the left ear. Blood oozed, but the local officials showed little urgency towards rushing him to the hospital. A short-of-the-length ball from Holder took the top edge of Brijesh Patel's bat and cut his lip open. Both men had to retire hurt.

Holding was himself not impressed by these tactics: 'On that surface, it was inevitable that some batsmen would be hit against such a pace-based attack as ours, especially as we adopted the tactic of bowling from around the wicket, aiming the ball at their bodies. I was not too keen on this method since it gives the batsman little chance of avoiding a bouncer, especially against bowlers with plenty of speed.'

Indian captain Bishan Singh Bedi declared the innings closed 'in disgust' at 306–6. He and Bhagwat Chandrasekhar, the only ones left, were not competent batters: 'Suppose we had got hit on the head?' That evening, Bedi received a 'message of concern for the Indian players, wishing them a quick recovery' from Indira Gandhi, the Indian Prime Minister.

There is some discrepancy over when exactly the West Indian fast bowlers switched to hostile bowling from round the wicket. In Sunny Days, *Gavaskar mentions immediately after lunch on day one. The* Hindustan Times *and the* Times of India *corroborate this. However, in* Caribbean Adventure, *Kishore Bhimani notes that it happened when Lloyd claimed the second new ball, on the second morning, with India on 199–1. The* Jamaica Gleaner *merely reported that Holding bowled 'extremely well' and Lloyd 'should have attacked more' on the first day. However, there is no discrepancy over the strategy, its extent, its impact and the injuries.*

India did well to restrict the West Indies to an 85-run lead, but they now had to bat without Gaekwad, Viswanath and Patel. Dilip Vengsarkar opened instead of Gaekwad. Holding got Gavaskar early, but Amarnath counter-attacked his way to 60, with seven fours and three sixes.

The farce began when Vengsarkar fell with India on 68. Madan Lal walked out at four, followed by S. Venkataraghavan and Syed Kirmani. The fifth wicket fell on 97, but no one else walked out to bat. The Indian second innings was over.

Bedi later clarified that he had not declared the innings. Both he and Chandrasekhar had been nursing finger injuries and were unavailable to bat. With five men absent, the innings had to be closed.

Bedi did not take the field as the West Indian openers got the 13 runs in 11 balls. 'The West Indian tactics in this Sabina Park Test were not part of the game,' he said.

'If you get hit you have to take it,' quipped Lloyd.

'The whole charm of the game is being lost,' lamented Indian team manager Polly Umrigar. West Indies manager Clyde Walcott called the Indians 'ill-equipped to play fast bowling'.

Walcott's words rankled Gavaskar, who recalled the 1948–49 series in India. West Indies wicketkeeper Walcott 'walked to the boundary, not once but time and again, to retrieve the ball and thereby wasting time in order to deprive India of victory in a Test [in Bombay]'.

The Indian team left the Caribbean wounded and bruised in every sense. At the Norman Manley Airport in Kingston in plasters and bandages, the cricketers—to quote *Wisden*—resembled 'Napoleon's troops on the retreat from Moscow'. But their battering was only the start of one of cricket's most formidable juggernauts.

Despite taking only 11 wickets, the West Indies won the Test and, with it, the series. Lloyd was named captain for that summer's England tour. But more importantly, he had found a blueprint for success.

Lance Gibbs's retirement had left the West Indies without a world-class spinner, but they had hostile fast bowlers in Roberts, Holding and Daniel. Joel Garner and Colin Croft would arrive soon, and others would follow. There would be an incessant supply of world-class bowlers of terrifying pace in the islands.

Thus equipped, Lloyd switched to four fast bowlers who would come at the opposition relentlessly, day in and day out. Viv Richards followed suit in the 1980s, as did Richie Richardson in the 1990s; the West Indies ruled supreme in the sport for nearly two decades.

There was predictable resistance from those who failed to accept this incredible dominance by a side that was neither England nor Australia. 'The West Indian methods are against the essence of cricket,' Robin Marlar did not hesitate to write in *The Sunday Times*. 'A reflection of the Caribbean society where violence is commonplace,' he called it. In 2015, Mark Nicholas referred to the Caribbean 'years of plenty' as 'something of a fluke'.

Both Marlar and Nicholas would become presidents of the MCC, who, as we have seen, had been swift to react when England's Bodyline strategy was called out as 'unsportsmanlike'.

'The bouncer ... when used as the West Indians have been using it—whether bouncing in on the heart, the collarbone or the temple—it is a curse on both the spirit of the game and as a spectacle,' David Frith added in the *Wisden Cricket Monthly*. 'The summer game, it had become something else. It had lost its romance, it had lost its sportsmanship, it had lost its lovely edge; it was now a place where people got frightened ... The escalation of their fast bowlers has reached a murderous crescendo which shrieks remorselessly throughout the innings.'

Over the years that followed, Frith would be consistent in his criticism of an approach similar to what England and Australia had used decades before Lloyd.

None of that mattered. Between 1979–80 and 1994–95, the West Indies did not lose a single Test series. That alone is likelier to stand the test of time than baseless criticism.

Chapter 64

'I INTEND ... TO MAKE THEM GROVEL.'

Tony Greig, to BBC, 1 June 1976.

Tony Greig was leading Sussex against the touring West Indians of 1976. On the last day, he visited the dentist. Upon return, he did not enter the pavilion but climbed on to the roof for an interview with the BBC.

There, he said: 'I think you must remember that the West Indians—these guys—if they get on top, they are magnificent cricketers; but if they're down, they grovel. And I intend, with the help of Closey [Brian Close] and a few others, to make them grovel.'

The first Test match would begin at Trent Bridge in less than forty-eight hours' time. Greig would lead England against a side that had, as we have seen, already figured out how to demolish a team with pace—and pace alone.

Greig's statement reached the West Indian camp after the BBC broadcast it on *Sportsnight*, leaving them 'stunned'. Greig being a White South African made the word 'grovel' even more unacceptable.

'It was now combat. It was now a battle where there was no way England could have won,' felt Gordon Greenidge. Viv Richards thought on similar lines: 'This was the greatest motivating speech the England captain could have given to any West Indian team.'

'We were angry and West Indians everywhere were angry. We resolved to show him and everyone else that the days for grovelling were over,' summed up Clive Lloyd.

Greig's teammates were not impressed either. Mike Brearley, who had stood up against the MCC when they had been reluctant to snub South Africa over the D'Oliveira affair, would debut in the first Test here. He thought that 'the words of a blond South African … carried an especially tasteless and derogatory overtone'. Chris Old felt that Greig 'wanted the press to be backing England'.

Even Greig's father, a former Royal Air Force (RAF) officer, asked his son whether he had a dictionary at home.

As the angry anonymous letters 'expressing everything from outrage to pure hatred' piled up, Greig realized the damage he had caused. He appeared in a London radio station popular among the West Indian community and tried his best to elaborate that he had not meant to insult anyone.

It was too late. The West Indians strode out with a vengeance. Richards slammed 232 in the first Test, but David Steele helped England secure a draw. Andy Roberts sized up Greig with two 'sharp deliveries which bounced and cut back into the body'. Greig fell for a 7-ball duck.

Richards missed the second Test, at Lord's, where the West Indies needed to chase 323 in about five hours. They slipped from 230–2 to 241–6 before time ran out.

Then came Old Trafford. The West Indies made only 211, but Roberts, Michael Holding and Wayne Daniel rolled over England for 71. Greenidge and Richards both made hundreds, and England needed 552 to win.

In the eighty minutes that remained on the third day, the Caribbean fast bowlers peppered thirty-nine-year-old John Edrich and forty-six-year-old Close relentlessly with bouncers. 'Our fellows got carried away,' admitted Lloyd. It was the first time England received the full blast of the West Indian pace.

England folded for 126, scoring fewer in the match than Greenidge (134 and 101). Roberts took 9 wickets in the Test, Holding 7 and Daniel 4. Albert Padmore, the lone spinner, bowled only 3 overs.

That set the tone. The West Indies left out Padmore at Headingley and got in Vanburn Holder, a fourth seamer, and Collis King, an all-rounder who bowled medium pace. Greenidge made his third consecutive hundred and the tourists won by 55 runs.

Richards slammed 291 in the fifth Test, at The Oval, and Holding got 14 wickets. The West Indies lost only 8 wickets en route to a 231-run hammering.

Greig had been 'barracked on sight' by the Caribbean contingent throughout the series, but the boos got louder at The Oval. The series had already been won before the match. Richards and Holding now toyed with England to push the West Indies to a 3–0 win.

When Holding knocked the leg-stump out of the ground to bowl Greig in the first innings, 'a huge section of the crowd, mainly West Indians, swept over the ground and trampled on the pitch'. It was their way of giving Greig a send-off.

The West Indies then declared on 182–0 after 32 overs of batting. During the innings, Greig sauntered towards the Harleyford Road side of the ground and … grovelled. 'I realise that I made a mistake in using that word at the start of the series,' he told the media that night. The next day, the *Sun* ran the image with 'Okay, so I'm grovelling now' in large font.

It was too late, of course. England would not win another Test series against the West Indies until 2000.

Chapter 65

'THERE IS A LITTLE BIT OF THE WHORE IN ALL OF US, GENTLEMEN. WHAT IS YOUR PRICE?'

Kerry Packer to the television subcommittee of the Australian Cricket Board (ACB), 22 June 1976.

There used to be little money in cricket back in the 1970s. It was difficult to secure a comfortable future by playing the sport. Some took up day jobs; some retired early; and some either played in or migrated to England, the only country that provided a reasonable income to the professional cricketer.

There was little effort to address this. Cricket was often run by privileged men (yes, only men) detached from these realities. No wonder Australian media tycoon Kerry Packer felt it was 'the easiest sport in the world to take over'.

Since he inherited Channel Nine from his father in 1974, Packer had his eyes on cricket coverage in Australia. He loved the sport, and 'nobody bothered to pay the players what they were worth'.

In 1976, Packer met the television subcommittee of the ACB. Despite being aware of this meeting, the board members had still gone ahead and renewed the rights for cricket in the country to the Australian Broadcasting Corporation (ABC) for AU$ 2,10,000. When Packer offered them $1.5 million for three years, they assured that they would consider *after three years*, when the ABC contract expired.

Thus snubbed, Packer turned to the Test and County Cricket Board in England. He proposed to cover the 1977 Ashes, in England, and a series between an Australian side and a World XI. Nothing came out of that. Not content with refusing Packer, the ACB had recommended that the TCCB acquire the rights from the ABC.

Packer called this the ACB's 'second knifing'. He responded by launching World Series Cricket (WSC), his private cricket competition between Australia and a World XI. He offered the players several times what they made from playing for the board.

He started by reaching out to, among others, Ian Chappell and Tony Greig. Former Australian Test captain Chappell had recently retired, but his teammates were still active. Greig, the present England captain, became Packer's chief recruiting officer.

To celebrate a hundred years of Test cricket, a Centenary Test was played at Melbourne in the summer of 1976–77. By the time it was over, Packer had discreetly recruited more than twenty players. Over the next few months, he signed up cricketers from England, Pakistan, South Africa and the West Indies. The Caribbean dominance in cricket was still in its early stages, but they were the biggest catch.

The news got leaked to the media during the England tour of 1977, sending ripples across the cricket fraternity. Cricket took a backseat. 'It is virtually certain that if a circus scheme were launched in competition to Test cricket, it would fail,' predicted John Arlott.

Two reports affected Greig the most. 'He is an Englishman, not by birth or upbringing, but only by adoption. It is not the same thing as being an Englishman through and through,' wrote John Woodcock in *The Times*, while Henry Blofeld blamed Greig's epilepsy medication for the 'treacherous decision'. Neither comment would have been acceptable today.

'Cricketers Turn Pirates', ran the *Daily Mail* banner, accompanied by Ian Woolridge's sensational piece: 'The new Dogs of Cricket include England captain Tony Greig and 13 of the Australian touring party now in England.' In all, thirty-five cricketers had already signed up.

But in the same piece, Woolridge also explained why the cricketers took the decision: 'Disenchanted by low pay and what they regarded as doormat treatment by cricket authorities throughout the world, they are to play exhibition "Tests" for television and 10 times the money.' Indeed, when the offer was explained to South African Eddie Barlow, he merely asked, 'Where do I sign?'

The boards, led by the ACB and the TCCB, tried to sue and ban the players. They lost. The court merely barred Packer from naming his cricket teams after the nations, calling them Test matches or using the MCC Laws of Cricket.

By then, Packer's plans had expanded to three teams. He called them Australia XI, West Indies XI and World XI. He branded the games as 'Supertests'. Richie Benaud, one of Packer's early recruits, wrote the rules and playing conditions.

The ACB banned every Packer cricketer even from domestic cricket. The TCCB wanted to follow suit, but the counties wanted the players. When the West Indies board banned some cricketers, their teammates opted out. Pakistan refused to pick the Packer cricketers until a defeat in England in 1978 forced them to change their stance.

Two Australian teams took the field in the summer of 1977–78: a nearly full-strength side for Packer, and a severely depleted side to play the official Test series against India. A decade into retirement, Bobby Simpson returned to lead the Test side.

Barred from the main grounds, Packer was forced to use Australian Rules Football venues. For that, he used drop-in pitches, one of his many contributions to cricket. He had the best cricketers in the world. Never had the fiercest fast bowlers in the world assembled for the same league. Channel Nine's telecast was of unprecedented quality.

Yet, the spectators largely stayed away from the Supertests in the first season. To lure them, Packer then added floodlit one-day matches to the itinerary. The novelty brought some crowd in, but the first season was a triumph for the board.

The wheels turned next summer, when a full-strength England won the Ashes 5–1 *in Australia*. This utter mismatch pushed the fans to the now-floodlit Supertests, played with a white ball in coloured clothing as catchy jingles reverberated across the venues and motorized drinks carts rolled in. Never in history had cricket of such quality been married to entertainment and innovations of this scale.

As we haves seen in Chapter 50, Packer did not introduce the white ball to cricket. Coloured clothing, too, was common until the late nineteenth century. Even after white apparel caught on, Tom Horan, the nineteenth-

century Australian captain, used to bat in black or brown pads. What Packer did was convert these long-lost entities into selling points.

The ACB invited Pakistan for two more Tests, but the crowd did not respond. Realizing they did not have the pockets to match Packer, they caved in.

On 30 May 1979, Channel Nine signed a ten-year contract for exclusive rights of cricket coverage in Australia. The ACB lifted the ban on the cricketers, who had got a taste of how much they deserved to be paid. WSC matches, however, still do not have first-class status.

Cricket also underwent many a change over this period, but more on that later.

Chapter 66

'THERE WAS SOME SHAKING OF HEADS WHEN MEMBERS LEARNED THE LADIES WERE ALLOWED INTO THE MALE-ONLY PAVILION.'

Evening News, reporting on the incidents of 4 August 1976.

The first cricket World Cup across genders was the 1973 Women's World Cup. The Women's Cricket Association had reached out to the MCC for hosting them for a match, but with little success. Despite organizing the World Cup and captaining England to title glory, Heyhoe Flint had still one goal to conquer: gaining access to Lord's.

The MCC Committee had discussed the idea of admitting women as members in 1967, but it was not until 1998 that the idea bore fruit. Of course, there were female staff members, but even they were 'expected to avoid popular areas like the Long Room' on match days.

The queen of England was the only woman exempted from such restrictions. She could enter the Long Room en route to meeting the cricketers and enjoy the Committee Room facilities. Even that did not go down well with a section of the members. A scandalized E.W. 'Jim' Swanton once burst out of the Committee Room and exclaimed, 'There's a woman in there!'

'Yes, Jim. Of course there is. It's the Saturday of the Ashes Test. It's the Queen.'

'Nevertheless!'

But Heyhoe Flint, no stranger to conquering hurdles, was in no mood to concede. As we have seen, her team stormed Lord's in 1976. The bastion of patriarchy had to open its gates to the women.

Of course, that came with a clause: they would get to play at Lord's if and only if Lancashire defeated Middlesex in their Gillette Cup second-round match. If Middlesex won, *they* would play at Lord's—and the ODI would have to be rescheduled to Sunbury Cricket Club. Thankfully, Lancashire won, preventing a potentially ugly scenario.

For that day, the English and Australian cricketers would be the only women allowed in the pavilion, but they got access to the same facilities the men enjoyed, including the Long Room.

Some MCC members took umbrage at the move. One Peter Curtis later admitted to praying for rain to prevent the sacrilege. Another believed that 'cricket is a game where concentration is very important, and women are the greatest distraction a man can have around'. *Evening News* reported 'some shaking of heads' when women entered the male-only pavilion.

But generally, everything went well. A pleasant surprise awaited the cricketers when they arrived at the dressing-room: it was decorated with red roses.

On a sunny day (poor Curtis!), Australian captain Anne Gordon won the toss and elected to bat. The English fielders took the field in, to quote the *Glasgow Herald* report, 'tailored mini-skirts, short-sleeved shirts, knee-length socks—irresistibly "upper fifth" in effect, so that the umpires in their douce, straight skirts below the knee, and the finger-tip length white coats are inevitably school mistresses'.

England quickly reduced Australia to 41–5. 'I think we were nervous; the occasion was too much,' Gordon later admitted. Heyhoe Flint was just as excited: 'I've got those old butterflies. It's so exciting to be here at last.'

Australia eventually made 161 largely due to Sharon Tredrea's 54. Enid Bakewell (50) and Chris Watmough (50 not out) then sealed an 8-wicket win for England.

Fittingly, Heyhoe Flint herself was at the crease when the winning runs were hit. As they got closer to the win, news got out and more people poured in, cheering every run scored.

Unsurprisingly, the TCCB did not send news feed about the match to the Post Office for transmission, though they sent updates of the Gillette Cup. 'The WCA, they said in effect, have nothing to do with us, so we don't know about them,' they explained.

Even after the match, the MCC stood steadfast in their decision to deny women membership. Unless there was a women's match, sections of Lord's were out of bounds for women. 'The MCC should change their name to MCP,' quipped Indian cricketer Diana Edulji, after being denied entry to the pavilion in 1986.

By 1990, Lord's was the only venue in the county circuit where the female members of the home team could not enter their own pavilion. Half the global population were denied entry to the self-proclaimed Home of Cricket.

In 1998, the WCA merged into the ECB, whose headquarters were at Lord's. In February, a motion to admit female members was carried, but not by a margin significant enough for a rule change. That finally happened in September, when the motion was passed by a two-thirds majority.

In 1999, the MCC granted ten women honorary life membership. Heyhoe Flint was among them.

In 2017, Lord's was packed to witness England beat India in the final to win the Women's World Cup. 'Seeing Lord's sold out for a women's match is something I never thought I'd see,' admitted home captain Heather Knight.

The momentous occasion did not lead to equality. Lord's (and most other venues) charge hefty entry fees for men's domestic cricket, but the corresponding women's games are often played in secondary grounds with free or nominal entrance.

In 2026, Lord's will host women's Test cricket for the first time.

Chapter 67

'ALL OF US SHOULD BE INDEBTED TO HER FOR TAKING THAT INITIATIVE.'

Anjali Pendharkar, Indian Railways cricketer, about an act by Diana Edulji, Delhi, November 1976.

For decades, women's cricket in India was played in pockets around the vast nation without a well-defined structure. The Women's Cricket Association of India, founded in 1973, changed that to some extent, but there was still no money in the sport—certainly not enough for anyone to turn professional.

India women played their first Test matches against the West Indies, in 1975–76. Debuting in the first game was Diana Edulji, whose father had been an employee of Western Railways. Playing with the local boys—mostly children of Railways employees—had not only sparked her interest in sports but had also kept her 'connected to the Railways family'.

Railways minister Kamalapati Tripathi attended the third Test of that West Indies series, at Delhi. His daughter-in-law Chandra Tripathi was the WCAI president at that point. Edulji walked up to him during the match with a simple request: her father was set to retire that same year, and she wanted a job with Railways.

Edulji thus became the first female cricketer to be employed by Indian Railways under their sports quota. She did not have to worry about her livelihood anymore. She could solely focus on playing cricket, but she did not stop at that. She went all out to ensure other Indian women earned the same privilege as well.

It was not the first time Indian Railways offered livelihoods to cricketers. Their men's team had been playing in the Ranji Trophy since 1958–59. However, this was different, for Edulji got a job despite there being no Railways women's team.

That initiative had to wait until 1984, when a group of female cricketers reached out to Railways minister Madhavrao Scindia for jobs through Edulji. Realizing the potential of women's cricket in the country, Scindia commissioned a triangular intra-Railways tournament with the Western, Southern and Eastern sectors of the organization. This served as a trial for the first-ever Railways Women team.

This was a significant moment. At a time when female cricketers—not only in India but around the world—often had to sustain themselves outside playing cricket, Indian Railways offered life-changing day jobs to their employees.

While not professionals in the truest sense, the cricketers were at least semi-professional. They could work until three in the afternoon and leave for training. They got time off work to play or to recover from injuries at a time when their counterparts had to balance livelihood and cricket. The employers tilted the balance even more: the Railways cricketers travelled in air-conditioned coaches to play when their counterparts across India often travelled by unreserved second-class.

But Railways did not stop there. They recruited cricketers who did well for other teams. It was not a big challenge, for they offered financial security at a time when the players earned practically nothing. When cricketers from other states came together only for or just ahead of the season, the Railways employees trained together around the year.

All this obviously resulted in Railways emerging as the strongest team in India by the proverbial mile. At the helm was Edulji herself, not only as cricketer but as captain, equipped with innovative strategies and a burning desire to win. They would steamroll oppositions, match after match, year after year …

This led to two problems. First, Indian cricket was reduced to a monopoly. Secondly, a young cricketer often impressed for another side and got recruited by Railways. While that sorted her livelihood, the competition at Railways was so stiff that she often got left out of the playing XI and fell out of national contention.

Air India's arrival as a rival in 1991 addressed both issues. Like Railways, they too began to recruit cricketers from other states to build their team. They provided stern competition to Railways, and not just on the field; their cricketers travelled *by air*.

The duopoly benefitted the national team. Between 1994 and 2005, India won six out of eight bilateral ODI series and a triangular tournament in New Zealand, which also featured Australia; and reached the World Cup final for the first time. The two organizations also recruited the two biggest names in Indian cricket: while Railways had Mithali Raj on their payroll, Air India got Jhulan Goswami.

The intense rivalry ended in 2006 when the BCCI took over women's cricket from the WCAI. Since Air India were not a registered BCCI member, they were ineligible to participate in any cricket arranged by the board. Air India had to disband their team, and the Railways juggernaut resumed.

As Edulji moved on to an administrative role for the side after retirement, Raj stepped in as her heir. Barring 2011–12 and 2018–19, Railways has won the Women's Senior One-Day Trophy every time it has been hosted. Even in the fickler T20 format, they have missed only thrice—in 2017–18, 2018–19 and 2023–24. There have been challengers from time to time, but there is little doubt over their sustained supremacy.

As per the Supreme Court's recommendations in 2018, Railways should have lost their vote at the BCCI. Yet, they stayed put. 'In view of the security of employment of the players from Railways as well as the ability to demonstrate playing skills and having regard to women's cricket as an integral part of Indian Cricket, it appears necessary to consider this as an exception,' elaborated amicus curiae Gopal Subramanium.

Today, the BCCI offers retainers to female cricketers. There is enough incentive for women to become full-time professional cricketers. The Women's Premier League (WPL) has brought unprecedented riches to women's cricket. But long before that, Indian Railways had become the first large-scale recruiters of women in the sport.

The Original English Lady Cricketers (OELC) had predated them by nearly a century (see Chapter 37). Unlike the OELC, however, the Railways team did not disappear overnight. They have not only stayed but are likely to dominate Indian cricket for some time.

Chapter 68

'YOUR BALL IS MOVING BUT MINE WON'T.'

Imran Khan to Sarfraz Nawaz, Albion, 16 March 1977.

Imran Khan was confused. He was unable to move the old ball in the air. Of course, old cricket balls are not supposed to swing, but his teammate Sarfraz Nawaz was doing exactly that at the other end.

Sarfraz was possessive about his craft. After all, he was the only one to have mastered the weapon at this level. To ensure no one picked it up, he had been scuffing up *both sides of the ball.* However, he assured Imran that he would teach him the next day—because he felt Imran was not going to be his rival: 'I only told Imran because he was not playing domestic cricket in Pakistan.'

Fielding sides had always tried their best to maintain the shine on the cricket ball for as long as possible. The ball stopped swinging as it got old. The spinners wheeled away, and even the part-timers rolled their arm over until the second new ball was due. Sarfraz changed that.

Shaharyar Khan, former PCB chair, credits Salim Mir of the Punjab Club with the invention of reverse swing and passing it on to Sarfraz, who sometimes used to play for the club. Sarfraz, on the other hand, told Peter Oborne that he picked it up on his own: 'One day I shone one side of a very old ball and it swung. It was rough on both sides, but I shone one side and it swung towards the shine—it should not have done this.'

Whichever version is true, there is little doubt over Sarfraz being the first to master reverse swing *at the highest level.* When England toured Pakistan in 1969–70, Sarfraz—yet to make his Test debut—bowled in the nets. Roger Prideaux, the first English cricketer to be stunned by this alien craft, promptly invited Sarfraz to play for Northamptonshire.

The English conditions assisted new-ball movement for longer. The ball did not roughen up either. Sarfraz stuck to conventional swing, but once back home, he perfected his secret weapon for years on the dry, abrasive, grassless surfaces of Pakistan.

Of course, he had the skills. Merely understanding the craft did not make one a master practitioner. Mir himself got only 8 first-class wickets, that too at 40.62. Sarfraz had 177 Test wickets.

His contemporaries around the world figured out this phenomenon as well. 'That's how I bowled [Tony] Greig out twice in the match [The Oval, 1976]! But all we knew then was that at a certain point the ball would tend to swing the opposite way to the newer ball, so we just switched it round in the hand,' Michael Holding later told Mike Brearley.

Unlike Sarfraz, however, they did not know *why* it worked that way.

Once Sarfraz passed on the secret, Imran evolved into a master of reverse swing. The most devastating example came on the Christmas evening of 1982 in Karachi. With a ball about 40 overs old, he claimed 5 wickets for 3 runs in 25 balls in a display of unplayable reverse swing. This included Sunil Gavaskar and Gundappa Viswanath (both bowled) and Mohinder Amarnath (leg-before).

The Indian batters were left shell-shocked—for they had not seen anything like this before. From 102–1 at one point, they finished the day on 118–7.

Wasim Akram took over from Imran later that decade. And while Imran was still active, along came Waqar Younis to form one of the most celebrated new-ball pairs of all time with Wasim.

Wasim had already unleashed reverse swing in England. In hot, dry weather at Old Trafford in 1989, he swung the old ball prodigiously to take 5–44 and 5–51 for Lancashire in the County Championship. Six of the batters were bowled and two leg-before. By the time Pakistan arrived in England in 1992, he and Waqar were ready.

A brilliant exhibition of reverse swing from the duo helped Pakistan clinch the Test series 2–1. Wasim and Waqar shared 47 wickets.

This led to an outcry. 'The ball suddenly started to swing, and I know why,' said England manager Micky Stewart, with vague elaborations at best. At Lord's, Allan Lamb complained to the umpires, who told match referee Deryck Murray that they would have to replace the ball in the aftermath of 'clear and obvious ball-tampering'. It was changed, but Wasim and Waqar swung it even more prodigiously …

Sections of the media tore into the Pakistan team and their captain, Javed Miandad. The *Daily Mirror* and the *Sun* insisted Pakistan be 'thrown out of world cricket'. Simon Heffer wrote an obnoxious article so laden with racist remarks that the PCB sued the *Sunday Telegraph*.

Yet, none of that hampered the spread of reverse swing. The Indians had picked it up on their 1989–90 tour of Pakistan, but their bowlers, while very good, were seldom quick enough to wreak havoc. After the 1992 tour of England, Wasim and Waqar's weapon was imitated, then mastered, by some of the finest fast bowlers in the world—and why not?

As Oborne noted, the reverse swing grants fast bowlers a threefold advantage. They can swing the old ball. Unlike the new ball, the batter finds it difficult to predict the direction of the movement based on the shine. And unlike conventional swing, they do not have to compromise on pace—in fact, the quicker the bowler, often the more pronounced the deviation.

The craft is mainstream today. No one challenges its legality or accuses the fast bowlers of anything anymore.

Chapter 69

'IT CAN'T BE DONE, TONY. THEY WANT US TO MAKE SOMETHING THAT CAN WITHSTAND HALF A HOUSE BRICK AT A HUNDRED MILES AN HOUR.'

Arthur Wallace of Coonan & Denlay to Tony Henson, 1977.

Back in 1870, Lord's used to have a notoriously undulating pitch where the ball would often take off at alarming angles. The authorities did not care until MCC fast bowler John Platts hit George Summers of Nottinghamshire with a ball that rose sharply. Only twenty-five, Summers succumbed to the injury four days later.

Richard Daft, the next man in, appeared from the pavilion with his head draped in a towel. It was an unusual sight, but in his own way, Daft became the first batter to don protective headgear in first-class cricket.

Fast-forward to 1933. In the aftermath of the Bodyline series, the touring West Indian fast bowlers peppered the English batters generously with bouncers. At Lord's, Patsy Hendren walked out in a cap with 'three peaks, two of them covering his ears and temples, lined with foam rubber' designed by his wife, Minnie.

The *Daily Mail* accused Hendren of 'cracking another glorious cricket tradition'. The *Daily Sketch* advised him to 'leave this ridiculous contraption in the pavilion, or better still, send it to Australia'. But having been hit on the head before, Hendren was not going to take any risk.

The 'send it to Australia' advice might not have been the usual Ashes jibe. In the same decade, Rene Shevill used to keep wicket with a baseball mask attached to her cap—although she had almost certainly not attempted it in Test cricket.

None of these, of course, was a helmet. The first Indian to be commissioned into the Royal Flying Corps, Hardit Singh Malik had played for Sussex on either side of the First World War. He donned a 'specially designed helmet, outsized to accommodate his turban'—but for the battlefield, not the cricket pitch.

Indian captain Lala Amarnath won a crash helmet at the Exhibition Speedway on the 1947–48 tour of Australia. He *jokingly* said that he 'might use it to field at silly mid-on' against Queensland, but there is no evidence of him actually doing that.

The honours for that should go to Dickie Dodds of Essex, who 'imaginatively wore part of a riding helmet under his cap' in the 1950s.

Bruce Miles of New South Wales, known more as a lawyer and activist, designed a protective headgear—a motorcycle helmet with steel bars welded across the face—in the late 1950s. Australian opener Jim Burke trialled it and declared it fit. Miles dispatched 'four or five' of these helmets when Australia toured the West Indies in 1964–65. No one used them.

None of them set trends. That nearly happened in 1971, when Warwickshire opener Neal Abberley struck a violent blow that smashed into the head of Roger Davis at short-leg. Thankfully, it was not fatal, but Davis's Glamorgan teammate Tony Cordle acquired an unusual-looking helmet on the rest day and wore it while fielding at short-leg.

Leicestershire's Barry Duddleston and Lancashire's David Lloyd acquired 'headgear of varying style' within a week after this. 'Fear found its outlet,' felt Glamorgan captain Tony Lewis, but it failed to catch on.

Half a century after the incident, it seems logical that bona-fide helmets were first used by close-in fielders and not batters. The ball does not travel 22 yards for the short-leg or the silly point.

The next generation of helmets began with an incident in 1976—yet again at Lord's—when Dennis Amiss ducked into a bouncer from Michael Holding in fading light and the ball hit him on the back of the head. At Old Trafford later that summer, the pace of Holding, Andy Roberts and Wayne Daniel instilled fear in the mind of England captain Tony Greig.

Bill Swanwick was a Nottingham-based manufacturer of protective equipment for epileptics. Upon request, he took a wax mould of Greig's head and designed a skullcap that the England captain wore under his cap. Mike Brearley hesitatingly adopted a Swanwick model from April 1977 with an eye on the Ashes. He had been initially hesitant, but after the summer Rod Marsh assured him that it had been the right thing to do. Sunil Gavaskar would use one under his famous floppy sunhat from the 1983–84 season.

David Frith had seen it coming. 'Crash hats with visors are a repugnant prospect, but if some batsmen decide to wear them, for the sake of their wives and children, no-one will have the power to stop them,' he had written in June 1976.

Amiss went a step further. With the help of business owner Peter Beniman and a Birmingham-based company, Vellvic, he got a motorcycle-style helmet made of Kevlar over conventional fibreglass with a polycarbonate visor. Amiss believed that this device would absorb a blow from 'a double-barrelled shotgun from ten paces'.

The helmet got noticed when he went to Australia for Kerry Packer's World Series Cricket and wore it in the first season amidst the where's-your-motorbike boos. That same season, Roberts hit Australian David Hookes with a vicious bouncer. As next man Ray Bright was greeted with the sight of blood on the pitch, Packer himself drove Hookes to the hospital. They diagnosed a double fracture of the jaw and the cheekbone.

The incident prompted Packer to order a consignment of Vellvic helmets. As news of the order got around, one Tony Henson heard the news on radio. Henson had recently acquired Coonan & Denlay, who manufactured equestrian caps. He now called his colleague Arthur Wallace.

Meeting Packer's team left Wallace disappointed, for he felt that their expectations were beyond the scope of the company. However, Henson was not discouraged easily. He realized that the helmet 'need only deflect impact rather than absorb' the blow.

Henson got a prototype made and approached Marsh. Initially apprehensive, Marsh opened the batting against Roberts and Daniel donning the helmet, much to Henson's shock (it was only a prototype!). It must have worked, for Rob Langer later borrowed Marsh's new helmet.

Encouraged by this, Henson approached Cyklas, a windscreen manufacturer, and Cadillac Plastics. He equipped the helmet with a pre-stressed visor and temple guards. The idea caught on.

At Bridgetown in March 1978, Graham Yallop became the first batter to don a helmet in Test cricket. He resembled an 'astronaut strolling into battle' and was barracked; but he was wise enough to choose safety.

The helmet received criticism in its early years, mostly from old-timers who believed that the batters of their time did not need to be protected as much. Thankfully, the new generation was more practical. Over time, helmets became the norm. Today, some boards have made them mandatory in domestic cricket.

The call for safety has, in fact, extended beyond batters and fielders. Umpire Bruce Oxenford attaches the Ox Block—a polycarbonate arm extender to protect his face—to his arm, while several bowlers have taken to protective masks.

Chapter 70

'UNTIL APARTHEID GOES, YOU CAN FORGET ABOUT GETTING BACK INTO WORLD CRICKET.'

Doug Insole to Ali Bacher, 1979.

It had been nearly a decade since South Africa had last played men's Test cricket. The cricketing world had shunned them since. Their apartheid policies had ensured that non-White cricketers like Krom Hendricks, Frank Roro, Eric Petersen, Taliep Salie, Cec Abrahams, 'Tiny' Abed, Goolam Abed, Denis Foreman, Eric Majola and Khaya Majola never got the limelight they deserved.

Basil D'Oliveira, the one who managed to break through—for England, not South Africa—ended up playing a crucial role behind their long-overdue exile.

South Africa's abnormal policies had also ended the Test careers of Mike Procter, the Pollock brothers—Graeme and Peter—and Barry Richards, though as we have seen before, their matches should have lost Test status as per ICC's own rules once the nation left the Commonwealth in 1961.

Not long after the Gleneagles Agreement of 1977, the ICC sent a fact-finding group to South Africa for feedback on the racial policies. They gave a positive report, whose authenticity was challenged by India, Pakistan and the West Indies. South Africa was not accepted back.

One cannot help but marvel at the ridiculous optimism of the group that submitted the positive report. Steve Biko was beaten to death in prison by security officers in September 1977. He had been the twenty-first political detainee to die in twelve months.

At this point, Dr Ali Bacher, the last man to lead South Africa before their ban and now a consultant at the South African Cricket Union, met TCCB chair Doug Insole in London. If England was willing to take South Africa back, surely the others would follow suit?

But Insole was firm: 'England cannot support you. If we did, it would be the end of English cricket. The Black nations would not play against us.'

Bacher knew that South Africa's abnormal policies were not going to change soon. Boards would not send their teams. But he also knew that he could lure the cricketers with money. Kerry Packer had done that.

Of course, this was going to be a steeper challenge. Packer's men never lost the sympathy of the fans. Playing in apartheid

South Africa might result in permanent stigmas. But Bacher took his chance.

He began with the English. When England toured Sri Lanka in 1981–82, twelve cricketers had agreed for amounts ranging from £40,000 to £60,000. Bacher meant business ('no one could pull out once they had signed up'). The English arrived in South Africa on 2 March to play under the name South African Breweries England XI.

The news sent ripples through England. It was even raised in the parliament. The TCCB banned the cricketers ('the dirty dozen', the tabloids called them) for three years, but Bacher had got what he wanted. He promoted the tourists as an England side, gave out Test caps to the South Africans, and called the games Tests.

He next got a team of Sri Lankans who ended up getting life bans. As the newest Test-playing nation, they were not expected to be tough competition—but the non-White Sri Lankans would boost South Africa's image.

For the first time, White cricketers played non-White cricketers in an official match in South Africa, in 1982–83. Since such contests were illegal under the apartheid rules, the government classified the Sri Lankans as 'Honorary Whites'. Yet, the intrigue of the spectacle did not compensate for the one-sidedness of the contests. Bacher realized he had to get stronger teams—and he aimed for the best.

The Guyanese government had revoked the visa of Robin Jackman in 1981–82: his wife was South African, and he used to spend his winters in the country. The West Indies boycotted the 1982 Women's World Cup in New Zealand because a South African rugby union team had toured the year before. Getting the West Indians was going to be difficult.

Bacher offered Viv Richards a huge sum (sources vary between 5,00,000 Eastern Caribbean dollars and a blank cheque), but Richards refused to accept 'blood money'. Realizing he would never get the big guns, Bacher took an alternative route.

So high was the standard of the West Indies of the era that even Colin Croft and Sylvester Clarke were not certainties in the national side; Alvin Kallicharran, Lawrence Rowe, Collis King and David Murray had fallen out of favour; and Franklyn Stephenson and Ezra Moseley could not break through. Since the cricketers were not paid well either, their future looked uncertain.

Bacher offered $1,20,000 to every capped Test player and $1,00,000 to the others. Yet again, he moved with discretion. On 6 January 1983, Allan Rae, president of the West Indies Cricket Board, praised Rowe and Croft for turning down Bacher's offer. Rae had no idea what was happening, for the squad left five days later, with Rowe as captain.

The rebels were lambasted by their now-former teammates. 'If they were offered enough money, they would probably agree to wear chains,' said Michael Holding. Clive Lloyd denounced the venture as an 'affront to the black man throughout the world'.

In South Africa, the West Indians were received by a cheering crowd of about a hundred, but among them were three Black people who stood silently with a poster: *Freedom first—cricket later.* Rowe had expected his team to inspire the non-White South Africans. The real picture was anything but.

On the tour, a conductor evicted Croft from the Whites-only carriage in a local train in Cape Town. A fellow White traveller called Raymond Roos protested, but Croft had to leave. His Honorary White status was of no use. Three days later, the news hit the local media. Bacher's mission almost fell apart.

But the cricket was outstanding. Local South Africans saw a non-White team of this quality for the first time in history. The fans—mostly White—poured in, even in the notoriously racist Pretoria. The West Indians returned next year for a 15 per cent bonus—but the board gave them a life ban. The ban was lifted in

1989—but not the stigma. Some left the Caribbean. Some found employment difficult. Some became destitute.

The coverage of the series makes an interesting case study of the cricketing world back then. The March 1983 edition of The Cricketer *ran the cover feature, 'South Africa vs West Indies: What Now for World Cricket', with a mere two-page coverage of three Test matches of India's coinciding tour of Pakistan.*

Meanwhile, Bacher got the Australians for two consecutive seasons. Kim Hughes led a squad that featured Terry Alderman, Rodney Hogg and Graham Yallop.

Finally, in 1989, the ICC declared that *any* involvement with South African cricket would result in a ban of three to five years. At the same time, things were changing rapidly off the field. President F.W. de Klerk had implemented a series of reforms. Nelson Mandela was about to be released from prison.

With change imminent, Bacher's idea of inviting an English team in 1989–90 was a blunder—especially as unlike its corporate-paid predecessors, this tour was sponsored by the South African government. The British media tore into the cricketers. Violent demonstrations received them throughout the tour.

Throughout the decade, Bacher had been able to convince many that the South African fans loved the rebel tours, but it was far from the truth. The adulation was not universal. The non-Whites did not want the tours to continue. 'No normal sport in an abnormal society,' believed activist and cricket administrator Hasan Howa. The many demonstrations conveyed the sentiments of the non-Whites about these tours. Visiting captain Mike Gatting's naïve efforts to address the protestors led Bacher to believe Gatting might be killed in Pietermaritzburg.

Mandela was released the day after the first unofficial 'Test'. The second 'Test' was cancelled after an explosion near Newlands. The tour was over.

The next year's rebel tour had to be cancelled—but there was no need for it either. The International Olympic Committee readmitted South Africa in 1991. Bacher helped form the racially unified United Cricket Board of South Africa (UCBSA) with Steve Tshwete. The ICC accepted the UCBSA as a Full Member.

Section 9

Squabbles and Triumphs

Chapter 71

'I'VE TAKEN VERBAL ABUSE AS AN UMPIRE, BUT I'VE NEVER BEEN STRUCK BEFORE. YOU DEAL WITH CROFT BECAUSE WE MEAN TO IN OUR WRITTEN REPORT TO THE NEW ZEALAND BOARD.'

Fred Goodall to Clive Lloyd, Christchurch, 22 February 1980.

Despite Viv Richards's absence, the Test series between the best and the weakest teams in the world was touted to be a mismatch.

'We've beaten the Aussies, *maan*: now we're gonna beat you,' declared Joel Garner on television after the team had flown over from Australia.

Not many eyebrows were raised even after New Zealand stunned them in the only ODI of the tour. 'We got carried away thinking we were God's children,' Michael Holding later admitted. True, they might have been complacent, but it was not a Test match …

The West Indians were jaded and homesick after their tour of Australia. In New Zealand, they found facilities inferior to what they had enjoyed across the Tasman Sea. They had to haul their own kits. The food was 'endless servings of sausages and beans'. Accommodation was in cramped motels.

They would probably have put up with all that—it was, after all, not a long tour—had the dogged resistance from the home side and some questionable umpiring not caught them off-guard. 'There is little doubt that if both sides suffered from difficult, debatable decisions, more went against West Indies than against New Zealand,' summed up the *Wisden Almanack*.

In the first Test, at Dunedin, Richard Hadlee scythed through the West Indies with 5–34 and 6–68—though most reports highlight the role played by the umpires, Fred Goodall and John Hastie. The only one to put up a fight was Desmond Haynes, who opened the batting and was last out in each innings, for 55 and 105.

The incident of this game came in the New Zealand first innings, when a ball from Holding whooshed past John Parker. It 'tore off the glove', recalled Colin Croft, but Hastie ruled Parker not out. A fuming Holding walked up to the striker's end and uprooted two stumps with a spectacular kick. It resulted in one of cricket's most famous photographs. Croft felt that the act should have earned his teammate a contract from Manchester United.

New Zealand needed only 104 to win, but Holding, Garner and Croft showed why they were the best attack in the world.

Reduced to 73–8, the hosts eventually scraped through by 1 wicket. Only Haynes showed up from the West Indies camp for the post-match presentations. As for Holding, he got only a 'talking-to' from manager Willie Rodriguez.

By the time the teams moved to Christchurch for the next Test, the local media had got behind New Zealand. A local radio station broadcast a satirical calypso: '*Mr Goodall, you're breaking our hearts/ You ain't seeing straight, and we're losing/ If you carry on going this way/ We'll pack up our bags and go home. Go on home.*' The West Indians were not amused.

In the second Test, Lance Cairns (6–85) bowled out the visitors for 228. Home captain Geoff Howarth then made a hundred. Just before tea on the third day, a ball from Garner brushed against Howarth's thumb and went to the big gloves of Deryck Murray. No, said Goodall.

The umpires and the home batters walked out after tea, but the West Indians stayed put. 'They can wait. We won't be joining them,' informed captain Clive Lloyd when an official came to inquire. The West Indians had agreed to return home.

They eventually took the field reluctantly, twelve minutes late. The session was spent in slow over rates and short-pitched bowling. Six West Indians cleared out the dressing-room when they left that evening. Play was supposed to resume after the rest day, but they were not returning.

That evening, the West Indians voted 13–2 in favour of leaving New Zealand straight away. That night, they had an end-of-tour party. When venerable local journalist Don Cameron found out about it, he called Jeff Stollmeyer, head of the West Indies board. Stollmeyer assured that the team would stay put.

They relented. Howarth even assured Lloyd that the New Zealand batters would walk if they edged.

But Hadlee tried to hook Croft and edged to Murray on the fourth day and did not walk. Not out, ruled Goodall. Croft responded with a volley of abuses. Goodall and fellow umpire Steve Woodward wanted to raise the matter—but Lloyd was simply not interested in a conversation. Goodall and Woodward had to walk to first slip to talk to Lloyd. It had no effect.

Croft unleashed a volley of bouncers at Hadlee in his next over. In the process, he overstepped the side of the crease, and Goodall no-balled him. On his way to the run-up, Croft deliberately knocked the bails off at the non-striker's end. As the crowd responded with loud boos, non-striker Jeremy Coney picked them up.

Croft had an unusual run-up. He used to start from behind the umpire and emerge to the umpire's left at the last moment. This late appearance made him very difficult to pick. This time, however, he ran in but did not veer away to his left. Instead, he went straight and barged into Goodall. Croft maintains that the act was not deliberate, but the video footage indicates otherwise.

Goodall walked up to Lloyd to complain. Lloyd did not act. The game fizzled out to a draw, as did the third Test. New Zealand had stunned one of the greatest sides of all time. Once back home, Lloyd admitted to the board that he should have been stricter on his team.

When Tom Lister interviewed several players for his seminal book *Fire in Babylon*, the popular opinion was Goodall and Co. were more incompetent than unbiased. They were, after all, amateurs with other day jobs, acquired by the New Zealand Board for these games.

This was the only Test series a full-strength West Indian side lost between 1975–76 and 1994–95. It also triggered a phase lasting nearly twelve years when New Zealand did not lose a Test series at home.

Unfortunately, the legacy of this historic series remains sub-par umpiring and the unsavoury incidents involving Holding and Croft.

Chapter 72

'HOW'S YOUR UNDERARM BOWLING?'

Greg Chappell to Trevor Chappell, Christchurch, 1 February 1981.

'I have been waiting, with trepidation, for the moment when, with six runs needed off the final ball and a lot of money at stake, the bowler informs the umpire of a change of action and rolls the ball along the ground,' David Frith had predicted in the *Wisden Cricket Monthly* in June 1979.

Frith's prediction had come in the aftermath of a brilliant ploy from Brian Rose that prompted the authorities to abolish declarations from limited-overs cricket. Little did Frith know that not only would his words come true in less than two years, but they would also send ripples across the world.

After eliminating India, Australia and New Zealand had made it to the best-of-five finals of the 1980–81 Benson & Hedges World Series Cup. They won once each before arriving at Melbourne for the third final. There, Australia posted 235–4, and with 2 balls remaining, New Zealand needed 7 to win.

Trevor Chappell clean-bowled Ian Smith. The strapping Brian McKechnie, who had also played rugby for New Zealand, walked out. Wicketkeeper Rod Marsh advised the youngest Chappell brother to stick to the basics. Trevor Chappell himself had set his eyes on a spot on the pitch: if he could hit that, the ball would keep low.

Captain Greg Chappell had had a long day. It was not about his 90 runs or 3 wickets or the strain of leading Australia. The first four finals were, in fact, scheduled across six days. Australia's home summer, set to feature six Tests and up to fifteen ODIs over twelve weeks, was approaching its end, but the cricketers were dreary.

Now he walked up from mid-on to meet Trevor, who was about to begin his run-up. Did his younger brother still bowl underarm? He did not know, confessed Trevor.

'Well, you're about to find out,' Greg informed him, then umpire Don Weser, who updated his colleague, Peter Cronin.

Meanwhile, Marsh was asked to stand back. When he realized what was about to happen, a horrified Marsh exclaimed, 'Don't do it, mate!' Ian Chappell, the eldest of the brothers, echoed Marsh's opinion on air: 'No, Greg, no. You can't do that!'

But Greg would have his way, and Trevor would oblige—and why not? Underarm bowling was legal, so why not exploit that loophole to prevent New Zealand from levelling the score?

So, Trevor walked four steps and rolled the ball along the pitch. McKechnie blocked it, threw his bat away in anger, and left. New Zealand captain Geoff Howarth ran on to the ground to talk to the umpires: for some reason, he had been under the impression that underarm was illegal.

Unfortunately, it turned out that Greg knew the Laws of Cricket and Howarth did not.

But the matter did not end there. As the players walked back, a little fan had two words for Greg as he jogged towards the players' gate: 'You cheated.' It was the first time he realized the enormity of his act.

'Fair dinkum, Greg, how much pride do you sacrifice to win $35,000? Because, brother, you sacrificed a lot in front of a huge TV audience and 52,825 people,' wrote Ian in his column the next day.

Most echoed these feelings. It escalated to even the two national leaders. New Zealand Prime Minister Robert Muldoon called it 'the most disgusting incident I can recall in the history of cricket'. More surprisingly, even Australian Prime Minister Malcolm Fraser described it as 'contrary to the traditions of the game'.

The Laws of Cricket were changed shortly afterwards. Underarm is *still* legal, but *only if* both parties agree ahead of a match. However, the bowler can neither roll the ball along the ground nor make it bounce more than once.

Australia toured New Zealand the following year. They played the first ODI of this return tour in front of 43,000 people in Auckland. As Greg walked out to bat, a spectator sent a bowling wood (the orb used in lawn bowls) across the turf, mimicking the incident. Greg responded with a dazzling 108 in 92 balls.

Years later, Greg Chappell regretted his decision.

Few incidents have demonstrated the change in mindset of the cricket fan over time. As we have seen before, there was an uproar when some bowlers decided to evolve from the underarm era. In 1827, the leading cricketers even filed a written protest. The definition of fairness took a U-turn over a century and a half to reach a point where underarm was considered unfair play!

In 2004–05, when the two teams met in the first-ever T20 International, Glenn McGrath rolled the last ball of the match, underarm, along the pitch. Umpire Billy Bowden showed McGrath a red card, and there was laughter all around. Everyone had mellowed down.

Chapter 73

'WHY CAN WE NOT PLAY THE NEXT WORLD CUP IN OUR COUNTRIES?'

Nur Khan to N.K.P. Salve, 26 June 1983.

One cannot blame BCCI president N.K.P. Salve for not making plans for the 1983 World Cup final on 25 June. He had planned to arrive in London just for the ICC annual general meeting on 27 and 28 June. Before that, Salve—also the minister of steel and mines at that point—had planned an official trip to Germany and Sweden.

He obviously changed his plans when India stunned everyone by reaching the final. As BCCI president, he and his spouse were obviously invited, but he requested the MCC for four extra passes or, alternately, four tickets against payment. The MCC arranged for neither.

'It is inconceivable in India that for four personal guests of the President of the Board of Control of a country playing [the] finals of the World Cup there would be any difficulty whatsoever,' felt Salve. 'In India such courtesy for the visiting dignitary would be simply taken for granted.'

More than the snub—which partly had to do with the logistics as well—the 'arrogance of the officials at Lord's' left an impact on Salve. The day after the final, he attended a lunch with Air Marshal Nur Khan and Gamini Dissanayake, the heads of the Pakistan and Sri Lanka boards. 'How wonderful it would have been if someday we could play the World Cup in India,' expressed Dissanayake.

Nur Khan proposed India and Pakistan co-hosting the World Cup. The seeds of the idea were sown, albeit casually. Having hosted the first three editions, England was unlikely to concede the World Cup rights anytime soon, but Salve set the wheels into motion.

In the 1980s, a vote from each of the seven Full Members counted for two votes at the ICC, while every Associate Member—there were eighteen—had the power of one vote. Salve knew that the three Asian sides and the West Indies would work 'effectively in concert', but that made only eight votes out of thirty-two. He needed more than that.

To undergo any change in rules, the ICC needed a majority of the votes *and* (not *or*) support from at least one of the 'Foundation Members', England and Australia. Since the MCC president and secretary served as the ICC chair (who held a casting vote) and secretary, the odds were stacked in England's favour.

However, Salve knew that unlike England, India had allies next door. He began with the idea of an Asian cricket bloc. Nur Khan and Dissanayake were keen, and the Asian Cricket Council (ACC) was formed on 19 September 1983, with the three Full Members and Bangladesh, Malaysia and Singapore as the founding members.

This was significant. The ACC became the first *regional* body outside the ICC to host international cricket as well as make money out of it. The first Asia Cup, at Sharjah in 1984, witnessed the first-ever international matches outside an ICC Full Member nation. The ACC assured Sri Lanka of hosting rights in the second edition and the third in another Associate Nation, Bangladesh.

With the help of lawyers, Salve figured out that the veto power of the Foundation Members was applicable only when something needed to be *changed*. India and Pakistan were not trying to *modify* a rule. Like England, they were merely one of the proposers.

Jagmohan Dalmiya, the young BCCI treasurer, helped draft a proposal that Salve presented at an informal meeting of the Full Members on 18 July 1984. It was superior to England's proposal on nearly every count. India and Pakistan offered every member—Full and Associate—significantly more than England. And while the TCCB claimed £3,00,000 for hosting the World Cup, the BCCI and the BCCP expected nothing.

There was still predictable resistance, largely on the grounds that India and Pakistan lacked England's infrastructure. Visiting teams had, over the years, returned from the Indian subcontinent with horror stories about food, accommodation and infrastructure. Why would this be any different?

At the formal meeting the next day, both parties presented their cases again. The TCCB chair called the subcontinental proposal 'reckless'. He was uncertain about the source of India and Pakistan's foreign exchange. An 'infuriated' Salve reminded that the BCCI 'was not only the best managed board all over the world but financially it was the soundest'. At this, the ICC chair paused the meeting and requested the board representatives to discuss.

Salve assured England, Australia and New Zealand that their cricketers would get the best accommodation. When the New Zealand President demanded a bank guarantee, Salve threatened to walk out. He offered to present the BCCI balance sheets and reminded everyone that England had not needed to submit any guarantee for the first three World Cups.

After the intermission, the matter was put to vote. India and Pakistan won by sixteen votes to twelve. The shift of power in cricket had begun.

Chapter 74

'IT IS OKAY TO HAVE BEEN PART OF HISTORY, BUT WE WOULD HAVE LIKED TO WIN THE MATCH.'

Kapil Dev about the ongoings of the evening of 22 September 1986.

Australia underwent a transition in the mid-1980s. They had lost to New Zealand at home, conceded the Ashes in England, and had somehow managed to hold India to a draw at home. Greg Chappell, Dennis Lillee and Rod Marsh had bowed out together. Jeff Thomson was also gone. With new captain Allan Border and new coach Bobby Simpson at the helm, they were embarking upon a new era.

India had different issues. They played thirty-one Test matches between December 1981 and October 1984: they lost nine and did not win even one. At home, they lost three of these, while their twelve draws were largely boring contests with slow over rates on dead pitches.

It was improbable that these two teams would play out one of the greatest Tests of all time. At the same time, both teams were getting better at one-day cricket, where aggressive play was the norm. India had won the World Cup in 1983 and the seven-nation World Championship of Cricket in Australia in 1984–85, while Australia were building a unit that would win the World Cup in 1987.

On a hot day in Madras, Border won the toss, batted first and did not declare until the third morning, on 574–7. David Boon made 122 and Border himself 106, but the highlight was Dean Jones's magnum opus—a marathon 502-minute 210 in excruciating heat and sapping humidity. A dehydrated Jones vomited on the pitch and lost 8 kilograms: it took him nine months to regain the lost weight.

At one point, he could not take it anymore and considered retiring ill, but Border would have none of it: 'You weak Victorian, I want a tough Australian out there, I want a Queenslander. Get me Greg Ritchie.' That did the trick. Jones continued.

The Indian response seemed doomed at 245–7 before captain Kapil Dev slammed 119 in 138 balls to help them avoid the follow-on. Having made 44 with the bat, Greg Matthews now picked up 5–103. He would later make a breezy unbeaten 27 in the second innings and take 5–94 on the final day.

But most spectacularly, he bowled a significant part of his 409 balls in sweltering heat *in a sweater*—and fielded *in two sweaters*. He had his reasons: 'Nomadic herders in the desert wore woollen coats because they kept the cool air in, thus acting as a kind of air-conditioner.' It must have worked.

Australia led by 177 in the first innings and extended that to 347 by stumps on day four. Border declared on the overnight score, much to the delight of Indian fans who had endured half a decade of dull Test cricket. And many braved the conditions to pour into the venue as India went for the chase.

Kris Srikkanth made a quick 39 before Sunil Gavaskar took charge, with Mohinder Amarnath for company. Neither was new to big chases. A decade ago, Gavaskar had made 102 and Amarnath 85 when India had famously chased 406 at Port of Spain. Gavaskar had also made 221 as India set out to chase 438 at The Oval in 1979, but fell short by 9 runs. Here, India wiped out 94 of the runs by lunch. They lost Amarnath, but Mohammad Azharuddin kept the tempo going. At tea, India needed 155 in 30 overs.

Jones caught Gavaskar at cover for 90 off left-arm spinner Ray Bright soon afterwards. Chandrakant Pandit, in only his second Test, then kept the scoreboard ticking with deft placements. By the time the last 20 overs began, India needed fewer than a hundred.

Azharuddin fell at this point. Kapil promoted himself above Ravi Shastri and fell cheaply, leaving India with 95 to chase. Shastri now joined Pandit—and immediately made it evident that the chase was still on.

As Border slowed the game down—it might have been strategic, but it could have been the scorching sun as well—umpire Dara Dotiwalla stepped in. Words were exchanged. Tempers flared. When Pandit fell, Matthews gave him a send-off. But the match continued.

India needed 57 with 4 wickets in hand, but now Shastri and Chetan Sharma added 40 to leave India to score 17 in nearly 5 overs. The Test was theirs to lose … but Bright turned the game on its head. He had felt unwell and left the ground earlier, but

Border had summoned him back. He now had Chetan caught at long-on and Kiran More leg-before.

The best bet was to give Shastri the strike, but Shivlal Yadav felt otherwise. When Matthews tossed up the ball, he stepped out—to the surprise of some—and cleared long-on, much to Shastri's delight.

India had to score only 4 from 9 balls, but for some reason Yadav wanted to get the runs in one go. He tried to sweep Bright—a shot he would later regret—and was bowled off the pad. Last man Maninder Singh, a batter of no repute, somehow survived the last 2 balls.

India still needed 4. As Matthews came to bowl the last over, Border pushed the fielders back. Shastri defended the first ball but went after the next. He inside-edged the slog, and as Geoff Marsh misfielded at deep square-leg, got the second run he needed.

Border kept the field spread out. Shastri had two alternatives: he could take a run to secure a tie or take 4 balls to play the winning hit. He chose the safer option and picked up a single from mid-wicket.

Maninder defended the fourth ball. That was okay, for he would get two more chances—and India could not lose anyway. Matthews ran in with a silly point and a forward short-leg but no slip. Both sweaters had come off, but he still had his cap on.

The ball hit the pad. Maninder, semi-tangled in his limited footwork, was still trying to ground his bat when umpire V. Vikramraju raised his finger with amazing alacrity. He felt it had been plumb. But Maninder maintains that he had got bat on ball. 'Before I even played the ball, I could see his finger going up … That shows he was nervous.'

A fuming Shastri gestured at Vikramraju, but he had to peel himself off the ground. The Indians had just been part of the second—and till date, last—tied Test match, but they were not happy. Especially their captain, who was disappointed at having to leave without a win.

Chapter 75

'YOU ARE WAVING YOUR HAND. THAT'S CHEATING.'

Shakoor Rana to Mike Gatting, 22 September 1987.

Brothers Shafaqat and Azmat Rana both played for Pakistan, as did their nephews, Mansoor and Maqsood. None of them was the most famous member of the family. That honour lies with Shakoor, brother of Shafaqat and Azmat.

Shakoor Rana did not regret the incidents of that day at Faisalabad. 'How can I regret? It made me the most famous umpire,' he later admitted.

Rana's umpiring career was marred by controversies. On *his* umpiring Test debut, in 1974–75, he called Lance Gibbs for overstepping. A fuming Gibbs—he took pride in not overstepping—was not quite polite in his response. Clive Lloyd had to issue an apology to Rana on the rest day.

Mohsin Khan once questioned a leg-before decision. Rana deliberately subjected him to 'outrageous decisions' in the next two matches. He stopped only once Mohsin apologized.

When India toured Pakistan in 1978–79, he had a run-in with Sunil Gavaskar, who pointed out that Rana had been ignoring the overstepping of Imran Khan and Sarfraz Nawaz. After India's next tour of Pakistan, in 1982–83, Ravi Shastri famously said, 'Imran and Sarfraz could make the ball swing, and then there were those two umpires, Khizer Hayat and Shakoor Rana. It was like playing a four-pronged attack.'

In 1984–85, New Zealand captain Jeremy Coney—usually a calm man—threatened to walk off when Rana did not rule Javed Miandad out leg-before.

Rana did not stand in the Lahore Test of 1986–87, but England were at the receiving end of some dubious decisions as Abdul Qadir (9–56 and 4–45) spun Pakistan to an innings win. There was some drama during the England second innings, when Chris Broad refused to leave after being given out caught behind ('I didn't hit it. I'm not going. You can like it or lump it, I'm staying').

Decades later, Broad became an ICC match referee, dishing out penalties to cricketers for questioning the umpire's decision. Different times.

Broad left only after Graham Gooch persuaded him to. He got away with only a 'stern reprimand' from the England camp. England captain Mike Gatting, manager Micky Stewart and tour manager Peter Lush all criticized the umpiring after the match. *Wisden* observed that 'not one of the three appeared to acknowledge that the batting had been woefully sub-standard'.

It was under these circumstances that the second Test began at Faisalabad. Rana had an unremarkable game until the second evening. With 3 balls left in the day, Pakistan were 106–5 after bowling out England for 292.

As Eddie Hemmings ran to bowl to Saleem Malik, Gatting asked David Capel to move in from deep square-leg (Gatting later said that he had informed Malik of this move earlier). At this, square-leg umpire Rana stopped play immediately and accused Gatting of cheating.

The conversation began in a civil manner. 'The language employed throughout the discourse was basic' (*Wisden*) until both men began to approach each other. They stood very close from one another, wagging their fingers at and showering each other with swear words in front of television cameras.

The photograph remains one of cricket's ugliest.

The day's cricket ended there. Rana refused to continue unless Gatting apologized: 'In Pakistan many men have been killed for the sort of insults he threw at me. He's lucky I didn't beat him.'

Gatting was in no mood to comply: 'It was not his job at square leg to inform the batsman what I was doing. I did nothing for which I need to apologise.' He later agreed to apologize, but only if Rana apologized as well. Rana refused.

Only when the match did not resume the next day did the magnitude of the matter become evident. Both boards stood firmly behind their members. Ijaz Butt, the Board of Control for Cricket in Pakistan secretary, abruptly left for Lahore that afternoon. Lush drove to Lahore to find BCCP president Safdar Butt (unrelated to Ijaz), but could not meet either until the next morning, the rest day of the match.

The matter was not sorted out until British ambassador Nicholas Barrington rushed to the scenario to prevent any straining of diplomatic relations. Gatting submitted a handwritten note to Rana on the fourth morning: 'Dear Shakoor Rana, I apologise for the bad language used during the 2nd day of the Test match at Faisalabad. Mike Gatting, 11th Dec 1987.' He had been threatened with being sacked as captain.

Two days remained. England requested for an extra day to make up for lost time, but the BCCP refused, and the match fizzled out to a draw. The BCCP now appointed Shakeel Khan, who had stood at Lahore, for the third Test as well. They eventually had to withdraw him after England protested.

The TCCB later paid a £1000 'hardship bonus' to every England cricketer. Gatting still lost his job six months later, over an incident involving a barmaid in Nottingham. Some speculate that he would have been sacked anyway after the Rana incident.

Rana himself stood in only three more Test matches. There is a story—probably apocryphal—about the duo bumping into each other in England later. 'Oh god, not you again,' uttered Gatting before leaving the scene.

Chapter 76

'LET US CLOSE IT AT FORTY.'

Ali Bacher to Amrit Mathur, end-October or early November 1991.

India had been firm in their anti-apartheid stance throughout the 1970s and the 1980s. When South Africa seemed to be emerging from the curse, the Indian government honoured Nelson Mandela with the Bharat Ratna, their highest civilian honour, rarely bestowed upon a non-Indian. And in 1991–92, India became the first country to host post-exile South Africa for a cricket tour.

Three ODIs were scheduled in November 1991, in Calcutta, Gwalior and Delhi. Dr Ali Bacher, the man behind the rebel tours in South Africa, was now in charge of cricket in the nation. He was keen on the matches being telecast back home. Not too long before the series, he reached out to the BCCI for the television rights.

Live telecast of cricket in India had started in 1966–67, with a game between North Zone and the touring West Indians at Delhi. The government-run Doordarshan telecast cricket over the next two decades and a half. With the exception of the 1987 World Cup, the BCCI made no money out of these games: they were not even aware that the rights were theirs to sell. Their only revenue sources were gate money and on-field advertisements. If anything, they sometimes *paid* the channel.

Bacher's question thus stumped BCCI spokesperson Amrit Mathur. This was the first time the board became aware that the rights were theirs to sell—but they still had no clue how much they should ask for. Mathur called Doordarshan: they were not sure either, but they suggested a vague $10,000 per game.

Mathur ran the figures past the BCCI officials. Secretary Jagmohan Dalmiya recommended twice that amount. Twenty-five, was the consensus. When they met the next time, Mathur *asked Bacher* to name an amount.

Thirty per game, offered Bacher. Mathur hesitated. Bacher raised it to forty. The deal was sealed. For the first time, the BCCI sold the television rights of cricket in India—for a measly $1,20,000 for a historic series. Still, it was a start.

England toured India the next winter for the first Test series in the country in over two and a half years. Now aware that they held the television rights, the BCCI sold them to Trans World International (TWI). Doordarshan had to pay TWI $10,00,000 to televise the games in India. The BCCI made $6,00,000 out of the deal.

The Hero Cup of 1993 was next. Doordarshan offered 10 million rupees (approximately $3,20,000 back then) to the Cricket Association of Bengal—substantially less than TWI's offer (17.6 million rupees ($5,63,200) and 70 per cent share of global revenue). Fearing defeat, Doordarshan refused to pay, and chose not to telecast the matches. As a result, millions were deprived of a free-to-air live telecast of the start of a tournament in their own country.

The Indian Information and Broadcasting Ministry then cited the Indian Telegraph Act (it dated back to 1885!), according to which the Indian government agencies were the only ones authorized to 'telecast any event live by uplinking signals from Indian soil'. This put Doordarshan at an advantage.

The customs departments at Delhi, Bombay and Calcutta airports seized TWI equipment for apparently not obtaining the required approval from government officials. These were not released until the Supreme Court issued an order.

The Hero Cup generated little interest in its early stages, especially once Pakistan opted out. On-field advertising was minimal when India and Sri Lanka played the opener at Kanpur. Things looked up only once the later matches were telecast, but Doordarshan remained a threat.

That was not resolved until Justices P.B. Sawant, B.P. Jeevan Reddy and S. Mohan passed an order in February 1995. While classifying 'the airwaves or frequencies' as 'public property', they added that 'the right to impart and receive information is a species of the right to freedom of speech and expression guaranteed by Article 19(1)(a) of the Constitution.

'A citizen has a fundamental right to use the best means of imparting and receiving information and as such to have access to telecasting for the purpose.'

The order thwarted Doordarshan's attempts to exercise monopoly as a government body.

Mark Mascarenhas, the owner of WorldTel, guaranteed the organizers of the 1996 World Cup, hosted by India, Pakistan and Sri Lanka, a whopping $1.4 million, 'unheard-of money in cricket back then'.

By then, India had also understood that cricket played in the evening could dominate prime-time slots in a nation when most households had one television set. Live cricket, thus, replaced news and soaps as the evening family show across India in the 1990s, a decade when Doordarshan was still the go-to option even as cable television spread its wings across the nation.

After not making any money out of television coverage for more than two decades, the BCCI had taken its first steps to become the financial powerhouse of the sport. In 2022, they sold the IPL rights for five years to Disney Star and Viacom18 for $6.2 billion.

Section 10

The Renaissance of Cricket

Chapter 77

'THERE WAS A 50 PER CENT CHANCE THAT I'D HIT THE STUMPS IF I THREW, AND A 100 PER CENT CHANCE OF HITTING THE STUMPS WITH BALL IN HAND.'

Jonty Rhodes, recalling an incident from 8 March 1992.

The 1992 World Cup revolutionized cricket more than any other edition. In many ways, it was a World Cup of firsts: floodlit cricket, coloured clothing, white ball, next-generation hi-technology television coverage. Realizing they could take advantage of the field restrictions inside the first 15 overs, several teams sent specialist hitters to go after the bowling from the onset.

Cricket had seen each of these before, but never *together* at a stage this grand, with satellite television sending the feed around the world. And of all great spectacles the World Cup had to offer, nothing matched that one moment at Brisbane that left the cricket fraternity in awe.

South Africa made 211–7 that day. It rained during the Pakistan innings, and their target was readjusted to 194 in 36 overs. At 135–2, with Inzamam-ul-Haq (48) and Imran Khan (34), they seemed on course. At this point, Inzamam (wearing Mushtaq Ahmed's shirt for some reason) tried to flick and missed a ball from Brian McMillan.

As the ball rolled towards Jonty Rhodes at point, Inzamam set off for a leg-bye. No, said an ageing Imran. Inzamam turned back.

Rhodes had debuted in this World Cup. This was his fifth game. He neither bowled nor kept wicket; and had made 61 runs in four innings until this point. But South Africa retained him despite these unremarkable numbers—and the world was about to see why.

Rhodes played centre-forward in the national field hockey side. He would have played at the 1992 Olympics in Barcelona, but South Africa did not qualify. Hockey almost certainly contributed to his amazing speed and agility.

Rhodes realized that he might hit if he threw it from that distance, but with one stump to aim at, he might miss as well. If he made a dash for the stumps, on the other hand, it would be slower but surer. He went for the one where success was significantly more probable: he sprinted.

Over the years, Inzamam would earn a reputation of being a slow runner between the wickets, but at twenty-two, he was as quick as most others of his age. At one point, it seemed he had a reasonable chance of making it.

'The fastest way I could cover the last metre-and-a-half was head-first,' felt Rhodes. He did.

Rhodes was not the first great fielder in history. Jack Hobbs and Don Bradman were exceptional at cover, Wally Hammond at slip, Tony Greig at silly point, Ashley Mallett at gully. Nip Pellew could make it to any side on fielding alone. Learie Constantine and Colin Bland could draw crowds. Eknath Solkar remains arguably the greatest at short-leg. Clive Lloyd, Gus Logie and Roger Harper lit up the field with dazzling displays.

But satellite television ensured that Rhodes's exceptional effort stunned a global audience in an unprecedented manner.

He made fielding sexy in an era when every young child wanted to bat, or, at best, bowl. Fielding was often considered menial. They would still await their turn to bat or bowl; yet, by the time the World Cup got over, children in faraway lands wanted to fling themselves on the uneven grounds as well.

All of them wanted to field like Jonty Rhodes. By the turn of the century, every side in the world showed a marked improvement in fielding.

In March 2023, the ICC ran an online poll to select the best among thirty-two 'ICC Men's World Cup Greatest Moments'. Rhodes's run-out of Inzamam won.

Chapter 78

'SURELY SOMEONE, SOMEWHERE COULD COME UP WITH SOMETHING BETTER.'

Christopher Martin-Jenkins on air, recalling an incident from 22 March 1992.

For centuries, the outcome of cricket matches was determined by runs and wickets—but not balls. Teams could bat for as long as they wanted to. Teams chasing targets won if they could get the runs. If not, the defending sides won if they could bowl out the chasing side within the target. If they could not, the outcome was called a draw. In a draw, both teams walked away with honours even.

Limited-overs cricket changed everything. Both teams now faced the same number of overs, and the draw was taken out of the equation. To win, it was no longer mandatory for the defending side to bowl out the opposition; just bowling the quota of overs was necessary.

This made things tricky, because cricket is halted when it rains. If Team A made 209–4 in 50 overs and Team B 130–2 in 30, Team A neither got 10 wickets nor bowled the full quota of overs, while Team B did not reach their target. Surely 80 overs of cricket deserve a result!

The administrators first tried to address this with the average run rate (ARR) method—the humble unitary method that we have read in school. In the same example, Team A had scored at a run rate of 4.18. Since Team B got only 30 overs, they needed more than (30 x 4.18) = 125.4—in other words, 126.

The flaw is easy to understand. Of the two resources available to the chasing side, the ARR considered one (balls) but not the other (wickets). It did not distinguish between 130–2 and 130–9. ARR favoured the chasing side. In this case, Team B had 10 wickets to squander over 30 overs, while Team A, with 10 wickets for 50 overs, had to bat more cautiously.

This was exposed during the third final of the 1988–89 World Series. Australia scored 226–4 in 38 overs. The West Indies, requiring 5.97 an over, were 47–2 in 6.4 overs when rain stopped play. Upon resumption, the target was adjusted to 108 in 18 overs. They needed 61 in 68 balls with 8 wickets in hand, which they got easily.

Australia improved on this with the 'most productive overs' (MPO) method. The least expensive overs bowled by the defending side were now deducted from the target. The purpose was to reduce the obvious advantage the chasing side used to enjoy under the ARR.

Thus, if Team A had scored 229–4 in 50 overs but had conceded 5 maiden overs, the target would be 230 in 45 overs after removing the five least-scoring overs from the equation. Just like the ARR, the MPO, too, failed to take the wickets into the equation, but it was probably an improvement.

The rule received flak after the semi-final of the 1992 World Cup. South Africa needed 22 in 13 balls against England when it rained for twelve minutes. Since South Africa had bowled 2 maidens, their target was reduced to 22 from 1 ball. To minimize the chasing side's advantage, the MPO had ended up favouring the side batting first.

The scorers later confirmed that the target should have been 21 in 1 ball. There had been a leg-bye in the 2 maiden overs.

Christopher Martin-Jenkins voiced his frustration on radio. British statistician Frank Duckworth heard the words on air. He and fellow statistician Tony Lewis devised a method. They combined the two resources, wickets and overs.

The Duckworth-Lewis Method assumed that sides used up 50 overs and 10 wickets at the same rate, and pools the two together to form one parameter, resources, and calculates targets based on that. Unlike before, the target considered how many wickets the chasing side had in hand.

Until this point, the rain rule had largely been built around hunch and common sense. There had been no science to it. Duckworth and Lewis, both statisticians, introduced precise science to it. It was first implemented during an ODI between Zimbabwe at Harare on New Year's Day, 1997, and has not looked back since.

Duckworth and Lewis later retired, leaving Steven Stern as the sole custodian. The Duckworth-Lewis-Stern (DLS) Method remains the official ICC 'rain rule' for both 50-over cricket and

T20, though the BCCI uses the V. Jayadevan Method for domestic matches in India (however, they use the DLS Method at the IPL). While the Jayadevan Method uses regression, DLS uses a robust exponential decay function, resulting in slightly different targets.

The DLS Method does receive periodic criticism, especially when someone feels their favourite team has been robbed, but there is seldom any science to these comments. The method has impressed most, especially in the ODIs.

However, its usage in T20 cricket has raised valid questions. There, overs run out quickly, and teams seldom get bowled out. DLS's assumption of the two resources being used up at the same rate may not work as efficiently here. Perhaps it is time to formulate a different table based on the same method but using only T20 data.

Chapter 79

'I FELT INSTANTLY THE GAME HAD CHANGED FOREVER–AND FOR THE BETTER.'

Kepler Wessels, referring to an incident from 14 November 1992.

The first Test match of South Africa's 1992–93 home series against India, at Kingsmead, Durban, was a historic occasion for several reasons. South Africa were hosting Test cricket for the first time since their exile. Their captain Kepler Wessels became the first to score Test hundreds for two countries (he had earlier got one for Australia).

But all that was on the field. Just outside the boundary, inside a small box sat Karl Liebenberg, who had been umpiring in South African domestic cricket since 1978–79 and had been on the panel in the World Cup in Australia and New Zealand earlier that year.

This was a new role for him. He would still have to keep an eye on the cricket, but with particular focus on the action replays in the television set in front of him. He was the first television umpire—third umpire, if you must—in the history of Test cricket.

The South African board had come up with the idea ahead of the series. Steve Bucknor, the neutral umpire, would stand on the field throughout the Test match, while the two local umpires would swap duties after every session. The Indian touring committee had agreed, but with one change: the South African umpires would switch after every day.

The home board had also suggested a third light—amber—to indicate 'undecided'. The touring party had not agreed to this either.

Cyril Mitchley and Liebenberg were the local umpires for the first Test match. After spending a day in the television room, Mitchley stood on the field on the second day. The long-awaited moment came when Sachin Tendulkar pushed a ball from Brian McMillan to backward point and set off for a single, but non-striker Ravi Shastri sent him back. By the time the throw from Jonty Rhodes had arrived, Andrew Hudson had run from short-leg to the wicket at the striker's end.

Tendulkar, nursing an ankle injury, took his time to return. Hudson took the bails off and appealed to square-leg umpire Mitchley.

Was Tendulkar out? Mitchley was 'almost certain' that he was. The members of the Indian squad who sat near the boundary, on the other hand, felt that Tendulkar was 'safely in'.

Until now, the onus for such decisions used to rest with the square-leg umpire, who would—if the need arose—consult with the umpire at the bowler's end. Some of Mitchley's predecessors would have ruled Tendulkar out despite the 'almost' certainty. Some would have given the benefit of doubt to the batter.

But now, there was a third option, superior to any of the other two. Despite being 'almost certain' that Tendulkar had fallen short of the crease, Mitchley signalled a giant television screen in the air to refer the decision to Liebenberg.

There was no fixed camera at square-leg, but the camera from the off-side confirmed what Mitchley had seen. Liebenberg pressed the relevant button, and the *green light* came on, signalling that Tendulkar could leave. Over time, they would switch the lights and use red for 'out' and green for 'not out'.

Not all umpires were as receptive to technology as Mitchley. In the next Test match, at Johannesburg, Javagal Srinath ran out Rhodes with a direct hit from mid-off. For some reason, Bucknor had been walking away from the stumps, and turned around only at the last moment. Despite not being in the best position to judge, Bucknor ruled Rhodes not out. The Indians 'pleaded with him' to refer to the television umpire, but Bucknor trusted himself too much to oblige.

Television replays revealed that Rhodes was 'some six inches' short of the crease. It turned out to be vital: Rhodes was on 28 at that point and South Africa 61–4 (they soon became 73–5). Rhodes went on to make 91 and South Africa 292.

But the experiment was an overall success. It was soon followed by cricket boards around the world.

Over time, the umpires became less resistant to the idea. The television umpire's authority soon expanded beyond the modes of dismissals involving the crease—run-out and stumped. The twenty-first century would equip them even more, but that is another story.

Chapter 80

'I WONDER HOW, WITH THIS INTELLIGENCE, YOU COULD HAVE RULED US FOR OVER TWO HUNDRED YEARS.'

Jagmohan Dalmiya to the British media, 2 February 1993.

We have seen how N.K.P. Salve had wrested the 1987 World Cup from England to the subcontinent. Australia and New Zealand co-hosted the next World Cup, in 1992. With no other major contender, the World Cup was set to return to England in 1996.

At this point, South Africa, fresh from their exile, put forward a proposal. They did not have any immediate realistic hopes for hosting, but they at least wanted the right to bid. The ICC accepted this perfectly normal request—but in the process, they opened the bidding procedure.

Salve's proposal had been drafted by the young BCCI treasurer, Jagmohan Dalmiya, who had by now evolved into a significant member of the board. Seeking an opportunity, he suggested to BCCI president Madhavrao Scindia that India bid for the 1996 World Cup.

As with 1987, the BCCI reached out to their counterparts in Pakistan and Sri Lanka. Together, they formed the Pak-Indo-Lanka Joint Management Committee (PILCOM).

It is important to understand the ICC's voting system back then. With the induction of Zimbabwe, the ICC now had nine Full Members, whose votes were worth two (eighteen in all) each. The nineteen Associates, on the other hand, accounted for one vote apiece. The PILCOM did the logical thing: they set out to woo the Associates.

'First, various Indian- and Pakistan-origin people controlling cricket bodies were identified,' noted Amrit Mathur, part of the PILCOM delegation. 'This was followed by an emotional appeal that sought to give PILCOM's bid an anti-white (we need to teach the racist nations a lesson) angle.'

Of course, that would not have sufficed, so they played their main card: they tweaked the World Cup payout. England's TCCB offered £2,50,000 as prize money; £3,00,000 to each of the nine Full Members; £1,50,000 to each of the three Associates who would qualify; and £65,000 to each of the sixteen others.

The PILCOM's respective sums were £2,00,000, £2,50,000, £1,25,000 and £1,00,000—in other words, they allocated some of the Full Members' money to the Associates. In *Wisden*, Jack Bailey, the secretary of the MCC (and hence the ICC: that was how it used to be) from 1974 to 1987, would describe this as 'politicking and favour-seeking among member countries by those from the sub-continent'.

Bailey's hollow frustration did not alter the fact that the PILCOM approach was not only legal but also more democratic than the TCCB proposal.

The TCCB were up against a threat, and their media sensed it. 'There was a time, before money and politics entered the equation, when the community of cricket nations looked no further than the United Kingdom to stage the World Cup,' lamented Christopher Martin-Jenkins in the *Daily Telegraph*. He felt that England's 'advantages cannot be matched by the rival bidders from a vast and frequently unruly subcontinent'.

These were curious claims. As we have seen, the World Cup had begun *because of a want for money*, and the ICC had largely been an extension of the MCC until this point. The first time an alternative to England had been available, in 1987, the 'community of cricket nations' chose India and Pakistan, and the 'frequently unruly subcontinent' had hosted an unanimously praised World Cup.

PILCOM's offers, clearly more in favour with more teams, should have clinched the deal, but there were still two problems. To arrive at a decision, two-thirds of the Full Members (six) had to agree; and at least one of England and Australia, the 'Foundation Members', had to be among the six.

The three Asian nations obviously voted for PILCOM, but the TCCB counted on the other six. However, not too long ago, the TCCB had tried to use their veto power to oppose Zimbabwe's Full Membership status. The BCCI, on the other hand, had supported Zimbabwe, and India were the first team to play a Test match against them. Zimbabwe naturally voted for PILCOM.

The Full Member votes read 5–4 (10–8) in the TCCB's favour. The Associate votes turned the verdict towards PILCOM, but the TCCB still had England and Australia's veto support.

PILCOM contested this. The 'destination for the World Cup' was not 'a binding decision' and should be decided by a majority vote, they argued. The meeting at Lord's went on until midnight. Finally, upon the insistence of Clyde Walcott of the West Indies and Ali Bacher of South Africa, and after the guarantee of hosting rights of the 1999 edition—the TCCB gave in.

As PILCOM convenor Dalmiya broke the news to the anxious media waiting outside, TCCB CEO Alan Smith was left fuming. At the press conference that followed, he minced no words after this 'fractious and unpleasant meeting … beset by procedural wrangling … by a long way the worst meeting I have ever attended'.

In the 1994 *Wisden*, Bailey called it 'the most acrimonious and shambolic meeting in the history of ICC … All that cricket used to stand for was thrown out of the committee-room window'. Curiously, all that was thrown out of anywhere were the TCCB's bid and greater share of profits for the Full Members, who anyway used to make more money than the Associates.

The English cricket fraternity had a meltdown. 'Whatever else may have been true about world cricket when it was in the hands of England and Australia, greed and political point-scoring never entered anyone's heads,' wrote Martin-Jenkins, choosing to ignore history altogether.

'The ICC is likely to become a commercial mess and a bazaar of backhanders,' commented Tony Lewis from India, where England were getting thrashed on field (*Anyone but England*, Mike Marqusee). 'Cricket is increasingly the province of Third World politicians whose concern for the good of the game is subservient to their lust for power and influence,' sighed Richard Hutton in *The Cricketer.*

'The TCCB has not got over the Raj hangover,' I.S. Bindra, another PILCOM delegation member, explained to Mike Marqusee the following year. 'They seem not to like their erstwhile colonial subjects coming to London and beating them at what they still consider their own game.'

In the 1980s, Salve had sown the first seeds of cricket's shift from the Old Boys' Club towards the subcontinent. In February 1993, Dalmiya & Co. took the next step towards making it a global sport.

But that was not all that happened at the ICC that year.

We have seen how, in 1909, Abe Bailey had founded the ICC with the vision of an imperialist, largely White cricketing world in mind. Teams had to be part of the British empire to become members of the Imperial Cricket Conference. In 1965, the ICC replaced 'Imperial' with 'International' in its name, but the MCC president and secretary continued to serve as the ICC president and secretary.

On 7 July 1993, England and Australia finally lost their veto powers at the ICC (International Cricket Council since 1989). The MCC also lost their control over the ICC: since then, they are merely the custodian of the laws and no more.

Walcott comfortably beat Raman Subba Row, his only rival, to become the first non-English, non-White ICC chair. David Richards of the Australian Cricket Board became the first chief executive. In 1997, Dalmiya became the ICC's first Indian chair, and cricket spread rapidly.

In 1998, the ICC reintroduced the Under-19 World Cup (expanded to sixteen teams) and launched the Champions Trophy. In 1999, they took the World Cup under their own aegis. Within the span of a year, the number of ICC trophies went up from none to three.

After being played in Sharjah, Toronto, Dhaka and Singapore over the 1990s, cricket ventured to Kenya and Morocco in the new millennium, though the claim to become a global sport was some distance away.

Chapter 81

'I BELIEVE HAIR'S ACTION–IN ONE OVER–TOOK THE DEVELOPMENT OF WORLD CRICKET BACK BY TEN YEARS.'

Don Bradman, referring to an incident from the Melbourne Boxing Day Test of 1995.

I shall use the spelling 'Muralidaran', as preferred by the man himself, but keep the spelling unaltered inside quotes.

Sri Lanka began their 1995–96 tour of Australia with a 273-run defeat against Queensland, but the buzz centred around their young spinner, who claimed 2–79 and 5–87 in the game. Muttiah Muralidaran had not been called for his bowling action until then, though two match referees—Peter Burge in 1993, Barry Jarman in 1995—had expressed their concern over his action behind the scenes.

Back in 1992, a debutant Muralidaran had beaten Allan Border's outside edge thrice. A bewildered Border turned around to ask *what* Muralidaran bowled. Off-spin, answered Romesh Kaluwitharana honestly from behind the stumps. One ball later, Border asked non-striker Dean Jones. Leg-spin, came the response. He was a mystery from the beginning.

Muralidaran could not straighten his bowling arm, and had an unusually flexible double-jointed shoulder. Nicholas Brookes, in *An Island's Eleven*, explained it eloquently: 'Those defending him were clear in their stance: yes, the arm was slightly bent at the point of release, but only because it cannot straighten.' Subsequent tests revealed that his action 'created an optical illusion of throwing'.

The Australian Cricket Board had made plans for him. Board CEO Graham Halbish had assured umpire Darrell Hair 'the full backing of the board' if he wanted to call Muralidaran. Coach Bobby Simpson 'commissioned photographs to be taken of Muralitharan's action and sent them to the ICC'. Umpire Steve Dunne noticed how 'at least one member of the ACB' was invariably present in the umpires' dressing-room.

'At least one high-ranking Australian official felt strongly Muralitharan be exposed as a "thrower" and had a lengthy bar-side conversation with a Test umpire three weeks ago forcibly expressing this point,' reported Robert Craddock in the *Herald Sun*.

To avoid media scrutiny, coach Dav Whatmore and captain Arjuna Ranatunga left Muralidaran out of the team in the Tasmania game. He played in the first Test, at Perth, where Australia duly thrashed Sri Lanka by an innings. Muralidaran bowled 54 overs without fuss.

Meanwhile, match referee Raman Subba Row requested the Sri Lankan camp to have a closer look at Muralidaran's action. Whatmore acquired a video camera, but neither he nor Muralidaran spotted any illegal action. Whatmore 'realised that might not be immediately clear to outsiders'.

In the Boxing Day Test match, Ranatunga opted to field in front of a 55,000-strong Melbourne crowd and gave Muralidaran 2 overs before lunch, from the Members End, where Dunne stood. After lunch, Muralidaran came on from the Southern End, where Hair stood further away from the stumps than usual.

Hair no-balled the third and fourth balls of Muralidaran's fourth over. The bewildered bowler asked whether it had been the side crease. 'No, it's your action,' came the response. 'You're chucking.'

Ranatunga had a conversation with Hair but kept Muralidaran on. Hair called Muralidaran thrice in his fifth over and twice in his sixth. Ranatunga switched him to the other end. Dunne did not no-ball Muralidaran, but by the fifth session, Hair was determined to call him irrespective of where he stood.

'His sudden disgust strikes as strange, given the fact that he had stood in four Sri Lanka ODIs in the past four months,' noted Brookes. 'For many, it is hard to escape the sense that the incident was timed to cause maximum humiliation.'

While calling Hair 'brave', Peter Roebuck felt that 'his action was also public and certain to catch the headlines'. Ron Reed of the News Limited Group reminded readers how Dunne had no issues with Muralidaran's action. Ashley Mallett, former Australian off-spinner and Muralidaran's former coach, was forthright: 'Some umpire goes back five metres to call him for chucking when he should be watching his feet instead of his arm. Who does this bloke think he is?'

The ICC requested the Sri Lankan board to take 'corrective action to save Muralidaran's career' and issued a statement that 'seemed to support Hair'. ICC chair Clyde Walcott outlined two years of official concerns.

We have seen the Australian board's insensitivity towards Ian Meckiff in the 1960s. In stark contrast, the Sri Lankan team management put their entire weight behind the youngster. 'If he had any other captain, I don't think he would have survived,' teammate Ravindra Pushpakumara later told Brookes.

The next ODI passed without fuss, but debutant umpire Ross Emerson called Muralidaran seven times in another ODI, at Brisbane on 5 January. Upon being called, Muralidaran switched to leg-breaks, which are not possible to bowl with a bent arm. When Emerson still no-balled Muralidaran, it became evident that these calls were not entirely based on cricketing reasons.

Emerson was booed by the crowd for the rest of the match. His colleague Tony McQuillan, who also no-balled Muralidaran, shook his hands with Emerson before leaving the field, but it did not improve the public mood. Emerson needed the police to escort him that day.

'He's just unorthodox. When I look at the slow-motion picture, I don't really think he chucks,' felt Richie Richardson, captain of the West Indies, against whom Muralidaran played these two ODIs.

Muralidaran did not play again on that tour but visited Daryl Foster in the University of Western Australia and got his action cleared by bowling in front of high-speed cameras. That, along with the farcical Emerson calls, helped clear his image temporarily.

Before that year's World Cup, he underwent biomechanical analysis in Hong Kong. He was reported again, by Emerson in 1999 and match referee Chris Broad in 2004, but he overcame both setbacks to finish with the most wickets in both Tests and ODIs. Over his career, the myriad tests convinced some of his early critics like Michael Holding and Jones of the legitimacy of his bowling action.

The impact of Ranatunga and the Sri Lankan board's decision to stand behind Muralidaran surpassed the latter's record-breaking career. For years, the umpires had been the sole authorities entrusted with the power of deciding legitimate actions. They could call bowlers whenever they felt, and their calls were seldom up for scrutiny. The subjective, human methods accommodated errors, and worse, bias.

Today, they can at most report an action to the authorities without humiliating the bowler in front of the public. The bowlers then need to appear for sophisticated tests—beyond the scope of the naked eye—before the official verdict. It will not be an exaggeration to call this progress a butterfly effect of Hair and Emerson's targeting of Muralidaran.

Chapter 82

'THE SERVER AT OREGON MELTED. LITERALLY MELTED. THE NETWORK GOT BURNT. WE HAD SO MUCH TRAFFIC, IT WAS SO HUGELY POPULAR ...'

Vishal Misra, recalling an incident from 14 February 1996.

In the early 1990s, it was impossible to follow live cricket if one's location did not have radio or television coverage of the match. Newspapers from overseas bearing cricket stories arrived days, even weeks later. In the US—a country with little interest in cricket but replete with expatriates from several cricket-loving nations—the only way to get *some* live cricket was on satellite television. Only 'a few select commercial establishments or universities' could afford that.

However, there was the internet. 'Cricket discussions, analysis, fights' happened primarily on Usenet in rec.sport.cricket (RSC). The admins could moderate, determine the topics (usually the latest available score of live games) and more. Everything was entirely voluntary.

In an era when browsing looked nothing like it does today, cricket fans around the world found a way to communicate. Among them was Kevin Roberts Elz, a senior systems programmer at the University of Melbourne; an ardent cricket fan who had been at the MCG for 'every minute of Test cricket' played for years and years. He also had access to the 'best internet connection in Australia'.

Elz watched the Boxing Day Test match of 1991–92 between Australia and India, returned home and filed a match report for RSC. Not only did he do this regularly, but he sent reports 'every hour rather than one long summary at stumps', he told Siddharth Vaidyanathan in an interview for ESPNcricinfo. As this became a habit, he was 'included in the "Usenet cabal"'.

Detached from live cricket for years, K. Sankara Rao, a professor at the North Dakota State University in Fargo, invested in a shortwave radio set. He had access to a 'large computer', from which he emailed cricket updates to his friends. This soon expanded to a mailing group, then a second—one of them exclusively for scores. Rao had to find moderators to help him out. Elz was one of them.

Elz's updates became more frequent over time. He covered the Australia–West Indies ODI on 12 January 1992, ball by ball. No one knew it back then, but he created history with the first ball-by-ball text commentary, though it would take a few years for it to become an organized, professional behemoth.

Over time, the community shifted from RSC to Internet Relay Chat (IRC) using the channel #cricket. University students around the world stepped in. There was no live cricket coverage in the US, but the volunteers resolved this. At Oxford, they left a radio set in front of a workstation, which captured BBC Test Match Special commentary and relayed it over a software utility called Vat to the American universities, where volunteers keyed in ball-by-ball commentary.

One of them was Simon King, a postdoctoral student at the University of Minnesota. On 15 March 1993, he incorporated a bot on the IRC channel #cricket to keep up with the rising demand of live scores for cricket-deprived fans. This bot went by the name Cricinfo. Over time, King modified the bot so that users could not only update scores but also archive existing scorecards.

Over time, eminent cricket statisticians reached out to the community: would they be interested in keying in scorecards of every international match ever played for posterity? Of course, volunteers were ready, but they needed a database. In 1995, Travis Basevi and Vishal Misra—'Travishal' to many—wrote the scripts to load the entire archive on the database.

Cricinfo struck an argument with PILCOM, the organizing committee of the 1996 World Cup. For the tournament, PILCOM would send live scorecards via FTP, which the volunteers would key in. Since Travishal had set a process in place, this seemed doable. After a press release, anyone with access to the internet but without access to live offline cricket waited in eager anticipation. The unexpected traffic caused the network card of the Oregon server to *literally* burn.

It turned out to be anticlimactic. PILCOM never sent the pre–World Cup sample scorecards Cricinfo requested for. The FTP credentials arrived 17 overs into the first match of the World

Cup. The first card took another 5 overs to show up. When it did, it was littered with formatting errors and inconsistencies ('caught' and 'ct' were both present, for example). To sum up, it was unusable.

Volunteers from the #cricket channel chipped in yet again. Availability around the many time zones helped, but it was never going to be sustainable. So, Misra turned to dougie, a 'sophisticated' cricket scoring program written in C by a South African graduate student called Jacques de Villiers—a curious portmanteau of two legendary compatriots of the future. Dougie was simple to use, for one command could update individual and team scores as well as bowling analysis.

But despite being 'great for nerds', dougie was not easy to use for all, especially in the early days. The available version was also an outdated one. Misra eventually fixed the problems and got it to work. Despite the odd hiccup (for example, it could not handle 'run out on a no-ball while taking the third run when the first one has been declared short by the umpire'), it generally worked fine.

That was not all. Since dougie updated ball by ball, every ball had to be keyed in with no room for lapses—never an easy job—to maintain continuity. The volunteers, thus, had to work for the entire duration of the match with utmost concentration.

On 1 March, Cricinfo provided ball-by-ball updates for the Australia–Zimbabwe World Cup clash—the first of its kind on a website. Misra himself scored in the final 'from a small college town in the US in the dead of the night with two feet of snow piled up outside'.

By India's tour of England later that year, the updates moved beyond the rudimentary bowler–batter–outcome stage. 'Javagal Srinath to Nasser Hussain, no run' became 'Javagal Srinath to Nasser Hussain, no run, rising ball on the rib cage defended to short square leg'.

Ball-by-ball commentary enabled anyone with an internet connection to follow live matches even in the most cricket-agnostic corners. Today, it is the greatest ally of cricket fans away from live television or streaming coverage. Unlike video services, it is also almost always free.

Basevi used the scripts for the scorecards to build StatsGuru at Cricinfo and later, the Wisden Wizard. Users could ask numerical queries on cricket and get their answers. This changed cricket writing and viewing forever, for the tools equipped fans with facts to question everything they came across.

No longer were words in print sacrosanct. Cricket journalists and writers were compelled to put facts before fiction.

Chapter 83

'THIS IS A LITTLE FAIRYTALE ... THEY'VE COME SUCH A LONG WAY IN SUCH A SHORT PERIOD OF TIME.'

Tony Greig on air, after the World Cup final, 17 March 1996.

School cricket traditionally played a major role in Sri Lanka. For decades, these games were two-day, two-innings affairs. This resulted in youngsters growing up with two attributes that were not common elsewhere. They knew that to win, they needed to score quickly enough to allow their bowlers enough time to take 20 wickets. And they were good at chasing targets at a rapid pace.

Cricket teams often played one-day games when they halted in the island, especially when England or Australia toured the other nation. There were visits from teams touring India or Pakistan as well. The batting exuberance of the locals often left them in awe. Garry Sobers and Frank Worrell were left in awe of Mahadevan Sathasivam. C.I. Gunasekara hit Lindsay Kline for 24 in an over. Michael Tissera was particularly harsh on Wes Hall as he blasted 'over 20 boundaries' in a belligerent hundred. In 1968–69 and 1972–73, the hosts had two successful chases against the MCC. The long list kept increasing once they earned Test status.

Sri Lanka were excellent chasers even before the 1996 World Cup began. They had won only four games across the five editions, but one statistic stood out: of the five instances of a team reaching 275 while chasing in World Cup cricket until then, four—including the top three—were by Sri Lanka.

In fact, until the 1996 World Cup, Sri Lanka won in 50 per cent of their chases (32 out of 64), but while batting first, that dropped to 27.4 per cent (17 in 62). Their run rate of 4.29 in chases was the fourth-best in the world. This may not sound too high on the list, but one must remember that they were perceived as one of the weakest sides in the world. Their bowling average (36.19) and economy (4.79) were the worst among all sides with 50 ODIs. Chasing was their strong suit.

For the 1996 World Cup, Captain Arjuna Ranatunga and coach Dav Whatmore now set out to get the most out of this unit.

To take advantage of the 15-over field restriction, teams had been using prolific hitters at the top for some time. Sri Lanka had already tried out all-rounder Sanath Jayasuriya, but now they went a step ahead by pairing him with wicketkeeper Romesh Kaluwitharana in the subcontinent, where the new ball seldom moved around. This enabled them to take on the bowlers without using their specialists.

No. 3 Asanka Gurusinha could both drop anchor and hit out. Aravinda de Silva, their best batter, was next. Ranatunga and Hashan Tillakaratne, experts in the middle overs and at the death, were five and six. At seven was Roshan Mahanama, a bona fide Test opener, ready for an emergency. The all-rounders, Kumar Dharmasena and Chaminda Vaas, gave them a near-bottomless batting lineup.

What about bowling? Some selectors did not want Muttiah Muralidaran after the recent controversy over his action in Australia. If the umpires called him at the World Cup, the fourteen-member squad would effectively be reduced to thirteen. But Ranatunga stayed firm, for Muralidaran and Vaas were his only truly world-class bowlers.

The support cast consisted of Dharmasena, Jayasuriya and de Silva—spinners who could bowl slow and straight on pitches conducive to their brand of bowling. All ten players played every match at the 1996 World Cup as Sri Lanka kept switching between Pramodya Wickramasinghe and Ravindra Pushpakumara, Vaas's new-ball partners.

It fell into place. Ranatunga averaged 120.50 and de Silva 89.60. Jayasuriya (132), Ranatunga (115) and de Silva (108) had the best strike rates at the World Cup. Gurusinha hit the most sixes (11). Tillakaratne got out only twice and Mahanama not even once. Kaluwitharana made only 73 runs but faced a mere 52 balls.

No bowler got more than 7 wickets, but they did not need to. Muralidaran (3.77), Vaas (3.93), Dharmasena (4.44) and Jayasuriya (4.52) choked one batting unit after another. Jayasuriya and de Silva also shared 11 wickets to add to their batting feats.

But Sri Lanka's campaign might have gone all wrong before the World Cup began. On 31 January, the Central Bank bombing in Colombo had killed 91 and injured 1400. Australia and the West Indies soon announced that they would not tour Sri Lanka for their league games.

'I'd like people to look at things from both sides. Put yourselves in our shoes and look at the way we live in Australia compared to the way other people live in the subcontinent,' Australian captain Mark Taylor would later try to explain. Mike Marqusee pointed out how Taylor assumed that 'mutilation and sudden death were intrinsic to south Asian culture and alien to Western culture'.

Both teams wanted full points from the games, but Sri Lankan board president Ana Punchihewa did not budge. One point each, suggested ICC chair Clyde Walcott. 'This is not a tie or anything,' pointed out Punchihewa. The matter was put to vote. Walcott's suggestion won, but Punchihewa insisted on re-polling.

This time Sri Lanka won by one vote. The local fans missed two home matches, but their team got four points. That left Zimbabwe and Kenya as the sides set to play in Sri Lanka. Sensing Kenya's apprehension, Punchihewa reached out to the co-hosts: India and Pakistan sent a combined team to demonstrate how safe it was to play in Sri Lanka. At his post–World Cup speech, Ranatunga thanked both captains.

Sri Lanka brushed aside Zimbabwe and Kenya and demolished co-hosts India in Delhi to finish the group stage unbeaten. In the quarter-final at Faisalabad, Jayasuriya pulverized the bowlers en route to a 44-ball 82 to make England's 235–8 look puny. Sri Lanka won over the Pakistani fans that day.

There was indecision in the camp ahead of the semi-final against India in front of an overpacked Eden Gardens. Whatmore wanted Sri Lanka to bat first on a 'soft, crusty deck' that was likely to crumble later, but Ranatunga was keen on the comfort zone of chasing. Fortunately, India won the toss and fielded—and caved in.

For the final, Sri Lanka found near-unanimous support at Lahore. No chasing team had won a World Cup until then, but Ranatunga backed his side's strengths. After a decent start, Australia found the Sri Lankan spinners difficult to put away.

Ranatunga did not recall his seamers at the death but used Jayasuriya and de Silva to keep the choke on. From 134–1 in 25 overs, Australia finished on 241–7.

Sri Lanka became 23–2 before de Silva followed his 3–42 and two catches with an unbeaten 107. The finishing touches came from Ranatunga. The day before the final, he had labelled Shane Warne an 'average spinner'. With the bat, he hit a ball back so hard that it burst through Warne's fingers and went to the straight boundary; and hoicked the next ball, a full toss, for six.

He then steered Glenn McGrath to bring up the winning runs. A cricket board with only $5700 at its disposal from a nation rocked by a civil war emerged as the world champions. And they did it their way.

Chapter 84

'WORDS CANNOT BEGIN TO DESCRIBE THE SHAME, HUMILIATION AND PAIN WHICH I FEEL IN THE KNOWLEDGE THAT I HAVE INFLICTED THIS ON OTHERS.'

Hansie Cronje as witness during the King Commission of Inquiry, 15 June 2000.

Already 2–0 up in the 1999–2000 Test series against England, South Africa could not lose when they went into the final Test, at Centurion. There, they made 155–6 amidst nearly four days of incessant rain. Ali Bacher, managing director of the South African cricket board, was 'anxious to save the game as a spectacle'. During a break, he met the two captains, Nasser Hussain and Hansie Cronje, the umpires and the match referee.

Converting the last day's cricket to an ODI was not feasible, for the Tests and the ODIs had separate sponsors. The only way to reach a result was a string of bold declarations. England were initially reluctant, but forty-five minutes into the final day, Hussain sent a message to Cronje that they were in.

Cronje declared on 248–8. England, without playing a ball (the Law enabling first-innings forfeitures came into place only later that year). South Africa forfeited their second innings. Set 249 in 76 overs, England won by 2 wickets with 5 balls to spare. 'It was a very special thing that Hansie did, and I hope he gets the credit he deserves,' exclaimed Hussain. His opinions would change in a few months' time.

Cronje's men then won the Test series in India 2–0. Till date, they remain the only team to clean-sweep India in India in a series of at least two Tests. South Africa lost the ODIs to India 2–3 and the final of the Coca-Cola Cup in Sharjah, but there was little to worry.

On 7 April 2000, a week after the Coca-Cola Cup got over, the Delhi Police Crime Branch revealed they had a recording of a conversation between Cronje and Sanjay Chawla, an Indian bookmaker. Cronje was implicated, along with teammates Herschelle Gibbs, Nicky Boje and Pieter Strydom.

Cronje rubbished these allegations the next day: 'I want to ensure every South African that I have made a hundred percent effort to win every match that I have played.' Bacher insisted on Cronje's 'unquestionable integrity and honesty'.

Yet, Bacher's phone rang at three in the morning on 11 April. Cronje had called to confess that he had not been 'entirely honest' about the affair. The board sacked him as captain with immediate effect. In May, national President Thabo Mbeki appointed a commission of inquiry, chaired by justice Edwin King, into the matter. The King Commission inquiries began on 7 June.

The details of every testimony are beyond the scope of this book. Perhaps the most significant was Gibbs's, on 8 June. Gibbs admitted that he and fast bowler Henry Williams had both accepted Cronje's offer of $15,000 for the fifth ODI, at Nagpur. Gibbs had to score 20 or fewer runs, while Williams had to concede at least 50 from his 10 overs.

As things turned out, Gibbs got carried away and reached 'thirty or forty' before realizing what he had done. When Cronje asked him to forget about the offer and 'enjoy', Gibbs made 74 in 53 balls. Williams, on the other hand, broke down after 11 balls and took no further part. Unsurprisingly, neither got their share. Williams corroborated Gibbs's testimony on 9 June.

Cronje appeared on 15 June. He declared that his initial letter to the board and the press statement had been 'untruthful in a number of respects'; admitted to approaching Gibbs and Williams with offers; requested the board to reinstate both to the squad; and laid down the timeline of his match-fixing involvements.

It had started with the best-of-three finals of the Mandela Trophy against Pakistan in January 1995. 'An Indian or Pakistani man who described himself only as John' approached him with $10,000 to throw the first final. Cronje did not accept the money and South Africa won the finals 2–0.

On South Africa's 1996–97 tour of India, Mohammad Azharuddin introduced Cronje to one Mukesh 'M.K.' Gupta, who offered him $30,000 if South Africa 'gave wickets away' on the final day of the Kanpur Test. Cronje did not speak to his teammates, but South Africa lost anyway.

Gupta then offered Cronje $2,00,000 to throw the final ODI. Cronje spoke to his team and received opposition from Daryll

Cullinan, Andrew Hudson and Crookes. 'The decision had to be unanimous or not at all,' was the consensus. Cronje told Gupta that the deal was off, but passed on some team information on injuries, albeit without payment.

When India next toured South Africa, Gupta requested for information for the first and second Tests. Cronje sent 'team selections and a daily forecast'. After the second Test, Gupta transferred $50,000 to Cronje's account, but Cronje turned down Gupta's $3,00,000 offer for throwing the third Test.

Three years later, one Marlin Aronstam called Cronje on the fourth evening of the fateful Centurion Test, urging him to request Hussain about an early declaration. He agreed to pay 5,00,000 rands (about £50,000) to a charity of Cronje's choice.

Since England were initially reluctant, Cronje messaged Aronstam that the declaration was off. When Hussain eventually agreed, Cronje asked Strydom to place a bet *on South Africa*—and texted Aronstam again. He had been too late, said Aronstam, but still gave 50,000 rands and a leather jacket. However, Cronje maintained that 'the match delivered a genuine result and was in no way manipulated'.

By the time he reached India, however, he had been 'increasingly pushed to manipulate results' and 'had got into something from which it was very difficult to get out'. Across the tour, he fraternized with Sanjay and Hamid 'Banjo' Cassim, two bookmakers he had met in South Africa.

Sanjay had been paying Cronje in exchange for information even before South Africa had arrived in India. They were now keen on South Africa throwing the odd match. Cronje approached Jacques Kallis, Mark Boucher and Lance Klusener during the Tests: the 'rebuffs were immediate, but I think they thought I was joking'.

Ahead of the first ODI, in Cochin, Cronje *lied to* Sanjay and Cassim about others coming on board. He assured that South

Africa would lose, which they did—though Cronje claimed to have 'honestly tried to win the match'. After 'intense, incessant nagging' from Sanjay and Cassim, Cronje agreed to throw the fifth ODI and roped in Gibbs and Williams, but that did not work out.

The hearings shook the world of cricket. *Cricket Talk* ran a full edition on the matter. The text on the cover—*You Too, Hansie?*—summed up the anguish of the fans, who rightfully felt betrayed by a much-loved captain of a truly fantastic team.

The South African board ruled Strydom innocent, but found Cronje, Gibbs and Williams guilty. On 28 August, they fined Gibbs 60,000 rands and Williams 10,000 rands and banned both from international cricket for six months.

On 11 October, they banned Cronje for life from playing or coaching cricket. He appealed the following year, but in vain. He died in a plane crash in 2002.

Chapter 85

'BY AGREEING TO A LIMITED BUT HIGH-PROFILE TRIAL, WE WILL BE BETTER PLACED TO JUDGE IF GREATER USE OF TECHNOLOGY IS THE WAY TO GO IN THE LONG TERM.'

Malcolm Speed, 18 March 2002.

As we have seen, the television umpire was first used in international cricket when India toured South Africa in 1991–92. It remained restricted to run-out and stumped, the 'line decisions'.

There was a departure from this in the final of the 1993 Hero Cup. As one of Anil Kumble's famous quicker balls whizzed past Roland Holder, the bails were left disturbed. Umpires Ian Robinson and Karl Liebenberg, unsure whether the ball had hit the stumps directly or was deflected off wicketkeeper Vijay Yadav, referred to television umpire Sekhar Choudhary. Bowled, was the verdict.

Despite being a significant moment, the Holder decision did not change one fundamental aspect. Choudhary gave the verdict based on what *had happened*, not what *would have happened.*

Later that decade, Paul Hawkins, a PhD in artificial intelligence, developed a technology where a cohort of cameras mounted 'around the ground's perimeter' tracked the ball's trajectory. Over time, this became a tool for the analysts, who can now assess the line, length, pace and movement of every bowler as well as the bounce every pitch produced.

But perhaps more significantly, the technology could *predict* what the ball would have gone on to do based on what the ball did before hitting the pad (or anywhere). This meant that it could validate the leg-before decisions—for it could not only tell where the ball had pitched but also predicted whether it would have gone on to hit the stumps.

The Hawk-Eye, it was named, after Hawkins. When Pakistan toured England in the summer of 2001, Channel 4 used it at the Lord's Test match—albeit not for actual decision-making.

Two years before that, Channel 4 had tried Alan Plaskett's Snickometer for England's Edgbaston Test match against New Zealand. 'Snicko' used the stump microphone to send a signal 'via a computer to an oscilloscope', enabling the viewer to see the soundwaves on the screen. A pronounced spike at the time of the ball passing the bat indicated an edge.

Over the years, this would be replaced by the more sophisticated Real-Time Snicko or Ultra-Edge.

Once technology became available, the ICC were surprisingly quick to experiment. At the 2002 Champions Trophy, they equipped the television umpire with the right to rule every possible decision, though this 'DRS before DRS' was solely an on-field umpire's decision ('Umpires will be able to consult with the third umpire *on any aspect* of a decision they are unsure of').

When Chaminda Vaas appealed for LBW in the tournament opener, Daryl Harper referred to television umpire Rudi Koertzen. Shoaib Malik 'made history by becoming the third umpire's first lbw victim'. Across the tournament, the umpires referred twenty times for LBW (8 out, 12 not out) and nine times for caught (all out).

Despite its success, the ICC shelved the experiment. Some broadcasters continued to use Hawk-Eye, but to enhance viewing experience: it did not influence decisions. Meanwhile, cricket's characteristic resistance to change was often echoed by those behind the microphone. In the Headingley Test of 2002, Asoka de Silva ruled Rob Key leg-before to Anil Kumble, but Hawk-Eye showed that the ball would have gone over the stumps. The glee in Navjot Sidhu's voice was unmissable when he quipped 'Hawk-Eye, two hoots!' much to the merriment of fellow commentators.

It was not until 2008 that the ICC finally reintroduced the Decision Review System—yet again in Sri Lanka—for their home Test series against India. Teams—while batting or bowling—could now challenge the umpire's decision.

This was significant, for it brought one of cricket's longest-running adages to an end. The umpire's decision, at least the on-field umpire's, was no longer final: there was a higher authority.

There was resistance from some quarters, most significantly from India until the mid-2010s. Not anymore.

Chapter 86

'WHEN WE ASKED ABOUT A SHORTER FORMAT, PLAYED ON MIDWEEK EVENINGS, WE HAD A MUCH BETTER RESPONSE FROM WOMEN, YOUNG PEOPLE AND FAMILIES.'

Stuart Robertson, 2002.

A ban on tobacco advertising brought the 50-over Benson & Hedges Cup to a premature end in 2002. It coincided with a 17 per cent decline of attendance across the five years, to 2001.

The time was ripe for a new competition—but it could not be the same format.

The ECB equipped marketing manager Stuart Robertson with £2,50,000 to investigate the reason behind the dwindling footfall. Robertson's survey, conducted across 4500 people across thirty focus groups, revealed that 'most cricket fans are middle-aged, middle-class white men'. Some of them even felt that 'they had to go to county games in a suit and tie'.

Cricket was perceived as 'posh' and 'socially inaccessible', and that was not the only complaint. The matches were often too long to fit into the schedule of busy fans—and there was no guarantee of a result despite that. The duration of the game and the futility of the draw might, while acceptable to the cricket fan, simply did not attract the neutral viewer enough to be converted.

The sport catered to 'members up and down the country who were dictating the programme and therefore, not really encouraging new people into the sport', felt Hampshire chair Rod Bransgrove. It needed a shorter format that fans could watch in the evenings, even on weekdays, with 'lots of excitement to go with it, colour and sideshows'.

In other words, a 20-over-a-side cricket competition—a format shorter than even the ODI. There were performances from Mis-Teeq and D-side, while Atomic Kitten performed on the Finals Day. The televised matches offered barbecue tents and karaoke stands. Sky Sports fitted microphones to selected cricketers playing in the match. The ECB packaged cricket as entertainment.

There was criticism and scepticism. 'Aimed at the sort of young philistine who prefers Britney Spears to a Beethoven symphony,' wrote Simon Briggs of this 'just-add-water recipe of instant cricket'. But Twenty20 appealed to the fans, drawing crowds by the thousands.

On 21 April 2002, the eighteen first-class counties and the MCC met to decide on whether the new limited-overs competition in England would be played in this format. The MCC abstained from voting. The counties voted 11–7 in favour of Twenty20 cricket.

Twenty20 inherited the players and the laws from Test cricket and ODIs, but that was about it. It changed some fundamental aspects of cricket.

The batting side still had 10 wickets for the 120 balls, which took defensive batting out of the equation altogether. The bowler, for centuries the attacker in every duel, had to adapt to a defensive role, for every run spent in going flat out for wickets was vital. The batter, conditioned to rebuild after collapses, could not afford to go for a long phase without attacking anymore.

Two-innings cricket often used to be about batting long. In ODIs, teams used to go after the bowling in the early overs with the field up, rotate the strike and minimize dot-ball count until the end, before cutting loose. This was different. The 'middle overs' were still there, but they lasted only 10 overs.

As was expected, specialists for the format emerged. Cricket training changed. Power hitters became the most valuable players (MVPs) of the format. Those who could hit without getting their eyes in were often used in the death overs. Bowlers learnt to master specific phases of the game and were forced to find rhythm early, for they knew they could be taken off after one over.

But that was not all Twenty20 did. Cricket had, over the years, eased into a comfortable geopolitical hierarchy, where quality performances in club cricket would be rewarded with a place in the state side, followed by national trials and the Holy Grail—a national cap. For larger talent pools, there used to be intermediate steps, but the structure used to be the same.

As Twenty20 soared in popularity and fetched significantly more cash than cricket had ever seen, these steps stopped being relevant to the players. A performance in a local league—even in another country—might get them lucrative deals in Twenty20 leagues. And since franchise cricket often paid them more than the boards, the national cap—despite the honour one associates with it—stopped being the ultimate goal for many.

Cricket's geopolitical hierarchy was irreversibly shaken to the core.

Section 11

Brave New World

Chapter 87

'H AND I HAVE WRITTEN A STATEMENT. I WANT YOU TO READ IT.'

Andy Flower to Zimbabwean teammates, 10 February 2003.

The brutal torture of MP Job Sikhala had shocked Zimbabwe at a time when they were preparing to co-host the 2003 World Cup with South Africa and Kenya. Based on a players' vote, England had opted out of their World Cup match against Zimbabwe at Harare to voice their protest against the Robert Mugabe regime.

About a month before the tournament, Andy Flower asked Henry Olonga to meet at the News Café in Harare. With full knowledge of the risk involved, they laid out a blueprint for their plan of action against the 'death of democracy'.

While Flower had established himself as the greatest cricketer from the nation, Olonga was a cultural icon, a role model. The first Black cricketer to play for Zimbabwe, he had released a hit song, 'Our Zimbabwe'.

'Andy Flower needed a black person, and a black person with some influence. I certainly had that,' admitted Olonga. 'Andy is world class, I'm not, but we'd got a combination of sport and music—Posh and Becks, if you like.'

The original plan for both men was to pull out of the World Cup, but that changed over some time. Olonga later said that he was influenced by Maximus, portrayed by Russell Crowe in *Gladiator*: 'I want to be the slave who defies an emperor.'

However, their teammates—except Andy's brother Grant—were unaware of their plan. Zimbabwe's first match at the World Cup was against Namibia, at the Harare Sports Club. Just before the game, they revealed their plan to the media: 'We have decided that we will each wear a black armband for the duration of the World Cup.

'In doing so we are mourning the death of democracy in our beloved Zimbabwe … We are making a silent plea to those responsible to stop the abuse of human rights in Zimbabwe … We pray that our small action may help to restore sanity and dignity to our nation.'

Olonga later admitted that he had been more nervous than he had been while playing Test cricket against Australia or facing Shoaib Akhtar: 'It was an exhilarating feeling, tinged with uncertainty about what the aftermath would be.'

Before they stepped on to the ground, Flower handed their statement to the rest of the squad. Neither coach Geoff Marsh nor manager Babu Meman was impressed. Zimbabwean Cricket

Union CEO Vince Hogg requested them to withdraw their statement. But they stayed firm.

The Zimbabwe openers added 107 in 21.4 overs after Heath Streak opted to bat. Then Lennie Louw caught Mark Vermeulen off his own bowling, and Flower walked out to join Craig Wishart. He wore a black armband. By the time he fell for a 29-ball 39, the world had seen him. Zimbabwe finished on 340–2. Wishart batted through the innings with an unbeaten 172. But all that paled into insignificance.

During the innings, Olonga was spotted with a black armband in the players' enclosure. In a hurry, neither man had acquired cloth armbands and had to improvise by strapping black insulating tapes to their arms, but it did not matter.

When he noticed Reuters photographer Howard Burditt zooming in, Olonga gave a thumbs-up and ensured the tape was prominent. The news had spread by then. Over the course of the match, 4000 fans were donning makeshift black armbands.

Namibia were 104–5 after 25.4 overs when rain washed out the rest of the match. Zimbabwe won by 86 runs via the Duckworth-Lewis System.

Before their next match, Flower and Olonga were asked not to wear black armbands. Flower was too good a cricketer to be dropped, but the management left out Olonga, ostensibly for ordinary form. He performed twelfth-man duties in black wristbands. Back home, the Takashinga Cricket Club expelled him.

The Mugabe government charged Olonga with treason and issued an arrest warrant. Had he been arrested he would perhaps have been killed, but rain came to his rescue. Zimbabwe's last league match, against Pakistan at Bulawayo, was washed out. That helped them qualify for the Super Sixes, which was scheduled entirely in South Africa. Olonga boarded the flight to Johannesburg with his teammates.

By then, his calls were being tapped. A well-wisher emailed him that the ministry was preparing to come for him after the World Cup. Ahead of the Pakistan match, his father had called him to alert him of a message he had received from the ministry: 'Tell your son to get out of Zimbabwe, now.'

Zimbabwe's last match was against Sri Lanka at East London, but things turned murky before that. Olonga received numerous hate emails ... including one from his girlfriend, who called off their relationship. Olonga's 'main reason to risk returning home' was gone.

Olonga requested to be left out of the XI for the Sri Lanka match. The team management obliged. The local security alerted him that there were six Zimbabwean police officials in the VIP box that day. Realizing that they were there to escort him back, Olonga issued a press release, announcing retirement from international cricket ('If I were to continue to play for Zimbabwe in the midst of the prevailing crisis, I would only be neglecting the voice of my conscience').

A fuming Ozias Bvute, a representative of the Zimbabwe Cricket Union, gave Olonga his air ticket, but made it clear that the board was severing all ties with him—including letting him use the team coach to the airport or pay for his hotel. Thankfully, a couple of his teammates convinced the board to foot the hotel bills.

The South African security personnel—one of whom used to be Nelson Mandela's bodyguard—gave Olonga a lift to the airport. Douglas Hondo carried his cricket kit back to Harare. Olonga stayed back in Johannesburg with only one change of clothes. He migrated to England later that year, and to Australia in 2015. Flower moved to England as well, where he became their national coach.

Over the next two years, Zimbabwean cricket plunged into a crisis that resulted in them being temporarily stripped of Test status. They have recovered some of their lost stature, but not entirely.

Chapter 88

'IN THE AIR ... SREESANTH TAKES IT!'

Ravi Shastri, on air, 24 September 2007.

Once the inaugural Twenty20 Cup became a success in England in 2003, the format did not take long to spread across the world. In 2004, South Africa hosted the Standard Bank Pro20 Series, while Sri Lanka had their Twenty20 Tournament. On their 2004–05 tour of Australia, Pakistan played a 20-over match against Australia A.

On 17 February 2005, New Zealand hosted Australia in the first-ever T20 International. The atmosphere was more carnival than hard-nosed. Both teams turned up in 'garish body-hugging kits last seen in the 1980s', and the New Zealand team 'sported all manner of outmoded facial hair, creating a cabaret feel'.

When Glenn McGrath tried to mock-bowl the last ball underarm à la Trevor Chappell, he was red-carded by Billy Bowden. Ricky Ponting, winning captain and Player of the Match, felt that it was 'difficult to play seriously'.

Yet, the ICC took this seriously. The short duration meant that the sport could finally be sold to countries where it had little presence. ICC CEO Malcolm Speed felt that if the ICC did not host a World Cup in the format, 'entrepreneurs, broadcasters, sponsors and multinational businesses' might beat them to it.

So, Speed and ICC president Ehsan Mani pitched their 'first-mover advantage' at an ICC meeting in March 2006. There was resistance from some quarters. Some felt—you can see they were right—that the format might corner Tests and ODIs. PCB chair Shahryar Khan 'disliked' the format altogether. BCCI honorary secretary Niranjan Shah was even more dismissive: 'T20? Why not Ten10 or Five5 or One1? India will never play T20.'

The tournament would be a financial disaster without India, who boasted of the largest fanbase in the sport. Speed and Mani knew that. At the same time, the ICC had with them a proposal submitted by India, Pakistan, Sri Lanka and Bangladesh for the 2011 World Cup, where the boards had not met with every necessary requirement—perhaps because there had been no rival bid.

Mani rejected this bid and, at the same time, convinced David Morgan of the ECB to submit a rival bid. Taken by surprise, the Asian bloc sought a solution. Participate in every ICC event, especially the inaugural T20 World Cup, said Mani. They agreed. Morgan was happy with the 2019 World Cup.

The World Cup was on, with twelve teams. The ten Full Members qualified directly. Kenya and Canada came after securing the top two spots in the 2007 ICC World Cricket League Division One—a *50-over* competition—an indication of how the world was coming to terms with T20.

In fact, the ICC were hesitant to call the tournament a World Cup to begin with. It started as the World Twenty20 and became the T20 World Cup only in 2016. The 'World TT', Ravi Shastri would call it on air.

By the time the tournament began, India were still rigid in their stance. They had been the last of the Full Members to play a T20 International. The inaugural Inter-State Twenty20 Tournament (now the Syed Mushtaq Ali Trophy), played in April 2007, was not televised. Sachin Tendulkar, Sourav Ganguly and Rahul Dravid opted out of the 'TT' World Cup.

But the tournament was brilliantly organized. It looked even better when pitted against the disastrous World Cup in the West Indies earlier that year—an affair marred by overpriced tickets, restrictions on the spectators, India and Pakistan's early exits, and to crown off things, a fiasco that resulted in the final moments being played under moonlight.

With a tighter schedule including double-headers, tickets being sold at about a tenth of the prices at the World Cup in the West Indies, and no restriction on the food or drinks they could bring, fans streamed in. But more importantly, the cricket was exhilarating.

Chris Gayle lit up the tournament with a hundred in the first match. South Africa chased down the target. Yuvraj Singh hit Stuart Broad for six sixes in an over. Bangladesh eliminated the seeded West Indies. Zimbabwe stunned Australia—who had just completed a hat-trick of 50-over World Cup wins—to demonstrate the fickleness of cricket's shortest format.

And then, there were two India–Pakistan classics. The league match was decided by a football-style tiebreaker where bowlers from either side had a go at empty wickets. And the final could have gone the other way had Misbah-ul-Haq got his scoop right.

The spectacular success of the competition was one of the two major reasons behind T20's popularity—around the world but especially in India—over the years that followed. The other, the official launch of a domestic league in India, took place during the tournament.

Chapter 89

'THERE CAN'T BE TOO MANY GAY ACCOUNTANTS WHO DISMISSED YOU TWICE IN A FIRST-CLASS MATCH.'

Alan Hansford, email to Michael Atherton, 2008.

The story should begin with George Cecil Ives, a poet, writer and LGBTQ rights activist long before the acronym had been coined. A friend of Oscar Wilde, Ives was one of the early voices in support of homosexuality. His life and works are beyond the scope of this book, but it is important to know that he did play cricket without being great at it.

Ives did turn out for the MCC a few times. One of these was against W.G. Grace's London County, which also boasted of Billy Murdoch, at Crystal Palace in 1902. Playing alongside the likes of Albert Trott and Arthur Conan Doyle, Ives batted at No. 11 in each innings, made 7 and 2, and neither bowled nor held a catch.

But since the match got first-class status, history remembers him as the first self-proclaimed homosexual cricketer at that level.

Cricket has shared an uncomfortable relationship with homosexuality. When the West Indies donned a coral-pink kit at Kerry Packer's World Series, Tony Cozier noted that the colour carried 'strong homosexual overtones in the Caribbean'. Sure enough, they switched to maroon soon afterwards.

The mindset barely changed by 2007. Middlesex's pink T20 shirts were not scoffed at—they were promoting breast cancer awareness—but when the MCC announced that they would experiment with pink balls, there was 'horror and derision' in some sections. 'Gaylord's', the *Sun* called them. Fewer eyebrows were raised when the Rajasthan Royals switched to pink a little over a decade later.

The traditionally hypermasculine world of cricket had little space for homosexuality. 'For young gay boys, sport can be a very scary area because it speaks to masculinity in a domain where being masculine and strong and brave is feted. It speaks to their fears, and they can feel unwelcome,' explained ECB media manager Henry Cowen, gay himself, to the *Wisden Cricket Monthly*.

The Grace's Cricket Club was founded in 1996 to 'promote enjoyment of the game of cricket amongst the LGBT community'. That was seven years after Sussex medium-pacer Alan Hansford had claimed 4–46 and 4–25 on first-class debut, against Cambridge University in 1989. His wickets included a young Michael Atherton in each innings.

Hansford retired in 1992. He wrote to Atherton in 2008. Unlike Ives, Hansford made his sexuality public well *after* his playing days were over. It was still a conservative world, but not as much as it used to be. In 2010, James Anderson posed naked for the gay lifestyle magazine *Attitude*.

By then, Steven Davies of Surrey and England had come out to his family. Davies debuted for England in 2009, confided to his teammates ahead of the 2010–11 Ashes tour, and went public in a 2012 interview with the *Telegraph*. He received support from the cricket fraternity, including Professional Cricketers' Association chair Vikram Solanki, coach Andy Flower, teammate Ian Bell, and … Hansford. Stephen Fry, who had come out as gay long before that, hailed Davies as 'brave, charming, modest, and inspiring'. In 2022, Fry would be named MCC president.

But Davies's interview did not lead to others following suit. Till date, he remains the only male international cricketer to have come out of the closet.

Out on the Fields (2015) and *OutSport* (2019) are the 'first and second international research on homophobia and transphobia in sport': 80 per cent of their participants 'witnessed or experienced homophobia in sport with homophobic language the most common', while 80 per cent 'believe gay people are "not at all accepted" or "accepted a little" or only "moderately accepted" in sporting culture'.

As with many cricketing aspects, the women have shown the way. In 2015, Alex Blackwell of Australia and England's Lynsey Askew had international cricket's first same-sex marriage. Australia's passing of the Marriage Amendment (Definition and Religious Freedoms) Act in 2017 made their marriage official in both nations.

Blackwell and Askew were followed by Amy Satterthwaite and Lea Tahuhu, Dane van Niekerk and Marizanne Kapp, Katherine Brunt and Nat Sciver (both Sciver-Brunt now), Ellyse Villani and Nicola Carey, Rachael Haynes and Leah Poulton … and several other cricketers who married same-sex non-cricketers.

At the same time, the authorities have become more stringent towards homophobia.

When Shannon Gabriel used a homophobic sledge during a Test match in 2019, Joe Root responded with 'there's nothing wrong in being gay'. The ICC fined Gabriel 75 per cent of his match fees and banned him for four ODIs for 'personal abuse of a player'. James Pattinson and Marcus Stoinis committed the same offence in the same year, respectively at Cameron Gannon and Kane Richardson. Pattinson was banned for a Test, while Stoinis got away with a fine.

Cricket has a long way to go, but perhaps things are looking up. At least homophobia is being evicted from the sport.

Chapter 90

'THANK YOU FOR MAKING MY TOURNAMENT A SUCCESS.'

Lalit Modi to Brendon McCullum, 19 April 2008.

During his days at Duke University in North Carolina, one Lalit Modi was arrested for trafficking cocaine. In a biography of Modi, *Maverick Commissioner*, Boria Majumdar noted that Modi pleaded guilty. He got a suspended two-year prison sentence and a five-year probation period with community service: he furnished a $50,000 bond, returned to India and inherited his family business.

This was in the mid-1990s. During his days in the US, Modi had seen the NBA basketball league. He now envisaged a cricket tournament on similar lines and drafted a proposal for the BCCI. Privately owned teams with Indian and foreign cricketers. Glitz. Entertainment. Glamour. Four to six weeks a year of evening cricket with extensive live coverage, targeting the only television set owned by middle-class families.

Jagmohan Dalmiya, then at the helm of the board, rejected the idea. The BCCI were not keen on sharing profit with franchises. They also found Modi's projected figures outlandish. This, despite Modi securing a ten-year contract for becoming the official distributor of ESPN in India in 1994. There was little doubt that he knew the viewership details.

The BCCI knew that there was money in televised evening cricket, but they had not realized *how much* money. But Modi was not one to relinquish his ambitions this easily. He played the right cards, found his way through the labyrinthine maze of the BCCI backroom politics, sided with Sharad Pawar, eventually ousted Dalmiya, and finally got the free rein he wanted.

But someone else beat him to it. In April 2007, media mogul Subhash Chandra announced the launch of the Indian Cricket League (ICL)—a tournament worth a hundred crore rupees (about $23 million back then) to be played in the new format of cricket, called the T20.

This was going to be Chandra's private league, independent of the BCCI. Privately organized 'masala matches' used to be a regular feature in India for decades, but that had been until the BCCI began to make serious money from television rights. By 2007, one could become very rich by playing for India.

Chandra was not new to innovations and bold decisions. He had founded Zee TV, India's first privately owned television channel, and launched Dish TV, the first satellite television provider in the country.

He had bid for the telecast rights of cricket in India and had not been amused when it went to ESPN-Star Sports. So, he returned with a plan. By owning the ICL, he would have the cricketers on his payroll, and telecast the cricket live on his own Zee Sports channel. The similarities with Kerry Packer are unmissable.

The six ICL clubs were expected to become sixteen in three years. Each club would have state-of-the-art facilities, mentors, media managers, psychologists, physiotherapists and an ombudsman. The scouts would look for talent in every state. Chandra got Kapil Dev to head the ICL executive committee. Ajit Wadekar, E.A.S. Prasanna, Madan Lal, Sandeep Patil, Tony Greig and Dean Jones came on board as well. The prize money was a million American dollars. Even 50-over tournaments were in the pipeline.

It was war. Chandra had challenged the monopoly of the richest cricket board in the world. Having accused the BCCI of being unable to create a 'reserve pipeline of players', he promised Indian cricket an 'ideal pool with killing instinct'.

The BCCI hit back. They banned every ICL cricketer *for life* from playing for India; used their clout at the ICC to ban the international signees as well; sacked Kapil as National Cricket Academy chair; and instructed the state associations to not let the ICL use their venues. They tried to crush the ICL in every possible way.

Chandra did get some big names. Brian Lara, Chris Cairns, Inzamam-ul-Haq and Lance Klusener were easy, for they had moved away from international cricket, but he also got active players like Andrew Hall, Daryl Tuffey, Abdul Razzaq and Ian Harvey.

The problem was Indian cricketers. He did get international cricketers whose chances of a comeback for India were fading away—Rohan Gavaskar, Hemang Badani, Deep Dasgupta, Reetinder Sodhi, J.P. Yadav—but the pool mostly consisted of domestic cricketers. Some were India prospects, but there was no guarantee that they would play. This was money ready to be made.

He could not get the men who mattered—the superstars of Indian cricket, the ones the largest fanbase in the world wanted to see the most. There was no Sachin Tendulkar, Rahul Dravid, Sourav Ganguly, Anil Kumble, Yuvraj Singh, Harbhajan Singh, M.S. Dhoni, Virender Sehwag, V.V.S Laxman, Zaheer Khan.

He did get a practice venue at the Mayajaal Complex, a resort near Chennai. Railways cabinet minister Lalu Prasad Yadav offered every ground owned by the Indian Railways around the country. Subhash Chakraborty, sports minister of West Bengal, even offered the Eden Gardens. But the first edition was eventually played out in its entirety at the Tau Devi Lal Cricket Stadium in Panchkula.

There were some advantages as well. Owning Zee granted Chandra access to Bollywood. As the ICL went on, more and more stars showed up at the matches. Popular singers performed between the innings. Chandra managed to win over the Indian audience.

But now the BCCI played their final card. Modi's plans that had been gathering dust for over a decade. Now they decided to unearth it. Two days after the 2007 T20 World Cup began, the BCCI—who had, as we have seen, not been keen on 20-over cricket—launched their own T20 tournament. This, the Indian Premier League, offered the Indian cricketers *even more money than they were getting.* Modi promised amounts at par with footballers and NBA players.

And since this would be the BCCI's own league, no cricketer would risk a ban. The Indian stars signed up. The BCCI had announced the IPL during the T20 World Cup. Once India won, the fans became curious about this bonsai version of cricket.

There were predictable speculations of the IPL being a direct response to the ICL. Modi, however, maintained that the

BCCI had been working on the concept 'for two years'. Perhaps they had. Perhaps they had not.

The BCCI worked with astonishing efficiency to make the IPL a success. Cricketers signed up to be auctioned, where franchises acquired them for astonishing prices. Eight teams would play in a home-and-away format. There would be cricket every evening. It did not matter if one missed the first thirty-five matches: the thirty-sixth was going to be a spectacle worth the evening. Cheerleaders would dance to the beats of DJs. The last introduction made many accuse Modi of hurting traditions, both Indian and cricketing. He did not care.

On the opening night, Brendon McCullum of the Kolkata Knight Riders smashed 158 not out against the home team, the Royal Challengers Bangalore. It did not matter to the fans at the Chinnaswamy Stadium that the local side was being thrashed. They cheered each of McCullum's thirteen sixes. The cameras spotted Shah Rukh Khan, owner of the Knight Riders and the biggest Bollywood star of the era, dancing. The celebrations in the stands became louder.

It was cricket like India had never seen before. The McCullum innings, the highest T20 score at that point, removed all doubts over the IPL's success. It revolutionized cricket.

Modi's prediction of the IPL being a recession-proof product turned out to be prophetic. The IPL TV rights sold at $25 million in 2007. By 2022, that had soared to $6.2 billion.

Copycat leagues sprang up around the world, but none of them matched the IPL's success. The sport is rapidly moving away from an era when international cricket, particularly Test cricket, used to be its pinnacle. Cricketers now forgo international careers to play franchise cricket. They do not care if they are labelled mercenaries.

The IPL and the many T20 leagues have ensured that many cricketers around the world do not have to take up day jobs for sustenance. Cricket had been evolving from an amateur pastime, but the IPL accelerated the process with an unprecedented push.

Far away from all this, the ICL sank rapidly. After the first edition, Chandra was left with six teams worth of cricketers banned from playing anywhere else. He had to pay the cricketers throughout the year. Had he sold the teams, the franchises would have footed their share, but he had decided to keep everything for his own. The only way to earn money was more matches.

Thus, Chandra had to cram in four tournaments in the space of four and a half months. The last of these ended just before the inaugural IPL, and had three teams—an India XI, a Pakistan XI and a World XI. The India–Pakistan clashes, something the IPL could not offer, was perhaps the last throw of the dice.

It did not work. The IPL's resounding success made the ICL fade from public memory. Chandra gave it a few months, then tried another edition. Few cared. He tried another. On the day of the third match, there was a terrorist attack in Mumbai and the tournament had to be called off, and that was that.

When the BCCI offered amnesty to the rebels in 2009, ninety cricketers (seventy-nine of them active) and eleven match officials accepted it. Some even played in the IPL.

But Chandra did leave a legacy. He made the BCCI realize that domestic cricketers were underpaid. The board increased the daily match fees for the Ranji Trophy from 16,000 rupees to 35,000 rupees. The amount has continued to rise since.

Chapter 91

'DO ME A FAVOUR. BOWL TWO NO-BALLS FOR ME.'

Mazhar Majeed to Mohammad Amir, Pakistan team hotel car park, London, 25 August 2010.

Pakistan toured England in 2010 to play six Test matches: two against Australia (teams refused to tour Pakistan in the aftermath of the terrorist attacks on the Sri Lankan team the year before), followed by four against the hosts.

Australia won the first game. Pakistan captain Shahid Afridi resigned and eventually retired ('with my temperament I can't play

Test cricket') after what was his first Test match in four years. Salman Butt, appointed mid-series, then led Pakistan to a 3-wicket win to level the series. Mohammad Amir, the teenage left-arm seamer, and Mohammad Asif, his senior right-arm new-ball partner, shared 12 wickets. All was well.

England went up 2–0 in the series that followed, but Pakistan clawed back with a victory in the third Test. As against Australia, Amir was named the Player of the Match in the triumph. The decider at Lord's was set up to be a classic.

There, Butt opted to field under a cloudy sky after bad light delayed the start of play until 1.40 p.m. The first two overs passed without event. Amir ran in to begin the third over. The first ball moved away, and Alastair Cook had little problem. A normal event—barring the no-ball, or rather the extent of it: replays revealed that Amir had overstepped by the proverbial mile.

Still, no one thought much about it at that point, or even after Asif did an encore with the last ball of the tenth over. The day's cricket ended amidst gloom, with England on 39–1.

No one was discussing the no-balls when Amir took 4 wickets in 8 balls next morning to reduce England to 47–5. At the other end, Asif induced an edge off Jonathan Trott. England seemed on the verge of a collapse.

At this point, Amir had a conversation with Butt, and bowled yet another colossal no-ball—the third questionable one of the innings. This one even got to the commentators. 'How far was that?' asked Michael Holding. 'Like net bowling,' quipped Ian Botham.

As before, the matter got buried when Amir struck twice in 2 balls. England became 102–7 before Trott and Stuart Broad hammered hundreds to lift England to 346–7 by stumps.

The next morning, *News of the World* ran a story—with a video—of a sting operation. Mazhar Majeed, a British sport agent and bookie, was seen predicting, in return for £1,50,000, the exact time of the no-balls and who would bowl them. His predictions matched Asif and Amir's suspicious overstepping.

It was fitting that the incident took place at Lord's, once the haven of betting and match-fixing. In his 1851 book *The Cricket Field*, James Pycroft described how 'Lord's was frequented by men with book and pencil, betting as openly and professionally as in the ring at Epsom', and how 'cricketers did take money to play badly at the latter end of the eighteenth century'.

'Silver Billy' Beldam, one of the greatest cricketers of the two decades on either side of 1800, noted that the betters 'had all sorts of tricks to make their betting safe'. He mentioned how, during a match at Lord's, 'for seven balls together, one would not bowl straight, and the other would not hit; but at last, a straight ball must come, and down went the wicket'.

The bookmakers at Lord's went to any extent to turn the odds in their favour. They even lied to major cricketers about their wives' deaths. In the archaic era of communication, these professionals were left with no choice but to return home, even if to verify, which was enough to weaken their respective sides.

This was the home of the MCC, where during his stint as club president between 1791 and 1825, Frederick Beauclerk abused his power to fix matches. Despite not being a professional, he made £600 a year from cricket matches alone. Jonathan Rice wrote that Beauclerk 'bought and sold matches as though they were lots at an auction'.

But let us return to 2010, where the news was all over the media the next morning, though that did not prevent Trott (184) and Broad (169) from taking England to 446. Pakistan folded for 74, followed on and were 41–4 when the day's play ended. Scotland Yard arrested Majeed the same day.

England won by an innings before lunch on the fourth morning. Under normal circumstances, few would have blamed Butt for completing an England tour with two wins and four defeats, or Amir and Asif for their outstanding summer with the ball.

But these were not normal circumstances. Amir accepted his Player of the Series cheque amidst awkward muted applause. 'The game of cricket was in the news not just for the wrong reasons but the worst ones,' reminded winning captain Andrew Strauss at the post-match presentations.

The police searched the hotel rooms of the cricketers to cross-check the currency notes paid by the *News of the World* to Majeed with the money they found on Amir, Asif and their captain, Butt. Having seen corruption unfold a decade ago, the ICC were prepared to dish out the harshest of penalties. Four days later, they suspended the trio.

Butt and Amir appealed. The ICC rejected their plea on 31 October. On 3 November, the PCB suspended their central contracts. Later, an ICC-appointed tribunal suspended Butt for ten years, Asif for seven and Amir for five.

For the first time in its history, the *Wisden Almanack* named four Cricketers of the Year instead of the traditional five. Editor Scyld Berry explained that they would 'reconsider the position' if the fifth candidate 'were exonerated'. While Asif had 23 wickets at 28.56, there is little doubt that Berry hinted at Amir (30 wickets at 19.80 on the tour).

Worse was to follow for the cricketers, as Angus Fraser predicted: 'It's not just a question of them losing their cricket careers, they can end up serving time.' The Crown Prosecution Service charged them. In his testimony at the Southwark Crown Court in October 2011, Sky Sports statistician Benedict Bermange put the probability of three no-balls happening exactly when predicted at 'one in a million' in general and, for specifically Asif and Amir, 'one in 1.5 million'. Not quite impossible but almost as good as.

Guilty, was the verdict on 3 November 2011. Majeed received a prison sentence for thirty-two months; Butt for thirty; Asif for twelve; and Amir for six. 'It is shameful that today Pakistan cricket is facing such a day,' noted Aamer Sohail, 'but this is what happens when you don't react quickly enough to fight corruption.' Unlike the fixers of cricket's so-called pristine past, all three cricketers served their sentences.

Once done, they returned to play at domestic level. Amir represented Pakistan as recently as in 2024.

Section 12

The Greater Game

Chapter 92

'IT WAS THE FIRST TIME THAT BOTH THE TALIBAN SIDE AND OUR SIDE WERE SHOOTING, BUT NOT AT EACH OTHER. THERE WAS SHOOTING IN THE AIR TO CELEBRATE THE SUCCESS OF THE AFGHANISTAN NATIONAL TEAM.'

An army commander to Afghanistan Cricket Board CEO Noor Muhammad, October 2013.

The English soldiers had failed to convert the Afghans to cricket during the First Anglo-Afghan War (1839–42). The 'chiefs and the people' initially took 'lively interest', but generally they merely 'looked on with astonishment' at the cricket. To quote George Robert Gleig from *Sale's Brigade in Afghanistan*, they were not 'tempted to lay aside their flowing robes and huge turbans and enter the field as competitors'.

Cricket did not take off there even during the Second Anglo-Afghan War (1878–80). Perhaps the long phases of inactivity did not attract the locals who grew up on the adrenaline rush of buzkashi. Or perhaps the rugged terrain and the harsh weather were not conducive for the sport.

Nearly a century after that, in December 1979, the Soviet Union attacked Afghanistan. We shall not get into the details of the decade-long conflict. For our book, it should suffice to know that the butterfly effect of the war produced one of cricket's greatest stories. It remains Russia's greatest contribution to cricket, albeit an inadvertent one.

The Soviet invasion forced many families to move across the Durand Line to Pakistan, where they saw this curious game that had failed to attract their ancestors. They began to play the sport and liked it. The Afghanistan Cricket Federation (ACF) was founded in 1995, *in Pakistan.*

When the Afghans returned home around 2001, they brought the game back with them. Among them was Taj Malik. He had barely played beyond tennis- or tape-ball cricket, but as coach, his 'insatiable enthusiasm and self-belief' was instrumental in Afghanistan's early success. For the latter stages of their remarkable journey, Afghanistan would replace him with a coach of greater credentials, but he helped them cross the initial hurdles.

The Afghan journey began with help from unexpected quarters. The Taliban, otherwise rigid in their stance against *any sport* (even the national sport of buzkashi for some time), had no problem with cricket. 'Cricket kits accommodated religious and cultural requirements,' theorized Tim Wigmore.

In fact, in January 2000, the Taliban urged the ACF to request the Pakistan Cricket Board to support their application to the ICC. This was an important alliance, for Pakistan was one of three states to 'recognise the Taliban as Afghanistan's official government'.

Afghanistan became an ICC Affiliate Member in 2001, and an Asian Cricket Council member in 2003. At this point, they were playing as a team in *Pakistan domestic cricket*. Nawroz Mangal, Karim Sadiq and the ageless Mohammad Nabi were all part of Afghanistan's earliest national teams.

At the 2004 Asian Cricket Council Trophy, Afghanistan beat Bahrain and the host, Malaysia. Matches with 'international' status were sporadic, and ODI status was out of the question, but by 2006, they had beaten Saudi Arabia, Kuwait, Qatar, Iran, Thailand, Nepal, and on an England tour, the Second XIs of Essex and Leicestershire. They also finished third in the ACC Trophy.

Afghanistan also beat an MCC side that year. Nabi impressed enough to earn an MCC Young Cricketers contract. So did Hamid Hasan, the broad-chested, war-painted fast bowler who would later bowl the first ball for Afghanistan at the 50-over World Cup and take cricket by storm with his pace and cartwheel celebrations. Both men toured the Netherlands with the MCC side that year.

Afghanistan had tasted as much success as any other team in the first two years of international cricket. Even then, harbouring the dream of a World Cup berth might have seemed outlandish. After all, they were in Division Five of the World Cricket League. Only the top teams of Division Three made it to *the Qualifiers*, let alone the World Cup.

It was an arduous climb, but perhaps not for cricketers who had spent their childhoods in refugee camps. In May 2008, they won the Division Five League in Jersey with a 2-wicket triumph against the hosts in the final. In October, they won the Division Four final as well, defeating Hong Kong by 57 runs at Dar es Salaam. Division Three was played in round-robin league format, in Argentina: Afghanistan topped the points table by April 2009.

Less than a year after entering Division Five for the first time, Afghanistan had zoomed through three divisions to make it to the World Cup Qualifiers. Of course, they had their share of luck. Had rain not denied Cayman Islands a certain win and forced a replay (instead of a resumption) the next day, they would not have made it. But despite everything, despite the odd defeat on the way, there have been few parallels to this in 500 years of cricket.

Cracking the World Cup at first attempt was too good a dream even for the Afghans, but they did come agonizingly close. Four teams qualified for the 2011 edition: they came fifth.

Yet, there was hope. As Afghanistan broke barriers at a dizzying pace, so did T20, cricket's newest format. The first World Cup had already been played, and the second was too close, but Afghanistan did make it to the third, in the West Indies in 2010. It had taken them only six years since they started playing international cricket.

Their dream run made news in unexpected corners. 'If we are searching for a model of how to meet tough international challenges with skill, dedication and teamwork, we need only look to the Afghan national cricket team,' suggested Hillary Clinton.

In the 2013 qualifiers, they eventually booked an ODI World Cup berth. The moment was celebrated with fervour back home. People even fired AK-47s. At the 2015 World Cup, Afghanistan reduced Bangladesh to 119–4 and pushed Sri Lanka to a point where they needed 55 in 52 balls with 4 wickets in hand. They lost both, but they did beat Scotland, who had been playing World Cup since 1999. The AK-47s were pressed into action back home yet again.

In 2017, Afghanistan became an ICC Full Member. In 2018, they played their first Test match. In 2023, they beat England, Pakistan and Sri Lanka to finish fifth at the World Cup. In 2024, they defeated New Zealand, Australia and Bangladesh en route to a maiden T20 World Cup semi-final berth. Rashid Khan, the greatest Afghan sportsperson and arguably the greatest cricketer in the brief history of T20 cricket, led them in the latter.

Had the ICC remained the Old Boys' Club it used to be until 1993, would the Afghan story have been different? Almost certainly. Perhaps their cricket would have been restricted to occasional matches against touring sides who would masquerade as the sport's great evangelists. Afghanistan's story is also the story of cricket's expansion, of its aspirations to become a global sport, and setting up processes accordingly.

Yet, Afghan cricket's peerless rise has been restricted to one gender. At one point, the Afghan Board had made attempts to promote women's cricket. In November 2020, they awarded professional contracts to twenty-five women and girls. Things were looking up. But the Taliban takeover of Afghanistan in 2021 ended everything.

In a country where the women were denied basic rights, their playing cricket was out of the question. Many contracted female cricketers were forced to burn their kits to erase all signs of their playing days. Some had to flee the nation to survive.

There is no immediate hope of a revival. Ahmadullah Wasiq, deputy head of the Taliban cultural commission, had made that amply clear shortly after the takeover: 'I don't think women will be allowed to play cricket because it is not necessary that women should play cricket.'

Australia have ended all bilateral cricketing ties with them on the grounds of Afghanistan's 'poor record on human rights for women and girls', but they really put nothing at stake. Given the World Cup qualification processes and the quality of the Australian team, the boycott is unlikely to harm them in any way. And they have no qualms in playing Afghanistan at the World Cups.

As per ICC's own operating manual, all Full Members are liable to organize 'club cricket—adult, youth cricket, schools cricket, women's cricket'. Afghanistan should ideally have lost their Full Membership status (and hence, revenue), but that has not happened.

If the journey of the Afghan men has been one of cricket's, and the ICC's, greatest success stories, the inability to address the peril of the female cricketers had been among their biggest failures.

An update arrived not too long before this book went to press. In April 2025, the ICC announced the formation of a 'dedicated task force' to support displaced Afghan women cricketers. They joined hands with Indian, English and Australian boards 'to assist these talented athletes in both their cricketing and personal development journeys' by providing financial help, advanced coaching, world-class facilities and 'tailored mentorship'. Perhaps there is hope, after all.

Chapter 93

'WITH HIM, THEN, MIGHT GO NOT ONLY AMONG THE MIGHTIEST OF CRICKETERS, BUT A WAY OF LOOKING AT THE WORLD–THE TRANSITION FROM A TIME IN WHICH INDIA SUCCEEDED IN SPITE OF TO AN ERA IN WHICH IT SUCCEEDS BECAUSE.'

Gideon Haigh, 2014.

There have been cricketing legends before Sachin Tendulkar. There will be more after him as well. Yet, in 500 years of the sport, no one else has been honoured with the tag of 'God' by as many people over a span of time as long. More than a decade after hanging up his boots, Tendulkar continues to dominate the first page of Google search results on the 'God of cricket'.

To understand this unprecedented impact, it is important to understand how India changed over Tendulkar's career. Television had arrived late in the nation. When it did, it took its time to expand beyond the large cities. Colour sets were rare. The state-owned Doordarshan was the only channel. Doordarshan did launch a second channel, but only in the large cities and not until well into the 1990s.

Of course, there was cricket, but live coverage of Test cricket was restricted to matches in India and Pakistan. The Doordarshan feed for home matches was ridiculously grainy even by the standards of the day: cameras used to be placed at one end for years, and it was common for the viewer to not watch the ball to the boundary.

Over time, Doordarshan borrowed feed of overseas ODIs (while welcome, it was also a sad reality check of the abysmal quality of coverage in India). But there was no live feed of Test matches—what generations grew up hailing as 'real cricket'—from outside Asia. The fans had to settle for highlights.

The economic policies of 1991 prompted three significant changes to this. Cable television arrived, and thanks to cable operators, spread at a rapid rate—even beyond the large cities over the next decade. Affordable television sets with improved quality flooded the Indian market. And the large brands went flat out in signing up famous names from India's most favourite sport. On their 1993–94 tour of New Zealand, India played a solitary Test match, at Hamilton. This drawn affair, Kapil Dev's last Test and Stephen Fleming's first, marked the first instance of Indians getting to watch a Test match played outside Asia live. When India travelled outside Asia again, in England in 1996, even some tour matches were shown live back home.

By then, there were more than fifty channels in the nation. India was consuming the sport like never before. Cricket, transitioning towards coloured clothing under floodlights, refused to restrict itself to daytime or 'seasons'. Fans could watch their heroes round the year, even after returning from work, from the comfort of their home. They did not have to take the day off to travel to the venue (that too, if they lived in a city with an international venue). Television made cricket a household show across the lengths and breadths of India.

Tendulkar's illustrious predecessors had diehard fans as well, but these fans had grown up without getting to *watch* their heroes perform against the best sides in the world at their den. They never got to see Sunil Gavaskar's hundreds in the West Indies, Kapil Dev's Test match heroics in England or Australia, India's sporadic Test wins outside Asia or even Tendulkar's early classics away from home. They had to rely on highlights, radio commentary and written reports.

Tendulkar's first great peak coincided with the great spread of television in India. Between the start of the 1996 World Cup and the end of the 2000–01 season, he amassed 4237 runs at 60.52 with seventeen hundreds in Test cricket. He headed the runs and hundreds charts, while among batters with 3000 runs over this period, no one else averaged even 54. He combined this with 6967 ODI runs at 46.13 and a strike rate of 89—no one matched these numbers—while his twenty-four hundreds were eight clear of anyone else's tally.

But that is not all. Throughout the 1990s, as Tendulkar went from strength to strength, India won a solitary Test match away from home, in Sri Lanka in 1993. His performances during this hopeless phase made him stand out as a superhuman among peers.

The greatest cricketers have dominated cricket over five-year phases—even more—to this extent. However, this was the first time the world's largest cricket fanbase could *watch* someone dominate the greatest bowlers anywhere on the planet, in *real time*. This was a hero whose deeds did not need to be exaggerated: everyone could *see* him at it.

Of course, the brands played their roles. With Gavaskar gone and Kapil on his way out, they had little problem in identifying Tendulkar as the face of cricket in a batting-crazy nation—this, despite the enigmatic Mohammad Azharuddin's presence at the helm.

It worked. In commercials, Tendulkar could switch between the impish youth and the superstar cricketer with ease. The appeal was universal. By the 1996 World Cup, he was already being touted as the best in the world, but in Pepsi's ambush marketing campaign ('Nothing official about it'), he was the prototype Indian youngster scared of breaking glass while playing street cricket.

The first Indian generation to grow up on satellite television, thus, grew up on Tendulkar playing one timeless classic after another in hopeless causes. Punctuating the innings—breaks between overs make cricket an advertiser's dream—were commercials, many of them featuring Tendulkar. In India in the 1990s, Tendulkar *became* cricket.

Passers-by queuing outside electronics showrooms to watch India play on television became common, as was the switching off of television sets as soon as Tendulkar got out. If Gavaskar had been Indian cricket's first supermodel—Thums Up, Dinesh Suitings, Air India, Sentry Soap, Iodex, Cherry Blossom shoe polish, Forhan's toothpaste; the list is long—Tendulkar was the first brand. He was in the newspapers, on the billboards, in school assemblies, in office discussions, on exercise book covers. He was everywhere.

'The coming of the market and the availability of hitherto unavailable options freed the spirits of a middle class burdened by the knowledge of its own inadequacies,' explained Santosh Desai, author and ad guru. 'In cricket and in Sachin, they found an accelerant of their growing aspirations, a symbolic assertion of the new confidence with which they felt ready to take on the world.'

One can see how he became God. A peerless genius in a struggling team with the added benefit of playing his cricket at the right place at the right time. Tendulkar became the face of Indian cricket when it embraced power and finances it had never known.

There are anecdotes aplenty. Of people—the driver included—insisting a train delay its start until Tendulkar got his hundred. Of Barack Obama wanting to know why productivity in the US dropped when Tendulkar was batting. Most are apocryphal, but fans hesitated to dismiss the stories, however outlandish they were. Had they not known the craze, experienced it first-hand? Given a choice, would they not have wanted to stop the train themselves? Had they not stealthily hit Alt + Tab, followed by F5, at work every now and then to check on the score?

Tendulkar's colossal career spanned the entirety of India's rise from a closed economy. As he went from strength to strength, state-owned channels gave in to satellite television, landlines made way for mobile phones, dial-up internet evolved to high-speed connections and social media arrived. Cricket changed over his vast career, but perhaps as significantly, the ways in which the sport was consumed changed just as much.

As a generation moulded itself to adapt to a rapidly changing world, Tendulkar remained their one constant companion, their one connection with the many pasts they had left behind on the way. Once he left the playing arena for one final time, the entire generation was—to quote Arunabha Sengupta—'faced with the unfamiliar task of walking alone'.

Ask them. Everyone has a Tendulkar memory.

Chapter 94

'GO OUT, HAVE A LOOK, BOYS. THEY'RE USING SOMETHING.'

Fanie de Villiers to the camera crew, 24 March 2018.

During the 1920–21 Ashes, England captain Johnny Douglas had demanded to inspect Australian leg-spinner Arthur Mailey's hands. Once he was done, he announced: 'You've been using resin. I'll report you to the umpire.'

In response, Mailey asked Douglas to produce *his* right hand; had a close look at it; and responded with, 'You've been lifting the seam, Johnny.' Douglas grinned, leaving onlookers clueless.

'Douglas and Mailey appear to be good friends again. They were shaking hands out in the middle yesterday,' reported the next day's newspapers.

Cricketers might have tampered with the ball before Mailey, but no high-profile player had been candid about it: 'I always carried powdered resin in my pocket and when the umpire wasn't looking, lifted the seam for Jack Gregory and Ted McDonald.' He felt that the use of resin was as fair as wicketkeepers applying birdlime on their gloves—as they often used to do—to make the ball stick.

Once, Mailey dropped a catch in the slips and requested captain Herbie Collins to move him to cover. But the shrewd Collins had other ideas: 'You've got a better chance of lifting the seams for Jack Gregory and "Stork" Hendry there.' The second role was just as important.

There was no guilt, for Mailey felt that the matter 'should be left to the umpire to decide. If his inspection of the ball reveals no damage, what right have the legislators to interfere? Seam-lifting and resin-dusting preserve but never destroy.'

Reverse swing was not there yet, but the fielding sides would often polish one side of the ball to assist conventional new-ball swing. Picking the seam to counter the gradual flattening of the seam as the ball grew old was not unheard of.

Yet, they seldom used to get caught. It is only in the era of high-quality video coverage that cricketers began to get exposed—though Shahid Afridi chomping on the cricket ball did not really demand a close-up shot.

On the 1976–77 Indian tour, John Lever swung the ball prodigiously to take 7–46 and bowl England to a win in the Delhi Test. Later in the series at Madras, umpire Judah Reuben found a Vaseline-doused gauze strip and reported the matter. Lever admitted to using the strip—but on physiotherapist Bernard Thomas's recommendation to keep the sweat off, not tamper with the ball. 'The whole thing was completely innocent, even though Vaseline inevitably got onto the ball, and that could make it swing,' summed up Bob Willis, who used a similar strip in that match.

An unconvinced Indian captain Bishan Singh Bedi found it 'disgusting that England should stoop so low'. Subsequent analysis by the Tamil Nadu Forensic Science and Chemical Laboratory found 'Vaseline on the gauze and traces on the ball'.

Wasim Akram and Waqar Younis put Pakistan into an early lead in the series against the touring New Zealanders of 1990–91 with an orb that, as per Martin Crowe, 'bore no resemblance to a cricket ball'.

Two down with one Test to play, the New Zealand bowlers experimented with an artificially roughened ball and were astonished to see it swing the other way. Chris Pringle generously used a quarter of a bottle cap with a corrugated edge. The umpires never inspected the 'grooves and lines and deep gouges' on one side. Pringle got 7–52 and 4–100, but Waqar (7–76 and 5–54) prevailed.

None of them got punished, though all of them would have been today. The first major penalty for ball tampering happened in 1994, when the television cameras focused on Michael Atherton. Aided by superior coverage, the ICC introduced stringent punishments over the years. If a cricketer was caught, the ICC Code of Conduct dished out objective penalties as per their Code of Conduct.

But all hell broke loose when commentator Fanie de Villiers noticed Australian Cameron Bancroft using a yellow object on the ball on day three of the Cape Town Test match of 2017–18. De Villiers alerted the crew, who took an hour and a half to finally spot it. Bancroft initially claimed it to be sticky tape, but after an internal investigation, Cricket Australia announced that he had been using sandpaper upon instructions from vice-captain David Warner.

Captain Steve Smith confessed that the 'leadership group' had planned the ball-tampering. The ICC banned Smith for a Test and fined him his entire match fees, and Bancroft 75 per cent of his match fees. The matter could have ended there, as it had in the previous and subsequent issues of ball-tampering.

It did not. Smith, Warner and Bancroft received backlash from the Australian cricket fraternity. The Australian Sports Commission called for Smith 'to be stood down immediately by Cricket Australia'. On 25 March, the day after the camera had caught Bancroft, Cricket Australia (CA) CEO James Sutherland confirmed that Smith and Warner had agreed to step down from their respective roles.

CA named Tim Paine the captain (unofficial, of course) for the rest of the Test. By then, Australian Prime Minister Malcolm Turnbull had weighed in: 'We all woke up this morning shocked and bitterly disappointed by the news from South Africa. It seemed completely beyond belief that the Australian cricket team had been involved in cheating.'

Australia lost the Test inside four days. Three days later, CA suspended Smith and Warner for twelve months, and Bancroft for nine months, from 'all international and domestic cricket' (though they were allowed to play club cricket).

Smith (Rajasthan Royals) and Warner (Sunrisers Hyderabad) had already resigned as captains of their respective IPL teams as well. The BCCI now barred them from participating in the 2018 IPL. The next day, the Somerset Cricket Club announced that the previously contracted Bancroft would not play for them that summer.

Keen on probing into the root of the matter, CA commissioned an independent panel, chaired by Rick McCosker and including Paine, Justin Langer, Rachael Haynes, Shane Watson, George Bailey, Pat Cummins and Peter Collins, to review the 'cultural, organisational and governance issues in cricket' in Australia.

After the McCosker Committee submitted its review, Dr Simon Longstaff composed a strongly worded report based on that: 'The leadership of CA should also accept responsibility for its inadvertent (but foreseeable) failure to create and support a culture in which the will-to-win was balanced by an equal commitment to moral courage and ethical restraint … The most common description of CA is as "arrogant" and "controlling". The core complaint is that the organisation does not respect anyone other than its own.'

The accusations included propagating beliefs including, but not restricted to, 'always be winning and ignore the costs'; 'collaboration is for losers'; 'bow to the alpha male'; 'power gets things done'; de-humanise your opponent'; and so on.

It is not clear what direct impact these recommendations had, but Cummins, Australia's current Test and ODI captain, is one of cricket's great ambassadors.

Chapter 95

'TO SEE THE QUEUES AND KNOW THEY ARE THERE FOR US—THAT'S JUST NOT SOMETHING I'D EXPERIENCED AS A PLAYER.'

Megan Schutt, recollecting an event on 8 March 2020.

The 2020 Women's T20 World Cup was the last major cricket tournament before the world went into a lockdown. The tournament began in spectacular fashion. Poonam Yadav spun India to a win against hosts and defending champions Australia;

debutants Thailand jolted the West Indies, albeit briefly; and South Africa beat England for the first time in the history of the T20 World Cup.

The tournament provided one classic game after another. Sri Lanka gave Australia a scare. India did well to win a thriller against New Zealand. Two days later, New Zealand made only 91 but shot out Bangladesh for 74. Rain denied Thailand a shot at history after they made 150–3 against Pakistan. There was enough reason for the fans to yearn for an expansion of the World Cup beyond the ten teams.

Semi-final day at Sydney turned out to be a damp squib. The first match, between India and England, was completely washed out, and India went ahead based on group-stage points. Australia triumphed over South Africa later that day as the match stuttered to a finish amidst bursts of rain.

In the end, Australia and India, the two best teams of the tournament, made it to the final. And the final was a night like no other. As the Australian team coach meandered along the short trip from their hotel to the Melbourne Cricket Ground, the cricketers saw a crowd like they had never seen before.

The Indian fans, of course, played their part, as they have been doing whenever and wherever India play cricket. And the mighty Australians were the home team. Between them, they had attracted 13,000 at the Sydney Cricket Ground when they had clashed in the group stage of the tournament. 'The most I'd played in front of,' recollected Megan Schutt.

This was different. The organizers had scheduled the match on International Women's Day. They invited Katy Perry to perform before and after the game. They had dreamt of the unthinkable—of filling up that colosseum of a stadium for a women's cricket match.

It is important to put some perspective to that target. Until 2016, the finals for the two T20 World Cups were held on the same day at the same venue as the men's—first the women's, then the men's. The record for the final day of a T20 World Cup was 66,000 at the Eden Gardens in 2016. Lord's held the record for the largest crowd for a Women's T20 World Cup match—12,717 in 2009.

What about any women's cricket match? Since entry was free, no exact data was available for the 1997 World Cup final, at the Eden Gardens. But the turnout for the day was estimated between 50,000 and 80,000. Between those numbers was 53,034, the highest attendance for any women's sporting event in Australia—the 2019 Australian Football League Women's Grand Final at the Adelaide Oval.

But the organizers aimed for a number far beyond any of these. The #FillTheMCG campaign aimed for 95,000—the full capacity of the venue. That would mean eclipsing 90,185, the attendance for the 1999 FIFA Women's World Cup final at Pasadena, US—though Mexico City would still hold the record for any women's sporting event: 1,10,000 to 1,12,500 fans had showed up for the 1971 FIEFF Women's World Cup final, the predecessor of its FIFA counterpart.

It seemed impossible, but the tickets sold at an astonishing rate. By the time the gates opened at three in the afternoon on match day, a crowd was waiting outside the turnstiles. When Perry began her show—she sang 'Roar' and 'Firework'—the ground had filled up.

That evening, the MCG fell short of Pasadena's numbers—but only just. During the match, the giant scorecard flashed the attendance—86,174—to one of the loudest cheers of the night. They roared when the team names were called out.

Alyssa Healy came out all guns blazing to smash a 39-ball 75. Once she was done pulverizing India, her opening partner Beth Mooney batted through the innings for an unbeaten 54-ball 75. Australia amassed 184–4.

Unlike Australia, India failed to do justice to the momentous occasion. The chase fizzled out once they became 30–4. India were eventually bowled out for 99 against Schutt (4–18) and Jess Jonassen (3–20), though not before Richa Ghosh became T20 cricket's first concussion substitute. But the cricket was—barring Healy's onslaught—too one-sided to be remembered.

That night, however, was not about cricket alone. For years, women's cricket was typified by empty stands, often at second-tier venues—and the cricket and the cricketers had been blamed for the lack of interest.

The World Cup final demonstrated that, with relentless promotion, the fans do show up. It had never been about gender. The empty stands for years before that had to do with poor marketing, not the gender of the cricketers.

Chapter 96

'WE ASK THAT YOU UNDERSTAND THAT THIS IS OUR VERY FIRST TIME LIVE STREAMING ANY OF OUR CRICKET MATCHES.'

Vanuatu Cricket Twitter account, 25 April 2020.

We have seen how 86,174 thronged to the MCG as late as on 8 March. Even at that point, no one had any idea that such gatherings would be deemed illegal in about a week's time, and sanitizer and mask sales would skyrocket as the world spiralled into arguably the greatest global crisis of the twenty-first century.

When Australia hosted New Zealand for the first ODI of the three-match series a mere five days after that final, it was 'behind closed doors'—in other words, fans were not allowed. The horror-struck faces of the captains, Aaron Finch and Kane Williamson, were all over social media shortly after the toss: forgetting to maintain 'social distance'—yet another phrase from the COVID-19 era—they had reflexively shaken hands.

The match had a surreal feeling to it. There was no applause as the sound of bat on ball reverberated across the vast Sydney Cricket Ground. 'Every time you tried to speak, it echoed around the ground,' reminisced Ish Sodhi. If a ball landed in the stands, the fielders had to retrieve it. The rest of the series was called off. The New Zealand players returned home just before their country closed the borders.

Both nations cancelled their respective domestic tournaments with immediate effect. New South Wales and Wellington, table leaders at that point, were named champions. The South Africa tour of the Australian women's team—cricket's newest world champions—was called off.

The first ODI between India and South Africa, at Dharamshala, had been washed out. The other two games had to be called off as well. The BCCI were forced to postpone the IPL indefinitely. The UAE eventually ended up hosting it … in the unusual months of September to November.

When cricket limped back into existence, the BCCI were forced to skip some domestic matches. The axe fell on the longest—and logistically least viable—competition: for the first time in its history, the Ranji Trophy had to be scrapped. Decades after being halted by both World Wars, the County Championship faced the same fate yet again. In the summer of 2020, it was replaced by the

Bob Willis Trophy, a curtailed version that featured all eighteen counties.

It took months for cricket to resume. When it did, it was invariably behind closed doors. Visiting teams had to arrive beforehand and spend a week, even a fortnight inside 'bio-secure bubbles'—yet another COVID-19 concept—to become eligible to take the field.

The world had meanwhile slumped into a crisis. The global recession threatened livelihoods. People became helplessly stranded at remote places, at times without income. Rumours and theories about the virus, some of them outlandish, did the rounds. Meeting people became illegal. Travel to work was replaced by Zoom calls. Essentials were rationed. For once, the 'frontline workers' attained the respect they deserved for years.

Cricket was not a priority, but fans yearned for live matches—for the sake of return to normalcy if not anything else. Retro videos filled some time, but they were not the same as real-time action. Unfortunately, there was not any for the rest of March, or for that matter, nearly all of April.

On 21 March, the *RSIVP Auki*, the Solomon Islands patrol boat, had arrived in Port Vila, the capital of Vanuatu. En route, it had harboured in islands with COVID-19 positive cases. Vanuatu declared a state of emergency on 26 March and closed the borders. On 6 April, they were devastated by a cyclone, but life moved on.

Then, towards the end of April, they made an announcement on social media that made the cricket fraternity take notice. Not only was their domestic tournament going on, but a full day's cricket would also be telecast on Television Blong Vanuatu and … *globally* streamed on Facebook.

The Vanuatu Broadcasting and Television Corporation set up 'four cameras for its first ever live cricket show'. Shane Deitz, their cricket association chief executive, helped with the commentary.

A 10-over men's exhibition match was followed by the women's domestic T20 final (the Mele Bulls won this). At the Vanuatu Cricket Grounds in Port Vila, fans brought food or clothes as donations for the cyclone victims.

Starved of live cricket, about 3,50,000—more than Vanuatu's population—tuned in to VCA's Facebook page. The ICC media channels boosted the streaming, and the views reached a staggering 793 million. The fans did not know the cricketers, but they could watch cricket being played somewhere on this planet, and that was all that mattered.

There was the odd issue. The live scorecard ticker was absent. When the fans complained on social media, the organizers acknowledged their inexperience. It did not matter. For that one day, Vanuatu had brought memories of a normal world, just like the wartime matches in England had rekindled hope amidst the atrocities.

Within the nation, the day's tremendous response laid the foundation for the Vanuatu T10 Blast. Members of the national women's team visited the cyclone-hit islands. Inspired by their initiative, Vanuatuan women took up cricket as 'their families were encouraged by how the sport can be a positive, safe space'. Fifty of them—between ages fifteen and fifty—joined the two-month national training camp. About thirty-five of them admitted to being inspired by the broadcast.

In 2021, the VCA won the ICC's Digital Fan Engagement Initiative of the Year honour.

Chapter 97

'UNTIL WE EDUCATE THE ENTIRE HUMAN RACE, THIS THING WILL NOT STOP.'

Michael Holding on Sky Sports, 8 July 2020.

On 26 February 2012, an American man called George Zimmerman shot Trayvon Martin, a Black teenager, to death in Sanford, Florida. On 26 July 2013, Zimmerman was acquitted of second-degree murder. As a form of protest, a group of activists began to post on social media with the hashtag #BlackLivesMatter. The activists also became involved in the 2016 US Presidential Election.

On 25 May 2020, Derek Chauvin, a White police officer, murdered a Black man called George Floyd in Minneapolis, Minnesota, by kneeling on his neck and depriving him of oxygen. The incident led to protests—often using Black Lives Matter (BLM) slogans and posters—that spilled over the national borders. By 6 June, an estimated 15–26 million in the US had participated in BLM demonstrations. In July 2022, Chauvin would be sentenced to twenty-one years in prison.

Meanwhile, the world limped back to normalcy after COVID-19. England hosted the West Indies for three Test matches from 8 July. Ahead of the series, the West Indians announced that they would don the BLM logo for the series. The English cricketers agreed to join in.

A BLM flag fluttered in the West Indies team balcony at the Rose Bowl that day. Their cricketers strode out on the ground wearing one black glove each. Before the first ball was bowled, the cricketers and umpires 'took the knee'.

As we have seen, the ICC had—for a long time—tried its best to stay non-political. True, they did ostracize South Africa—but not when they refused to play the non-White nations or left the Commonwealth in 1961, but when England, then Australia, declined to play against them. Afghanistan continues to retain its Full Membership status despite not having any infrastructure for women's cricket.

The ICC also prevented individuals from conveying political messages on the field. They had issues with Moeen Ali's 'Save Gaza' and 'Free Palestine' wristbands and the army insignia on M.S. Dhoni's wicketkeeping gloves, and even Imran Tahir accidentally revealing an image of singer Junaid Jamshed from under his shirt.

In 2020, however, they had no problem with the BLM messages. It was a refreshing change from their don't-mix-sports-and-politics stance, but it turned out to be temporary. In 2023–24, they would bar Usman Khawaja from using 'All lives are equal' and 'Freedom is a human right' messages on his shoes, and even from donning a black armband.

Given their shared history, cricketers from England and the West Indies taking the knee together was one of cricket's most impactful moments. As we have seen, theirs is a unique shared history on and off the field.

On the first day of the Test match, Sky Sports ran a programme on BLM. It featured, among other poignant moments, the memories and thoughts of Ebony Rainford-Brent, the first Black woman to play for England, and Michael Holding, member of the all-conquering West Indian side of the 1970s and 1980s.

Holding, also a Sky commentator, then delivered a monologue on the subject on air. He spoke about White privilege; the importance of education; going back in history to understand the 'dehumanisation of the Black race'; the universal portrayal of Jesus Christ as a White man but Judas as Black; the obliteration of Lewis Howard Latimer (a Black man who invented the carbon filament that makes light bulbs shine continuously) from school curriculum; and more.

Latimer was not the only forgotten Black person with a significant impact. John Edmonstone was born into slavery. After being freed, he set up a shop as a 'bird-stuffer' and taught taxidermy at the nearby University of Edinburgh. Among his students was a teenaged Charles Darwin, who famously put the skill to use while preserving his famous Galapagos finches. There are several other examples.

As Holding's speech went viral on social media, support poured in. As it often happens, a section of the audience, cocooned by privilege, voiced their displeasure at their cricket being ruined. Fellow commentator Nasser Hussain stepped in: 'All I'll say to those people who say "not again" is that a few weeks ago I watched a Black man being killed in front of my eyes on Channel 4 news, and my natural reaction was to look away. Next time that footage came on, I forced myself to watch because I felt something inside of myself say: "You've been looking away too long."'

Of course, average cricket fans on social media were not the only ones unhappy about Holding calling a spade a spade on live television. 'I was saddened to read the comments of Michael Holding … I have found it difficult that they glorify somebody like Floyd. I don't know whether you heard but there were rumours that he actually died of self-inflicted barbiturate poisoning rather than the result of the actions of the police,' Mihir Bose quoted Tim Lamb as saying in an interview for *Dreaming the Impossible*. The former cricket secretary of the TCCB and chief executive of the ECB, Lamb was an honorary life member of the MCC.

One can argue that Chauvin's verdict was yet to be out. However, in the same interview, Lamb insisted on the existence of 'reverse racism by non-White people towards White people' and refused to acknowledge the racial assaults Bose had faced in England ('You can be assaulted as a White person walking down the streets in town').

But generally, Holding's words had an impact. Several cricketers around the world, especially in England, spoke up against racism in the years that followed. Many recounted dreadful experiences. Cricketers had spoken up against systemic racism before, but this time it refused to die down.

The most significant recollections came later that year, when former Yorkshire captain Azeem Rafiq spoke explicitly about the racism he had encountered at the club. In November 2021, Rafiq appeared in front of the Digital, Culture, Media and Sport select committee.

Ten days later, the ECB committed to launching the Independent Commission for Equity in Cricket (ICEC), which they established in March 2021. The ICEC's objective was to help the ECB assess 'the evidence of inequalities and discrimination of all forms within cricket' and recommend 'the actions needed to tackle these issues'.

They reached out to the cricket fraternity in England and Wales. They received responses from over 4400 individuals and organizations. These included Heather Knight, Ben Stokes, Joe Root and Eoin Morgan—all former or present England captains—as well as the MCC and several county clubs.

The 317-page ICEC report, submitted in June 2023, included forty-four recommendations. They demanded 'the ECB makes an unqualified public apology for its own failings and those of the game it governs', acknowledging that 'racism, sexism, elitism and class-based discrimination have existed, and still exist, in the game'. The ECB obliged.

The report discussed in some detail English cricket's systemic racism, sexism and 'elitism and class-based discrimination', and provided elaborate explanations on improvement.

There is still a long way to go, but at least a process has been initiated. It is perhaps not overly optimistic to hope that at some point, every board will commission similar committees.

Chapter 98

'IT'S A VERY SPECIAL FEELING, THE FIRST TIME IN OUR HISTORY WE'VE COME AWAY WITH A WORLD TITLE.'

Kane Williamson at the post-match presentations after the World Test Championship final, Southampton, 23 June 2021.

There is a running meme about New Zealand's consistent omission from cropped Eurocentric world maps. Of course, the island's geographical position is the reason for that, but in the world of cricket, they can claim that they had to earn respect at every point.

New Zealand played their first-ever Test match at Christchurch from 10 January 1930. The calendar date is important here, because the next day, the West Indies began a Test match at Bridgetown. Both Tests were against teams that bore the name 'England', who had taken neither New Zealand nor West Indies seriously enough to send a full-strength side.

That attitude persisted when New Zealand toured England in 1931. They had initially been assigned one Test. So, New Zealand bowled out the MCC for 132 and 48 *on the same day* to win by an innings. Then, in the lone Test match, they set England a target of 240. England finished on 146–5.

Since both matches were at Lord's, the organizers' folly became evident to the men who mattered in English cricket. The home board hastily replaced New Zealand's tour matches against Surrey and Lancashire with Tests at The Oval and Old Trafford. New Zealand, thus, *earned* a longer series through performance.

In 1948, Don Bradman's team famously finished an England tour without losing a single match. In the following year, 1949, Walter Hadlee's New Zealand visited England with only four men with prior experience of playing in that country. They returned from English shores without losing a Test or to a county (their only defeat came against Oxford University).

They drew all four Tests, but unlike the previous year's Ashes, these were three-day matches. Had they been five-day affairs, New Zealand might have won one or more of them.

Bradman's team earned the moniker of the 'Invincibles'. Hadlee's unit, the '49ers'—a tag so neutral that no one would take second notice.

It was not England alone. Given their geographical proximity and isolation from the rest of the Test cricket world, Australia should have been New Zealand's most frequent opposition in the latter's early days. Just like Pakistan's first-ever series was in India, New Zealand's could have been in Australia. Logistically, if not for any other reason, especially in the days of sea travel.

Yet, until 1973–74, the two teams had played only one Test match, in New Zealand in 1945–46, and even that did not get Test status until 1948. Australia bowled out New Zealand for 42 and 54 on a pudding of a wicket in Wellington to win by an innings. The game did not last even nine hours, but the 'record gate-takings' were worth £3000.

The elated New Zealand officials wanted to pay the Australian cricketers a bonus of sorts—the 'nice guys' tag was not built in a day—but the ACB declined the offer. As mentioned, the teams did not play another Test for twenty-eight years.

In between, when Australia launched their domestic one-day tournament in 1969–70, they invited the *New Zealand national team* to participate—not to play against the champions but just as another team. In six attempts, New Zealand won thrice including the first edition, and came runners-up twice.

New Zealand's first golden era was between 1978–79 and 1991–92, when they went unbeaten for thirteen consecutive Test series at home and won Test series in Australia and England. Yet, during that phase, in 1986, Graham Gooch infamously described their bowling attack as 'the World XI at one end, and Ilford Second XI at the other'—a reference to Richard Hadlee and his colleagues. New Zealand responded by winning their first-ever series in England.

Gooch's statement was as derogatory as it was surprising, for New Zealand had beaten England at Headingley in 1983—their first win in the country—despite Hadlee not getting a single wicket. Fans recite Gooch's quote more than recollect that Test match, but that is hardly surprising. Cricket, after all, thrives on a baseless claim of having, without any scientific or even clerical verification, the greatest literature among all sport.

Since 1999, New Zealand have qualified for the top four in every edition of the World Cup, including runners-up finishes in

2015 and 2019. In the latter, they lost the final on boundary count. Until 2022, they also qualified for the T20 World Cup semi-finals every time, including the final in 2021.

And in Test cricket, they emulated their own performance in the 1980s. Yet again they went thirteen home series unbeaten; beat England in England and Pakistan in the UAE; and scaled the top spot in the ICC rankings. They were not merely showing up. They were being consistent over a sustained period across formats.

The journey began in 1995, when New Zealand Cricket had appointed a committee chaired by John Hood to help improve the sport in the country. In tune with the 'drastic step' recommended by the Hood Committee, the NZC developed a streamlined domestic system and worked on conscious improvement of the infrastructure (including playing conditions). In 2005, they issued a 'warrant of fitness' for every ground to be considered fit for playing.

When franchise-based T20 cricket arrived, the NZC adopted a more pragmatic approach than other boards. Unlike them, the NZC did not bar their players from playing in the leagues. Nor did they try to mimic the IPL by creating an expensive city-based T20 competition. Instead, they stuck to a tournament based on their existing domestic teams.

The cricketers were fine with this arrangement, for they made money and gained experience around the world at the same time. The improved conditions in domestic cricket, along with a well-functioning T20 league, helped New Zealand thrive across formats. Slowly, they built a deep talent pool.

Despite their consistency in global tournaments, despite their runs in the 1980s and the 2010s, despite their triumph in the 2000 Champions Trophy, New Zealand were seldom hailed as one the greatest sides in the world.

They finally earned that respect when they won the inaugural World Test Championship.

Chapter 99

'I CAME TO THE REALIZATION THAT I WAS TRYING TO FAKE MY INTENSITY A BIT RECENTLY.'

Virat Kohli in an interview with Star Sports, August 2022.

In *Silence of the Heart*, his seminal volume on cricketers who had died by suicide, David Frith calculated that six out of 339 dead male English Test cricketers had taken their own lives until 1 July 2000. For Australia, it was five in 182. For South Africa, seven in 170. For New Zealand, two in 52. Individually, these were higher than the English national average of 1.07 per cent in 1998.

From 'Drewy' Stoddart to Sid Barnes, from Aubrey Faulkner to Graham Thorpe, the list of suicides is long among Test cricketers. Among eminent cricket journalists, they include Berry Sarbadhikary and Peter Roebuck.

True, there is no published evidence of this rate being higher than other sports, let alone being the highest among all sports. At the same time, one must remember that these were the ones who had been driven to the extreme. Some, like Brad Hogg and Praveen Kumar, were fortunate enough to not succumb to their suicidal urges. And for decades, even centuries, many silently suffered without broaching the subject in public.

There was an era when cricket used to be restricted to one home season and one overseas. Quicker international transport has changed that. The constant routine of travel, practice, playing, living out of a suitcase often gets to the players, making them yearn for the comfort of families.

Yet, relationships can seldom be taken for granted. Few understood this better than Herschelle Gibbs: 'I wasn't at home long enough to actually work on the relationship. If one partner in marriage is home only for a few months of the year, it follows that the relationship is going to struggle.'

The impact has been obvious. In his research for the University of Chester in 2013, Shaun McNee noted that 'the rising percentage divorces unduly high divorce rate in cricket compares only to that of Hollywood'.

Mental health used to be a taboo for years (it still is, for many), milder bouts often went unchronicled, but some records survive. At least four famous nineteenth-century cricketers had to be admitted to the Kew Asylum near Melbourne: Tom Wills, the first outstanding Australian cricketer and co-founder of Australian Rules Football; Billy Midwinter, who played in the Ashes for both Australia and England; Harry Trott, whom we have met in this book before; and Test cricketer Paddy McShane. Their case files make sad reading, for medical science of the era was not equipped to handle them.

Things did not improve much over the next few decades. Baqa Jilani, who played one Test for India, in 1936, used to demonstrate, in the words of teammate C. Ramaswami in *Ramblings of a Cricket Addict*, 'quixotic and queer behaviour on the field', from 'viciously hurling' the ball at teammates to 'kicking the ball towards the boundary instead of fielding it'. Ramaswami added: 'Knowing full well that he was slightly off his head, I ignored his presence in the field.'

The Jamaican Roy Gilchrist, one of the fastest bowlers of the 1950s, had to be deported from an India tour after he failed to control his temper and hurled beamers in a tour game. Gilchrist allegedly pulled a knife on his captain, Gerry Alexander. Gilchrist failed to control his temper on numerous occasions, both on and off the field. With empathy, diagnosis and treatment, he would have played much more than thirteen Tests.

Patrick Patterson, the terrifying fast bowler of the 1980s and early 1990s, had gone missing for years. When journalist Bharat Sundaresan found him after a long quest in 2017, Patterson admitted to being 'mentally disturbed for twenty years'.

Rowland Bowen, the venerable cricket historian, used a hacksaw, a hammer and a chisel, to amputate his own right leg … just because it could be done. Today, they would have diagnosed apotemnophilia in time and prevented the damage. No one knows why eighty-nine-year-old C. Ramaswami, who had played Test cricket and Davis Cup for India, disappeared one day from his home and never returned.

In his autobiography *Playing It Straight*, the legendary Ken Barrington spoke about the inner demons he coped with in the summer of 1966: 'I felt no emotion about anything … I had frightening attacks of the "shakes"—an uncanny, unstoppable trembling of the fingers and hands … I was strangely irritable; would blow up at the slightest provocation.'

Benzodiazepine, the most common remedy of the era, could make the patient drowsy—never a great idea while facing the fastest bowlers of the era. They left him in a 'dreadful haze'. A six-day break seemed to have put him back on track when he signed off the season with 117 against Lancashire. The next summer, he made 2059 runs at 68.63 to finish third on the runs chart and topping the averages. The old Barrington seemed to be back … until he suffered a heart attack while playing a double-wicket match at Melbourne in end-1968. That ended serious cricket for him.

Incidents were aplenty, but—barring the odd exception—very few cricketers spoke about mental health. Cricket's uncomfortable relationship with mental health continued until Marcus Trescothick wrote about the 'black wings' of depression in his 2008 autobiography, *Coming Back to Me*.

Stress had got to Trescothick on the India tour of 2005–06. ('I was a shell. You could have taken all my kit, all my money, taken my life away. I didn't care.') He flew back, made an excuse about a virus, made a Test hundred at home against Sri Lanka and seemed to be back on track when he left with the team for Australia for the Ashes. Nine days before the first Test, however, he flew back again. This time he had no qualms about telling the world about his battles.

The response, barring the odd exception, was positive. Somewhat prophetically, Geoff Boycott called Trescothick 'the first victim of this greedy game', blaming the administrators for working the players 'into the ground'. Trescothick did not play for England again but continued for Somerset until the age of forty-three. He also paved the way for many cricketers speaking publicly about mental health.

Suzie Bates, who had led New Zealand at cricket and played basketball for them at the 2008 Olympics, called cricket 'one of the worst sports for mental health'. After being hit by Mitchell Johnson on the helmet in the Edgbaston Test match of 2013, Jonathan Trott had to cite 'back spasm' as a reason for skipping the next game. He cited anxiety when he left the Ashes tour of 2013–14 early. Anxiety also forced Sarah Taylor first to take a break, then eventually end her illustrious career.

Ben Stokes took six months off cricket to cope with panic attacks. Meg Lanning took a break from cricket to work in a café and travel. She returned to cricket but retired shortly afterwards. 'I was over-exercising and under-fuelling,' she admitted. 'I was in denial. It became a bit of an obsession. It was because I could escape mentally.'

When Glenn Maxwell took an indefinite mental health break from cricket in 2018, he found support from Virat Kohli. In a candid interview four years later, Kohli himself spoke about having to 'fake the intensity'. He addressed it by—among other things—not touching a cricket bat for a month for the first time in a decade.

Kohli's words were significant, not only because he is easily the most popular contemporary cricketer but also because mental health remains a taboo in these parts of the world. Even Kapil Dev, no less, dismissed depression and pressure as 'American words' in a talk show, 'Chat with Champions', barely two months after Kohli's earnest confession.

Chapter 100

'THE PREAMBLE IS WELL-MEANING BUT WISHY-WASHY: NO ONE REALLY KNOWS WHAT IT IS. I ALSO THINK IT'S BEEN USED TO VILIFY PEOPLE WHO ARE PERCEIVED TO BE IN BREACH OF THE SPIRIT OF CRICKET WHEN THEY'RE ONLY FOLLOWING THE LAWS OF THE GAME.'

Heather Knight, Wisden Almanack, 2024.

James Dance (under the pseudonym James Love) used the words 'Hail Cricket! glorious, manly, British game! First of all Sports! be first alike in Fame!' in *Cricket! An Heroic Poem*, describing a match between 'England' and Kent. This poem, written in 1744, is usually considered the first-ever written on cricket.

In English, that is. William Goldwin's In Certamen Pilae, *published in 1706, describes a cricket match—but it was in Latin.*

More than a century later, in *The Cricket Field* (1851), often considered the first major cricket book, James Pycroft dedicated an entire chapter to demonstrate how the 'highly intellectual' sport was England's 'noble and national pastime'.

A man of the cloth, Pycroft can be called cricket's first notable evangelist. He was one of the first ones to try to establish cricket as a British sport. 'The English settlers and residents everywhere play at Cricket, but of no single club have we ever heard dieted either with frogs, sour-krout, or maccaroni,' he wrote.

The idea would take root. Despite having seen more of the world than Pycroft, Neville Cardus would adopt a similar tone nearly a century later: 'Where the English language is unspoken there can be no real cricket.'

One wonders how they would have reacted to the ICC's membership expanding to over a hundred. Or to the stunning rise of Afghanistan, where only 6 per cent speak English. Or to Mike Hesson, who—when working in the IPL—tries to speak in Hindi: 'It's a bit of a respect thing … I don't think it's right if someone doesn't feel comfortable expressing themselves in their own country.'

The Cricket Field is also considered the first book to use the phrase 'not cricket'—not once but twice. 'Mere stopping balls and poking about in the blockhole is not cricket, however successful,' wrote Pycroft. Later in the book, we find: 'Why then, we will not say that any thing which that hardest of hitters and thorough cricketer [Fuller Pilch] does, is not cricket, but certainly it is anything but play.'

Over time, the sport aligned itself to the concept by establishing a self-proclaimed sense of moral superiority over other sports. There is obviously no basis to this claim. The entire thing has been artificially concocted, to an extent that even today, 'not cricket' is used for anything unfair, be it in dictionaries or popular culture. While translating *Astérix chez les Bretons* (*Asterix in Britain*), the brilliant Anthea Bell and Derek Hockridge used 'that's not cricket' for '*ils n'ont pas ete franc jeu*' (that's not fair).

Of course, it was not Pycroft's work alone. The 2023 ICEC report notes how, in the Victorian era, cricket 'began to embody and epitomise an idealised version of middle and upper class, "manly" Englishness', and of how the Victorian cult of athleticism and 'muscular Christianity' became central to the idea.

In 1841, Rowland Hill, commander in chief of the British Army, ordered that every military barrack in England should be equipped with a cricket pitch. Over the next two decades, cricket became an important part of the curriculum at public schools, the 'nursery for national and imperial ruling elites'. They used cricket as 'a primary device … to write a cultural code upon their youthful charges'.

In *Tom Brown's School Days* (1857), Thomas Hughes hammered the message further in. Tom, the protagonist, tells his master that cricket is 'more than a game … an institution'. George Arthur, another boy, adds that it is 'the birthright of British boys, old and young, as habeas corpus and trial by jury are of British men'. The book would become required reading in schools of several British colonies.

It is worth a mention that Benjamin Aislabie, a real person, makes an appearance in Tom Brown's School Days. *He is shown in reasonably good light. Aislabie was a slaver and a joke of a cricketer—but was, after all, born into wealth.*

The Gentlemen's Book of Etiquette and Manual of Politeness (1860) reminded the readers that 'a good player is not always a gentleman, and the difference in cultivation may always be distinguished'. In a letter to a friend, Edward Cracroft Lefroy, the late nineteenth-century poet and cleric, wrote 'the whole edifice of the Christian virtues could be raised on a basis of good cricket'. In his 1892 poem '*Vitaï Lampada*', Henry Newbolt described how, on the cricket field of Clifton College, schoolboys learn duty, valour, commitment and camaraderie expected of future soldiers.

Contrast this with the attitude towards other sports. Samuel Butler, headmaster at the Shrewsbury School up to 1836, was hell-bent on preventing the students from playing football: 'More fit for farm boys and labourers than for young gentlemen'.

Butler eventually relented, but in the 1913 *Wisden*, editor Sydney Pardon wrote that cricket 'must not be tampered with to please people who vainly think that it can have the concentrated excitement of an hour-and-a-half's football'.

In 1923, A.P. Herbert wrote in *Punch* how he thought 'with pity of the effeminate dagoes who can only play pelota, basket-ball and lawn-tennis'. Cricket's snobbery was entrenched so deeply that in 1975 Prince Philip, the Duke of Edinburgh, wrote about the existence of 'a widely held and quite erroneous belief that cricket is just another game'.

Why did Pycroft, Hill, Hughes and their ilk choose to promote cricket and not another sport? Perhaps, when they were active (the mid-nineteenth century), cricket was the only 'properly organised' sport at that point. As we have seen (Chapter 4), the first Laws had been made in 1744 and by 1850, they were more than a century old. Cricket had already witnessed bat shapes transform; defensive strokes evolve; bowling migrate from underarm to roundarm and takes strides towards overarm; and so on.

Cricket, thus, had the early mover's advantage and little else. For perspective, association football had its first set of rules only in 1863, when carrying the ball (in the hands) and hacking (kicking in the shins) were outlawed. Only then was it formally distinguishable from rugby.

This made cricket the sport of choice to be lionized. Since it was perceived as the 'ideal' sport of platonic perfection, any change was considered detrimental to start with. Cricket remained a stagnant sport for decades, for it resisted change. The great innovators were often looked down upon. In 1924, former England captain Archie MacLaren went as far as warning the young players against the innovating cricketer. He wanted 'the Bolshevist of the cricketing world' to be 'suppressed'.

Once the narrative took root (long before MacLaren, of course), innovations were often looked down upon. The Grace brothers—first E.M., then W.G.—broke new barriers by using cross-batted strokes to send off-side balls to the vast uncharted territory on the leg-side. There is a story (probably apocryphal) of a bowler pointing out that such a shot was not cricket. 'I know,' responded W.G, 'but it's four runs'. If the story seems convincing, it is because there are too many stories of W.G. not caring for cricket's moral supremacy.

Of course, the Graces were not the first to be criticized for *presumably* unfair acts on the cricket field. A century before them, William Fennex, the great player of the front-foot shot, was chastised by his father for attempting the same. In fact, the words ('Do you call that play?') bordered on 'It is not cricket'. The early reverse-sweeps met with similar reactions.

Fielding sides face worse. After all, for a long time, the best bowlers were almost invariably professionals. As we have seen, they were accused of playing unfairly when they did not bowl underarm in 1827; and in 1981, when they did bowl underarm. Innovations—the googly, swing bowling—were looked upon with suspicion in their early days. The Pakistani fast bowlers were accused of ball tampering when they used the reverse swing to great success, particularly in 1992.

And of course, we have discussed how running out the non-striker without bowling the ball went from being just another dismissal to a controversial one. Some feel the bowler should issue a warning—and no one knows why.

In the Lord's Test match of 2023, Jonny Bairstow ducked at a ball from Cameron Green and left the crease. For some reason, he was under the impression that the ball had been dead. Taking advantage, Alex Carey stumped Bairstow. Though Carey had not broken any Law, the incident led to a furious spate of (partly drunken) abuse by the MCC Members in the Long Room. The custodians of the Spirit of Cricket, who had—as we have seen—kept their premises secluded from half of humanity until 1998, were up in arms to rescue the game from the decadence of playing by the Laws of Cricket they had themselves prescribed.

Later that year at the World Cup, Shakib Al Hasan appealed for timed-out against Angelo Mathews and got the decision in his favour. Neither Carey nor Shakib broke any Law of Cricket, but both were branded villains for reasons that remain mysterious. The 'Spirit of Cricket', some would say.

It is difficult to tell when the term was first used. In 1888, the MCC had referred to pad-play as 'contrary to the spirit of the game'. At Lord's in 1896, Oxford were 9 wickets down when they needed 12 to avoid the follow-on—not optional back then. Cambridge did not want to bat last, so Eustace Shine bowled two deliberate no-balls. Wicketkeeper Edward Bray let these (and a third ball) run to the boundary.

After lecturing the readers on why this was 'not cricket', *The Times* noted: 'All things may be lawful. Yet all things are not expedient.' The Spirit of Cricket, in other words, without spelling it out—perhaps because the phrase had not been in vogue yet.

In the twentieth century, the term continued to appear in cricket literature. Since cricket's status as the grand British sport had also been established, the colonies imbibed the same mantra. Spirit of Cricket, the tag-phrase of the sport's moral superiority, began to be recognized. While fair play was common in most sports, cricket attempted to establish itself as holier than the others.

The period between the two World Wars marked an era when several British colonies strove for independence. During this period, the spirit and ethos of the British game became a major vehicle for spreading the moral superiority of the rulers. This was the time when the Plum Warners and the Neville Carduses wrote volumes on the intangible values that the game supposedly embodied.

It continued while England was the centre of the cricketing world. By the end of the twentieth century, however, the geopolitics of cricket had changed significantly. The British empire was a thing of the past. At the ICC, England and Australia had lost their veto powers, while the MCC no longer had the grip they used to enjoy. The sport had been tilting towards the Indian subcontinent at a rapid rate. It was turning into a sport unfamiliar to the old guard.

Acting upon the suggestion of former England captains Ted Dexter and Colin Cowdrey, the MCC added a preamble to their Laws of Cricket that remains to this day. It began with 'cricket owes much of its appeal and enjoyment to the fact that it should be played not only according to the Laws, but also within the Spirit of Cricket'.

This is followed by vague LinkedIn-type instructions like 'create a positive atmosphere by your own conduct', 'show self-discipline, even when things go against you' and so on. These would not be out of place in moral science textbooks and

Sunday schools, but their intangibility makes them too open to interpretation to be of any real use.

Rule 1 of Golf mentions a Spirit of the Game as well. It covers 'following the Rules, applying all penalties, and being honest in all aspects' along with 'showing consideration to others' and 'taking good care of the course'. However, the same Rule assures that there is no penalty for the same, though the Committee may disqualify players for if someone commits 'serious misconduct' ('player behaviour that is so far removed from what is expected in golf').

As a result, everyone continues to interpret the Spirit of Cricket in their own way. In the diverse world of cricket, one person's definition of how to play the sport cannot be applicable to the others. It is often forgotten that the laws work as an objective, robust bridge between nations, cultures and individuals in the world of cricket. There is little ambiguity over their interpretation.

There is little place in a professional sport for an entity above the Laws. As Simon Taufel noted in the aftermath of the Carey–Bairstow controversy, 'My experience is when people don't like a dismissal under the Laws of Cricket, they cite the Spirit of Cricket to support their view.'

There was a time when the 'British sport' needed its image of spiritual superiority. In Britain, cricket was run by the elites. For decades, they were the only ones eligible to hold positions off the field and even on it. The image helped the amateurs establish their moral supremacy in a sport where they were almost never a match for the professionals. Across the empire, the Spirit of Cricket had helped spread the notion of British moral superiority.

It is not the same world anymore. The Spirit of Cricket has run its course. To determine how to play a global sport, or how not to, is no longer the burden of one nation.

Acknowledgements

The list should begin with my favourite cricket writers. Stephen Chalke to David Foot, Gideon Haigh to Sharda Ugra, Gerald Brodribb to Shehan Karunatilaka, Christian Ryan to Tim Wigmore—the list is long and diverse. I wish I could name everyone. The bibliography has the list, but it does not tell how they have touched my life.

This book began with a message from Karthik Venkatesh, who probably believed in it more than I did. Patient with the deadlines and astute with the recommendations, he made the collaboration thoroughly enjoyable.

Saba Nehal was impossibly meticulous with her copy-editing. Sparsh Raj Singh captured the essence of the book with an astonishing cover design. And the Penguin Random House marketing team is the reason you are holding a copy of this book.

Arunabha Sengupta, my university senior, mentor, friend, co-author of my first book and patient listener to many a cricket rant over the years, chipped in with invaluable inputs and suggestions that made the book what it was.

It is established in cricketing circles that if B. Sreeram checks a fact, it remains checked. What is not as well-known is the patience with which he has—for more than two decades now—been accommodating questions from me.

Mayukh Ghosh has always been there to help with material from his enviable library. Jarrod Kimber and Joy Bhattacharjya have been kind enough to take out time from their busy schedules to help out. Vishal Misra was prompt and elaborate with his inputs on a rather niche subject.

My colleagues at Wisden help me stay in touch with every avenue of cricket and find new perspectives.

Shakuntala and Prodipto-*da* had seen me through a very dark phase of my life. The Sobuj Songho WhatsApp group is a safe space for venting out, while the Hardcore Sports Quiz group has consistently prevented me from being complacent..

My parents have shaped me in their characteristically different ways. My brother and sister-in-law have been unwavering in support. Rubu and Uju fill up my life in ways they are probably not aware of. Koi continues to be absurd in her canine exuberance.

Finally, Rituparna, comrade and confidante, I fall in love with you a little bit more with every passing day. Thank you for believing in me.

Bibliography

Books

Albone, Tim; *Out of the Ashes: The Extraordinary Rise and Rise of the Afghanistan Cricket Team* (Virgin, 2011)

Altham, Harry and Swanton, Ernest William 'Jim'; *A History of Cricket* (Allen & Unwin, 1948)

Arlott, John; *Arlott on Cricket: His Writings on the Game* (Willow Books, 1984)

Ashwin, R. and Monga, Siddharth; *I Have the Streets: A Kutti Cricket Story* (Penguin, 2024)

Baldwin, Mark; *The History of the Cricket World Cup* (Sanctuary Publishing, 2003)

Bandyopadhyay, Kausik; *Mahatma on the Pitch: Gandhi & Cricket in India* (Rupa Publications, 2017)

Barrington, Ken; *Playing It Straight* (S. Paul; 1968)

Baucom, Ian; *Out of Place: Englishness, Empire, and the Locations of Identity* (Princeton University Press, 1999)

Baxter, Peter; *Test Match Special—50 Not Out* (Random House, 2012)

Benaud, Richie; *A Tale of Two Tests with Some Thoughts on Captaincy* (Hodder and Stoughton, 1962)

Benaud, Richie; *My Spin on Cricket* (Hodder & Stoughton, 2006)

Bhimani, Kishore; *West Indies '76: India's Caribbean Adventure* (Nachiketa, 1976)

Birley, Derek; *A Social History of English Cricket* (Aurum Press, 1999)

Birley, Derek; *The Willow Wand: Some Cricket Myths Explored* (Aurum Press, 2000)

Bonnell, Max and Sproul, Andrew; *Tibby Cotter: Fast Bowler, Larrikin, Anzac* (Walla Walla Press 2012)

Boock, Richard; *The Last Everyday Hero: The Bert Sutcliffe Story* (Penguin Random House, 2011)

Booth, Keith; *Knowing the Score: The Past, Present and Future of Cricket Scoring* (Two Head Publishing, 1998)

Bose, Mihir; *Dreaming the Impossible: The Battle to Create a Non-Racial Sports World* (Arena Sport, 2022)

Bose, Mihir; *The History of Indian Cricket* (Welbeck Publishing Group, 1990)

Bose, Mihir; *The Nine Waves: The Extraordinary Story of Indian Cricket* (Aleph Book Company, 2019)

Bose, Mihir; *The Spirit of the Game: How Sport Has Changed the Modern World* (Constable, 2012)

Bowen, Rowland; *Cricket: History of Its Growth and Development Throughout the World* (The Book Service Ltd, 1970)

Bowes, Bill; *Express Deliveries* (Stanley Paul, 1950)

Bradman, Don; *Farewell to Cricket* (Hodder & Stoughton, 1950)

Brearley, Mike; *On Cricket: A Portrait of the Game* (Constable, 2018)

Brearley, Mike; *The Art of Captaincy: What Sport Teaches Us about Leadership* (Hodder and Stoughton, 1985)

Brittenden, Richard Trevor 'Dick'; *Great Days in New Zealand Cricket* (Bailey Bros & Swinfen, 1958)

Brittenden, Richard Trevor 'Dick'; *Silver Fern on the Veld* (A.H. & A.W. Reed, 1954)

Brookes, Nicholas; *An Island's Eleven: The Story of Sri Lankan Cricket* (The History Press, 2022)

Brooks, Tim; *A Corner of Every Foreign Field: Cricket's Journey from English Game to Global Sport* (Pitch Publishing, 2020)

Buckley, George Bent; *Fresh Light on 18th Century Cricket: A Collection of 1000 Cricket Notices from 1697 to 1800 AD Arranged in Chronological Order* (Cotterell & Co., 1935)

Booth, Lawrence; *Arm-Ball to Zooter: A Sideways Look at the Language of Cricket* (Penguin, 2007)

Box, Charles; *The Theory and Practice of Cricket, From Its Origin to the Present Time* (Palala Press, 2015)

Brodribb, Gerald; *Next Man In: A Survey of Cricket Laws and Customs* (Putnam, 1985 edition)

Brodribb, Gerald; *The Lost Art: A History of Under-Arm Bowling* (Boundary Books, 1997)

Cardus, Neville; *Cardus on Cricket* (Souvenir Press, 1977)

Cashman, Richard; *The 'Demon' Spofforth* (New South Wales University Press, 1990)

Case, Roy; *The Pebble in My Shoe: An Anthology of Women's Cricket* (Authorhouse UK, 2018)

Chalke, Stephen; *Summer's Crown: The Story of Cricket's County Championship* (Fairfield Books, 2015)

Chalke, Stephen; *Tom Cartwright: The Flame Still Burns* (Fairfield Books, 2007)

Chappell, Greg and Knox, Malcolm; *Greg Chappell: Fierce Focus* (Hardie Grant, 2012)

Crowe, Martin; *Out on a Limb: My Own Story* (Raupo Publishing, 1995)

Dawson, Marc; *The A–Z of Everything Cricket* (ABC Books, 1996)

De Mello, Anthony; *Portrait of Indian Sport* (PR Macmillan Limited, 1959)

Dexter, Ted; *The Little Cricket Book* (Bloomsbury, 1996)

Dhole, Pradip; *The Postman Who Delivered the Ashes: The Life and Times of Harry Trott* (CricketMASH, 2022)

Duckworth, Leslie; *S.F. Barnes: Master Bowler* (Sportsman's Book Club, 1968)

Duncan, Isabelle; *Skirting the Boundary: A History of Women's Cricket* (Biteback Publishing, 2013)

Felix, Nicholas; *Felix on the Bat* (Baily Brothers, 1845)

Fingleton, Jack; *Cricket Crisis: Bodyline and Other Lines* (Pavilion Books, 1946)

Fingleton, Jack; *Masters of Cricket: From Trumper to May* (Sportsmans Book Club, 1959)

Foot, David; *Sunshine, Sixes and Cider: The History of Somerset Cricket* (David & Charles, 1986)

Fox Bourne, Hery; *English Newspapers: Chapters in the History of Journalism, Volume 1* (Chatto & Windus, 1887)

Frindall, Bill; *Bearders: My Life in Cricket* (Orion, 2006)

Frith, David; *Archie Jackson: The Keats of Cricket* (Pavilion Books, 1987)

Frith, David; *Bodyline Autopsy: The Full Story of the Most Sensational Test Cricket Series* (Aurum, 2003)

Frith, David; *Silence of the Heart: Cricket Suicides* (Mainstream Publishing, 2011)

Frith, David; *Stoddy's Mission: The First Great Test Series, 1894–1895* (Allen & Unwin, 1994)

Frith, David; *The Fast Men* (Allen & Unwin, 1982)

Frith, David; *The Slow Men* (Allen & Unwin, 1984)

Gale, Frederick; *The Game of Cricket* (Swan Sonnenschein, 1887)

Gavaskar, Sunil; *Sunny Days* (Rupa, 1976)

Gibbs, Herschelle; *To the Point: The No-Holds-Barred Autobiography* (Penguin Random House South Africa, 2010)

Gleig, George Robert; *Sale's Brigade in Afghanistan, with an Account of the Seizure and Defence of Jellalabad* (John Murray, 1846)

Gooch, Graham; *Out of the Wilderness* (HarperCollins, 1986)

Greig, Tony and Lee, Alan; *Tony Greig: My Story* (Stanley Paul, 1980)

Greig, Joyce and Greig, Mark; *Tony Greig: Love, War and Cricket* (Macmillan Publishers, 2013)

Guha, Ramachandra; *A Corner of a Foreign Field* (Macmillan Publishers, 2002)

Giffen, George; *With Bat and Ball: Twenty-five Years Reminiscences of Australian and Anglo-Australian Cricket* (Ward, Lock and co., 1898)

Grace, William Gilbert; *'W.G.': Cricketing Reminiscences and Personal Recollections* (James Bowden, 1899)

Haigh, Gideon; *Game for Anything: Writings on Cricket* (Aurum Press, 2005)

Haigh, Gideon; *The Big Ship: Warwick Armstrong and the Making of Modern Cricket* (Aurum Press, 2002)

Haigh, Gideon; *The Cricket War: The Inside Story of Kerry Packer's World Series Cricket* (Performing Arts, 2007)

Haigh, Gideon; *The Summer Game: Australia in Test Cricket 1949–71* (81allout Publishing, 2023 reprint)

Hamilton, Duncan; *Harold Larwood: The Ashes Bowler Who Wiped Out Australia* (Hachette UK, 2017)

Hamilton, Duncan; *The Great Romantic: Cricket and the Golden Age of Neville Cardus* (Hachette UK, 2019)

Hall, Wes; *Pace Like Fire* (Pelham Books, 1965)

Harris, George (Lord); *A Few Short Runs* (John Murray, 1921)

Hartley, Cecil B.; *The Gentlemen's Book of Etiquette and Manual of Politeness Being a Complete Guide for a Gentleman's Conduct in All His Relations Towards Society* (G.W. Cottrell, 1860)

Hartman, Rodney; *Ali: Life of Ali Bacher* (Penguin Random House, 2012)

Harvey, Adrian; *Football: The First Hundred Years—The Untold Story* (Psychology Press, 2005)

Haynes, Richard; *BBC Sport in Black and White* (Springer, 2016)

Heller, Richard and Oborne, Peter; *White on Green: Celebrating the Drama of Pakistan Cricket* (Simon and Schuster, 2016)

Heyhoe Flint, Rachael; *Heyhoe!: The Autobiography of Rachael Heyhoe Flint* (Pelham, 1978)

Holt, Richard; *Sport and the British: A Modern History* (Clarendon Press, 1990)

Hobbs, John 'Jack'; *My Cricket Memories* (Heinemann, 1924)

Holding, Michael with Cozier, Tony; *Whispering Death: The Life and Times of Michael Holding* (Andre Deutsch, 1993)

Howson, Edward W. and Warner, George Townsend (edited); *Harrow School* (Edward Arnold, 1898)

Hughes, Simon; *And God Created Cricket* (Random House, 2010)

Hughes, Thomas; *Tom Brown's School Days* (Macmillan, 1857)

James, Alfred and Roberts, Michael; *Crosscurrents: Sri Lanka and Australia at Cricket* (Walla Walla Press, 1998)

James, Cyril Lionel Robert; *Beyond a Boundary* (Hutchinson, 1963)

Jones, Ben and Leamon, Nathan; *Hitting Against the Spin: How Cricket Actually Works* (Constable, 2022)

Keshav, Karunya and Patnaik, Sidhanta; *The Fire Burns Blue: A History of Women's Cricket in India* (Westland, 2018)

Khan, Shaharyar M. and Khan, Ali; *Cricket Cauldron: The Turbulent Politics of Cricket in Pakistan* (I.B. Tauris, 2013)

Knox, Malcom; *Never a Gentleman's Game* (Hardie Grants Books, 2012)

Law, Michael John; *1938: Modern Britain: Social Change and Visions of the Future* (Bloomsbury, 2017)

Lazenby, John; *Edging Towards Darkness: The Story of the Last Timeless Test* (Bloomsbury, 2017)

Lazenby, John; *The Strangers Who Came Home: The First Australian Cricket Tour of England* (Bloomsbury, 2015)

Lee, Alan; *Lord Ted: Dexter Enigma* (Gollancz/Witherby, 1995)

Lester, John Ashby (edited); *A Century of Philadelphia Cricket* (University of Pennsylvania Press, 2016)

Levison, Brian; *Amazing & Extraordinary Facts: Cricket* (David and Charles, 2012)

Lewis, Tony; *Playing Days* (Arrow, 1985)

Lincoln, Bob; *Reminiscences of Sport in Grimsby* (Grimsby News Company, 1912)

Lister, Simon; *Fire in Babylon: How the West Indies Cricket Team Brought a People to Its Feet* (Yellow Jersey Press, 2016)

Lister, Simon; Worrell: *The Brief but Brilliant Life of a Caribbean Cricket Pioneer* (Simon and Schuster, 2024)

Lloyd, Grahame; *Six of the Best: Cricket's Most Famous Over* (Celluloid, 2008)

Lyttelton, Robert Henry and Steel, Allan Gibson; *Cricket* (Longmans, Green & co., 1888)

Lyttelton, Robert Henry; *The Crisis in Cricket and the Leg Before Rule* (Longmans, Green & Co., 1928)

MacLaren, Archie; *Cricket Old and New: A Straight Talk to Young Players* (Longmans, Green & Co., 1924)

Mailey, Arthur; *10 for 66 and All That* (Sportsmans Book Club, 1958)

Maitra, Jagadish Chandra; *Indian Sports Flashback* (The Commercial Printing Press Ltd, 1965)

Major, John; *More than a Game: The Story of Cricket's Early Years* (HarperCollins, 2007)

Majumdar, Boria, *Eleven Gods and a Billion Indians: The On and Off the Field Story of Cricket in India and Beyond* (Simon & Schuster India, 2018)

Majumdar, Boria, *Maverick Commissioner: The IPL–Lalit Modi Saga* (Simon & Schuster India, 2022)

Manley, Michael; *A History of West Indies Cricket* (Carlton Books Limited, 1988)

Mann, Roger and Musk, Stephen; *Bart King of Philadelphia* (Matador, 2022)

Mant, Gilbert; *A Cuckoo in the Bodyline Nest* (Kangaroo Press, 1992)

Marshall, John; *The Duke Who Was Cricket* (Frederick Muller, 1961)

Martin-Jenkins, Christopher; *Ball by Ball: The Story of Cricket Broadcasting* (HarperCollins, 1990)

Mason, Peter; *Learie Constantine* (Macmillan Caribbean, 2008)

Mathur, Amrit; *Pitchside* (Westland Sport, 2023)

McCann, Liam; *Cricket: Facts, Figures & Fun* (Facts, Figures & Fun, 2006)

McCann, Timothy John; *Sussex Cricket in the Eighteenth Century* (Sussex Record Society, 2004)

Meredith, Anthony; *W.G. Grace: In the Steps of a Legend* (Amberley Publishing, 2015)

Midwinter, Eric; *The Lost Seasons: Cricket in Wartime, 1939–45* (Meuthen Publishing Ltd, 1987)

Moorhouse, Geoffrey; *Lord's* (Hodder and Stoughton, 1983)

Mortimer, Gavin; *A History of Cricket in 100 Objects* (Profile Books, 2013)

Mote, Ashley; *The Glory Days of Cricket: The Extraordinary Story of Broadhalfpenny Down* (Robson, 1997)

Mujtaba Ali, Syed; *Bangladesh* (Bishwo Shahityo Kendro, 2015)

Mukherjee, Abhishek and Kimber, Jarrod; *Overthrowing Cricket's Empire: How Every Team Beat England for the First Time* (Pitch Publishing, 2024)

Mukherjee, Abhishek and Sengupta, Arunabha; *Sachin and Azhar at Cape Town: Indian and South African Cricket Through the Prism of a Partnership* (Pitch Publishing, 2021)

Nyren, John; *The Hambledon Men* (Henry Frowde, 1907)—includes *The Young Cricketer's Tutor* and *The Cricketers of My Time*

Oborne, Peter; *Basil D'Oliveira: Cricket and Conspiracy: The Untold Story* (Little, Brown Book Group, 2017)

Oborne, Peter; *Wounded Tiger: A History of Cricket in Pakistan* (Simon and Schuster, 2015)

Olonga, Henry; *Blood, Sweat and Treason: My Story* (Vision Sports Publishing, 2011)

Pearson, Harry; *First of the Summer Wine: George Hirst, Schofield Haigh, Wilfred Rhodes and the Gentle Heart of Yorkshire Cricket* (Simon & Schuster Ltd, 2022)

Pearson, Harry; *Slipless in Settle: A Slow Turn around Northern Cricket* (Little, Brown Book Group, 2012)

Peebles, Ian; *Spinner's Yarn* (Readers Union, 1977)

Pollard, Jack; *The Formative Years of Australian cricket 1803–1893* (North Ryde NSW: Argus and Robertson, 1987)

Porter, Dilwyn and Wagg, Stephen; *Amateurism in British Sport: It Matters Not Who Won or Lost?* (Routledge, 2015)

Pringle, Chris; *Save the Last Ball for Me* (Celebrity Books, 1998)

Pycroft, James; *Cricketana* (Longman, Brown, Green, and Longmans, 1854)

Pycroft, James; *The Cricket Field: Or, the History and the Science of Cricket* (Longman, Brown, Green, and Longmans, 1851)
Rae, Simon; *It's Not Cricket* (Faber & Faber, 2012)
Rae, Simon; *W.G. Grace: A Life* (Faber & Faber, 1999)
Raiji, Vasant; *L.P. Jai: Memories of a Great Batsman* (Tyeby Press, 1976)
Ramaswami, C.; *Ramblings of a Cricket Addict* (Sremati, 1966)
Robinson, Ray; *On Top Down Under: Australia's Cricket Captains* (Cassell, 1976)
Rosenwater, Irving; *Sir Donald Bradman: A Biography* (Batsford, 1978)
Ross, Alan; *Through the Caribbean: The MCC Tour of the West Indies, 1959–1960* (Hamish Hamilton, 1960)
Ross, Gordon; *A History of Cricket* (Barker, 1972)
Ryan, Christian; *Kim Hughes and the Bad Old Days of Australian Cricket* (Allen & Unwin, 2010)
Salve, Narendra Kumar Prasadrao; *The Story of the Reliance Cup* (Vikas Publishing House, 1987)
Samiuddin, Osman; *The Unquiet Ones: A History of Pakistan Cricket* (Harper Sport, 2014)
Sandford, Christopher; *The Final Over: The Cricketers of Summer 1914* (The History Press, 2015)
Sengupta, Arunabha; *Apartheid: A Point to Cover—South African Cricket 1948–70 and the Stop the Seventy Tour* (CricketMASH, 2020)
Sengupta, Arunabha; *Cricket across Dark Waters: The Colourful Story of India–West Indies Tussles* (Royards Publishing Company, 2025)
Sengupta, Arunabha and Maha; *The Ashes: This Thing Can Be Done* (CricketMASH, 2022)
Sharpe, Graham; *Gambling's Strangest Moments* (Portico, 2015)
Speed, Malcolm; *Sticky Wicket: A Decade of Change in World Cricket* (HarperCollins Australia, 2011)
Swanton, Ernest William 'Jim'; *Cricketers of My Time: Heroes to Remember* (Andre Deutsch Ltd, 1999)

Swanton, Ernest William 'Jim'; *Swanton in Australia with MCC, 1946–75* (Collins, 1975)

Tendulkar, Sachin and Majumdar, Boria; *Playing It My Way: My Autobiography* (Hachette, 2014)

Thomson, Arthur Alexander; *Hirst and Rhodes* (The Epworth Press, 1959)

Tibballs, Geoff; *No-Balls and Googlies: A Cricket Companion* (Michael O'Mara Books, 2013)

Tossell, David; *Grovel!: The Story and Legacy of the Summer of 1976* (Know the Score!, 2007)

Trescothick, Marcus; *Coming Back to Me: The Autobiography* (HarperSport, 2008)

Trott, Jonathan; *Unguarded: My Autobiography* (Sphere, 2016)

Trueman, Fred; *Ball of Fire: An Autobiography* (London Dent, 1976)

Underdown, David; *Start of Play: Cricket and Culture in Eighteenth-Century England* (Allen Lane, 2000)

Vahed, Goolam and Desai, Ashwin; *Empire & Cricket, The South African Experience 1884—1914* (Unisa Press, 2009)

Vambe, Maurice Taonezvi and Zegeye, Abebe; *Empire & Cricket: The South African Experience, 1884–1914* (UNISA Press, 2009)

Ward, Andrew; *Cricket's Strangest Matches: Extraordinary but True Stories from Over a Century of Cricket* (Robson Books Ltd, 1980)

Warner, Pelham 'Plum'; *Cricket* (Longmans, Green, and Company, 1920)

Warner, Pelham 'Plum'; *Lord's, 1787–1945* (G.G. Harrap & Co. Ltd, 1946)

Waugh, Steve; *Out of My Comfort Zone: The Autobiography* (Penguin, 2005)

Weekes, Everton and Beckles, Hilary; *Mastering the Craft: Ten Years of Weekes 1948–1958* (Universities of the Caribbean Press Inc., 2007)

Wigmore, Tim and Miller, Peter; *Second XI: Cricket in Its Outposts* (Pitch Publishing, 2015)

Wigmore, Tim and Szymanski, Stefan; *Crickonomics: The Anatomy of Modern Cricket* (Bloomsbury Sport, 2022)

Wigmore, Tim and Wilde, Freddie; *Cricket 2.0: Inside the T20 Revolution* (Penguin, 2020)

Wilcock, Giles; *Forgotten Pioneers: The Story of the English Lady Cricketers* (Pitch Publishing, 2024)

Wilde, Simon; *Ranji: The Strange Genius of Ranjitsinhji* (Aurum Press, 2005)

Williams, Charles; *Bradman* (Hachette, 2013)

Willis, Bob with Murphy, Patrick; *The Cricket Revolution: Test Cricket in the 1970s* (Sidgwick & Jackson Ltd, 1981)

Winder, Robert; *The Little Wonder: The Remarkable Story of Wisden* (Wisden, 2014)

Woolley, Frank; *The King of Games* (Stanley Paul, 1936)

Wynne-Thomas, Peter; *The Complete History of Cricket Tours at Home and Abroad* (Hamlyn, 1989)

Wynne-Thomas, Peter; *The History of Cricket: From the Weald to the World* (Stationery Office Books, 1997)

Wynne-Thomas, Peter; *William Clarke: The Old General* (ACS Publications, 1997)

PhD Theses

McNee, Shaun; *Suicide in Cricket: A Sociological Explanation* (submitted to the University of Chester, 2013)

Threlfall-Sykes, Judy; *A History of English Women's Cricket, 1880–1939* (submitted to De Montfort University, 2015)

Web Pages: Without Bylines

About Wisden: 20 Facts
(https://www.bloomsbury.com/in/discover/wisden/about-wisden/20-facts)

BCCI Hikes Domestic Match Fees
(https://www.rediff.com/cricket/2007/aug/21hike.htm)

Boots, Bat and Joy Bangla: In Talks with Raqibul Hasan

(https://thefinancialexpress.com.bd/sports/boots-bat-and-joy-bangla-in-talks-with-raqibul-hasan-1576479737)

Cameroon's Maeva Douma Sees Running Out Non-Striker as Great Opportunity to Dismiss Batters

(https://www.womenscriczone.com/cameroons-maeva-douma-sees-mankad-as-great-opportunity-to-dismiss-batters)

Charles II, 1664: An Act Against Deceitfull Disorderly and Excessive Gameing (https://www.british-history.ac.uk/statutes-realm/vol5/p523)

East Pakistani Leaders Assail Yahya on Cyclone Relief (https://www.nytimes.com/1970/11/24/archives/east-pakistani-leaders-assail-yahya-on-cyclone-relief.html)

Letters from George 'Gubby' Allen, 1932–33, 1936–37 (Page 3) (https://www.sl.nsw.gov.au/pg3-sir-walter-allen-letters-george-gubby-allen-1932-33-1936-37-0)

How Men in Suits Won Two World Cup Matches in 1996 (https://www.pressreader.com/sri-lanka/sunday-times-sri-lanka/20171105/282364039947109)

Huge MCG Crowd Turns Up for World T20 Final but Anger at 'Disgusting' TV Decision (https://www.theguardian.com/sport/2020/mar/08/huge-mcg-crowd-turns-up-for-world-t20-final-but-anger-at-disgusting-tv-decision)

ICC Development Awards: Cricket, Camera, Action! Vanuatu Puts on a Show for the World (https://www.icc-cricket.com/news/icc-development-awards-cricket-camera-action-vanuatu-puts-on-a-show-for-the-world)

It Started with a Perfume Jar (https://www.lords.org/lords/our-history/the-ashes)

Journal of Olympic History (https://isoh.org/journal/)

Mitcham Cricket Club—9. Molly Hide (https://www.pitchero.com/clubs/mitchamcricketclub/a/past-players-48834.html?page=9)

Sinhala Language Radio Cricket Commentaries Are 58 Years Old (https://www.themorning.lk/articles/122500)

The Game, Player Conduct and the Rules (https://www.randa.org/en/rog/the-rules-of-golf/rule-1#1_2)

The Impossible Footsteps: The Children of W.G. Grace (https://oldebor.wordpress.com/2021/11/03/the-impossible-footsteps-the-children-of-w-g-grace/)

Translators Without Borders: Language Data for Afghanistan (https://translatorswithoutborders.org/language-data-for-afghanistan)

Web Pages: With Bylines

Aldred, Tanya; Cricket's Diversity Problem: Chasing the Rainbow (https://www.wisden.com/cricket-features/crickets-diversity-problem-chasing-the-rainbow)

Berry, Scyld; We Should Salute the Wonder of Devon Wanderers, Olympic Cricket Champions for 112 Years (https://www.telegraph.co.uk/sport/cricket/9187124/We-should-salute-the-wonder-of-Devon-Wanderers-Olympic-cricket-champions-for-112-years.html)

Blackmore, Jeremy; Reminiscing about a Revolution (https://www.cricbuzz.com/cricket-news/117467/reminiscing-about-a-revolution)

Booth, Lawrence; 'I Put on This Helmet and Fans Shouted "Where's Your Motorbike?"': Former England Batsman Dennis Amiss on the Customised Cricket Headgear That Changed the Game, Aussie Hecklers, ODI Heroics ... and Hypnosis! (https://www.dailymail.co.uk/sport/cricket/article-9419897/Dennis-Amiss-helmet-fans-shouted-Wheres-motorbike.html)

Boycott, Geoff; Trescothick First Victim of This Greedy Game (https://www.telegraph.co.uk/sport/columnists/geoffreyboycott/2350363/Trescothick-first-victim-of-this-greedy-game.html)

Brown, Oliver; Alan Hansford Is Finally Able to Pass the Baton on to 'Brave' Steven Davies after England Cricketer Announces He

Is Gay (https://www.telegraph.co.uk/sport/cricket/8352855/Alan-Hansford-is-finally-able-to-pass-the-baton-on-to-brave-Steven-Davies-after-England-cricketer-announces-he-is-gay.html)

Buchanan, Larry, Bui, Quoctrung, and Patel, Jugal K.; Black Lives Matter May Be the Largest Movement in U.S. History (https://www.nytimes.com/interactive/2020/07/03/us/george-floyd-protests-crowd-size.html)

Bull, Andy; Rachael Heyhoe Flint: The Reluctant Feminist Who Could Talk Lord's Language (https://www.theguardian.com/sport/2017/jan/24/heyhoe-flint-womens-cricket-lords-mcc)

Bull, Andy; What's Not Cricket? (https://www.espncricinfo.com/story/andy-bull-traces-the-origin-of-the-phrase-it-s-not-cricket-604449)

Chappell, Greg; Dear Tim, I Learnt from My Mistakes as Captain and I Have No Doubt You Will, Too(https://www.smh.com.au/sport/cricket/dear-tim-i-learnt-from-my-mistakes-as-captain-and-i-have-no-doubt-you-will-too-20210115-p56uet.html)

Coverdale, Brydon; Bowler Non Grata (https://www.thecricketmonthly.com/story/793569/bowler-non-grata)

Coyne, James; World Cup Moments—No.48: 1975, Prudential Cup and How *The Cricketer* Played a Part (https://www.thecricketer.com/Topics/news/world_cup_moments_-_no.48_1975,_prudential_cup_and_how_the_cricketer_played_a_part.html)

Cozier, Tony; A New World Cup Is Born! (https://www.espncricinfo.com/story/a-new-world-cup-is-born-128065)

Fernando, Andrew Fidel: The Lion's Fairy Tale (https://www.thecricketmonthly.com/story/834255/the-lion-s-fairy-tale)

Friend, Nick; Bernie Coleman: An Excellent Man, a Ground-Breaking Administrator and a Life Well Lived (https://www.thecricketer.com/Topics/news/bernie_coleman_

obituary_surrey_wimbledon_cricket_administrator_life_well_lived.html)

Gollapudi, Nagraj; Amicus Curiae in Favour of Five-Member Selection Panel, Vote for Railways (https://www.espncricinfo.com/story/amicus-curiae-in-favour-of-five-member-selection-panel-vote-for-railways-1146811)

Gollapudi, Nagraj and Ugra, Sharda; Mortal Combat (https://www.thecricketmonthly.com/story/942005/mortal-combat)

Gordon, Harry; Edward Hugh Buggy (1896–1974) (https://adb.anu.edu.au/biography/buggy-edward-hugh-5419)

Griffiths, Gareth; Malcolm Nash: The Glamorgan Bowler on the End of Sir Garfield Sobers' Six Sixes (https://www.bbc.com/sport/cricket/45341168)

Haigh, Gideon; Ken Barrington's Demons (https://www.thecricketmonthly.com/story/1220189/ken-barrington-s-demons)

Haigh, Gideon; Like 'The Simpsons', the Ashes Is Long Past Its Prime (https://www.thetimes.com/sport/cricket/article/like-the-simpsons-the-ashes-is-long-past-its-prime-7rrqndj2w)

Haigh, Gideon; 'So Much Done, So Little to Do' (https://www.espncricinfo.com/story/so-much-done-so-little-to-do-259254)

Hashim, Taha; The Extraordinary Life of Azeem Rafiq (https://www.wisden.com/cricket-features/the-extraordinary-life-of-azeem-rafiq)

Heyn, Lawrence; 'Lanka Minus Murali a Financial Disaster Down Under?' (https://www.sundaytimes.lk/040530/sports/7.html)

Hopps, David; I Was Tricked into Spot-Fixing—Amir (https://www.espncricinfo.com/story/spot-fixing-i-was-tricked-into-spot-fixing-mohammad-amir-557991)

Iyer, Aditya; How History's First Reverse Sweep Passed the Titmus Test (https://indianexpress.com/article/news-archive/print/how-history-s-first-reverse-sweep-passed-the/)

Jackson, Russell; Cricket Historian, Writer, Surgeon, Spy: The Mad World of Major Rowland Bowen (https://www.theguardian.com/sport/2017/jul/22/cricket-historian-writer-surgeon-spy-the-mad-world-of-major-rowland-bowen)

Keane, Daniel; Electric Light Cricket: The Game Adelaide's Alf Stone Invented 85 Years before First Day-Night Test (https://www.abc.net.au/news/2015-11-25/electric-light-cricket-invented-by-adelaide-digger/6972582)

Keating, Frank; Radio Just in Time for England's Batting Collapse (https://www.theguardian.com/sport/2000/jan/10/cricket4)

Keating, Frank; Taking a Leaf from Evergreen Myrtle (https://www.theguardian.com/sport/blog/2009/mar/24/myrtle-maclagan-womens-cricket)

Keats, John; To George and Georgiana Keats (http://www.john-keats.com/briefe/140219.htm)

Khan, Shahriar; Straight Man (https://www.theguardian.com/sport/2004/jul/11/cricket.theobserver)

Malcolm, Alex; 'I Was in Denial'—Meg Lanning Reveals Health Battle That Caused Her International Retirement (https://www.espncricinfo.com/story/australia-news-i-was-in-denial-meg-lanning-reveals-health-battle-that-caused-her-international-retirement-1429696)

Maume, Chris; Channel 4 Reveals the Sensational Snickometer (https://www.independent.co.uk/sport/cricket-channel-4-reveals-the-sensational-snickometer-1102323.html)

McGlashan, Andrew; Finch, Sodhi Reflect on 'Unique' Experience of ODI in an Empty Stadium (https://www.espncricinfo.com/story/finch-sodhi-reflect-on-unique-experience-of-odi-in-an-empty-stadium-1219309)

McGlashan, Andrew; To See the Queues and Know They Were There for Us, It Almost Brought a Tear to My Eye (https://www.thecricketmonthly.com/story/1253073/aus-vs-ind-women-s-t20-world-cup-final-2020---beth-mooney-megan-schutt-and-matthew-mott-look-back)

Meacham, Steve; Panoramic View of an Old Rivalry: How Ashes Fervour Was Stoked by a Famous SCG Victory (https://www.smh.com.au/sport/cricket/panoramic-view-of-an-old-rivalry-how-ashes-fervour-was-stoked-by-a-famous-scg-victory-20210101-p56r7e.html)

Miller, Andrew; Pretty in Pink (https://www.espncricinfo.com/story/pretty-in-pink-320291)

Misra, Vishal; One Night in 1996 (https://www.espncricinfo.com/story/vishal-misra-the-birth-of-proper-ball-by-ball-commentary-on-cricinfo-637331)

Monga, Sidharth; Were South Africa Really Unlucky in the 1992 World Cup? (https://www.espncricinfo.com/story/were-south-africa-really-unlucky-in-the-1992-world-cup-sidharth-monga-1219634)

Mukherjee, Abhishek; Alfred Mynn Scores 125 on One Leg: Pads Come into Vogue (https://www.cricketcountry.com/articles/alfred-mynn-scores-125-on-one-leg-pads-come-into-vogue-292576)

Mukherjee, Abhishek; The Duckworth-Lewis-Stern Method Does Not Work for T20I. A Look at Its Evolution (https://www.moneycontrol.com/news/cricket/2022-t20-world-cup-how-crickets-rain-rules-evolved-over-decades-and-why-the-duckworth-lewis-stern-method-doesnt-work-for-t20-8805981.html)

Mukherjee, Abhishek; Opinion: The Rules Are Clear, the ICC Should Strip Afghanistan of Their Full Member Status (https://www.wisden.com/cricket-news/icc-full-member-afghanistan-cricket-board-women)

Narayan, R.K.; When India Was a Colony (https://www.nytimes.com/1984/09/16/magazine/when-india-was-a-colony.html)

Nicholas, Mark; Is It Time for West Indian Nations to Go It Alone? (https://www.espncricinfo.com/story/mark-nicholas-is-it-time-for-the-west-indian-nations-to-go-it-alone-952847)

Oldfield, Tara; The Cricketers of Kew Asylum (https://prov.vic.gov.au/about-us/our-blog/cricketers-kew-asylum)

Paracha, Nadeem F.; Calling on the Game: History of Cricket Commentary in Pakistan (https://www.dawn.com/news/1128357)

Ramsey, Andrew; Trailblazers Who Set in Motion the Women's Ashes Rivalry (https://www.cricket.com.au/news/4157441)

Rice, Tim; Romantic Veil Tale Brings New Twist to Ashes Saga (https://www.espncricinfo.com/story/t-rice-romantic-veil-tale-brings-new-twist-to-ashes-saga-6-may-1998-76171)

Roller, Matt; Lost in Translation: How Does the IPL Overcome Its Many Language Barriers? (https://www.espncricinfo.com/story/how-the-ipl-overcomes-its-many-language-barriers-1478622)

Schofield, Daniel; Batting Collapses, Coach Crashes and Nonplussed Frenchmen: Cricket's First and Last Appearance at the Olympics (https://www.telegraph.co.uk/cricket/2020/08/20/batting-collapses-coach-crashes-nonplussed-frenchmen-crickets/)

Selvey, Mike; The Rankling History of our Vaseline Incident (https://www.theguardian.com/sport/2008/dec/11/cricket-englandinindia200809)

Sengupta, Arunabha; England's Gold Medal at the Summer Olympics 1900 (https://cricmash.com/tournaments/englands-gold-medal-at-the-summer-olympics-1900)

Sengupta, Arunabha; Gubby Allen: Refused to Bowl Bodyline, but Why? (http://cricmash.com/pen-sketches/gubby-allen-refused-to-bowl-bodyline-but-why)

Sengupta, Arunabha; Sachin Tendulkar Retirement: The Morning After, the Gloom of the News Still Has a Funereal Ring to It (https://www.cricketcountry.com/articles/sachin-tendulkar-retirement-the-morning-after-the-gloom-of-the-news-still-has-a-funereal-ring-to-it-31990/)

Sengupta, Arunabha; United States Take on Canada in the First Ever International Cricket Match (https://www.cricketcountry.com/articles/united-states-take-on-canada-in-the-first-ever-international-cricket-match-191081)

Seshadri, Badri; A Bot Called Cricinfo (https://www.espncricinfo.com/story/badri-seshadri-looks-back-at-the-origins-and-evolution-of-cricinfo-part-one-1139946)

Sundaresan, Bharat; Patrick Patterson: The Story of an Unquiet Mind (https://indianexpress.com/article/sports/cricket/patrick-patterson-an-unquiet-mind-4762590/)

Vaidyanathan, Siddhartha; Growing Up with Sachin (https://www.espncricinfo.com/story/siddhartha-vaidyanathan-growing-up-with-sachin-598402)

Vaidyanathan, The Unforgiven (https://www.espncricinfo.com/story/the-unforgiven-286356)

Vaidyanathan, Siddhartha; The Wizard Elz (https://www.espncricinfo.com/story/siddhartha-vaidyanathan-on-online-cricket-text-commentary-pioneer-robert-elz-666085)

Weaver, Paul; English Rebels Who Ignored Apartheid Cause Still Show a Lack of Shame (https://www.theguardian.com/sport/2010/jan/11/rebel-tour-1990-england-players-south-africa)

Whimpress, Bernard; Whimpress on 'The Controversy'—Part 1 (https://web.archive.org/web/20080703213924/http://www.muralitharan.org/murali/bernard.htm)

Wigmore, Tim; How the World T20 Was Made (https://www.espncricinfo.com/story/tim-wigmore-how-the-first-world-t20-tournament-in-2007-came-to-be-971333)

Wigmore, Tim; Taliban Will Cheer the Loudest for Afghanistan at Cricket World Cup (https://scroll.in/article/705274/taliban-will-cheer-the-loudest-for-afghanistan-at-cricket-world-cup)

Williamson, Martin; The Evolution of Bowling (https://www.espncricinfo.com/story/the-evolution-of-bowling-248600)

Williamson, Martin; Mynn's Majestic Innings—and the Birth of Leg-Guards (https://www.espncricinfo.com/story/mynn-s-majestic-innings-and-the-birth-of-leg-guards-135983)

Wilson, Andy; Cricket Backs Steven Davies after Player Announces He is Gay (https://www.theguardian.com/sport/2011/feb/28/steven-davies-gay)

Witney, Katya; 'If They Come for Me, Will They Kill Me?'—How a Cricket Dream Became a Nightmare for Afghanistan's Women's Team (https://www.wisden.com/cricket-features/if-they-come-for-me-will-they-kill-me-how-a-cricket-dream-became-a-nightmare-for-afghanistans-womens-team)

Podcasts

Managing Cricket, Feat. Amrit Mathur: 22 Yarns with Gaurav Kapur (https://open.spotify.com/episode/7DEdPJ jTmz3AhbhWUgcUZ7)

Videos

Hawk-Eye's Origin Story
(https://www.youtube.com/watch?v=EYI0t-OyNEE)

Social Media Posts

Simon Taufel: https://www.linkedin.com/feed/update/urn:li:activity:7082096054409576448/

Sky Sports: https://x.com/SkyCricket/status/128080987 0766284800

Vanuatu Cricket: https://x.com/vanuatu_cricket/status/1254157404624707584

Others

Wisden Almanacks, Wisden India Almanacks, Wisden Cricket Monthly, Wisden website
ESPNcricinfo (including StatsGuru)
CricketArchive (including Player Oracle)
Women's Cricket
The Gentleman's Magazine
Cricket and *The Cricketer*
Between Wickets
The Lady and Gentleman's Magazine
The Association of Cricket Statisticians and Historians
Z-Score's Cricket Stats Blog: Charles Davis (https://sportstats.com.au/bloghome.html)
Solidarity Online (https://solidarity.net.au)
National Army Museum (https://www.nam.ac.uk/explore/sport-and-morale-british-army)
Various newspaper archives
International Cricket Council website (https://icc-cricket.com)
The Independent Commission for Equity in Cricket (https://theicec.com/wp-content/uploads/2023/07/HOLDING-UP-A-MIRROR-TO-CRICKET-REPORT-ICEC-2023.pdf)